QUICK ACCESS CONTENTS

Amanda Hollingsworth

Writing Research Papers

A Guide to the Process

Writing Research Papers

A Guide to the Process

SEVENTH EDITION

Stephen Weidenborner

*Late of Kingsborough Community College,
The City University of New York*

Domenick Caruso

*Kingsborough Community College,
The City University of New York (retired)*

Gary Parks

Shoreline Community College

Bedford/St. Martin's   Boston   ◆   New York

For Bedford/St. Martin's

Developmental Editor: Karin Halbert
Editorial Assistant: Stefanie Wortman
Senior Production Supervisor: Dennis J. Conroy
Production Associate: Chris Gross
Senior Marketing Manager: Richard Cadman
Project Management: Books By Design, Inc.
Text Design: Books By Design, Inc.
Cover Design: Billy Boardman
Cover Art: Computer Mouse and Binary Digits © William Whitehurst/CORBIS;
    Pencil © Marvy!/CORBIS; *Computer* © Yasuhito Nakagawa/Photonica
Composition: Books By Design, Inc.
Printing and Binding: Haddon Craftsmen, an RR Donnelley & Sons Company

President: Joan E. Feinberg
Editorial Director: Denise B. Wydra
Editor in Chief: Karen S. Henry
Director of Marketing: Karen Melton Soeltz
Director of Editing, Design, and Production: Marcia Cohen
Manager, Publishing Services: Emily Berleth

Library of Congress Control Number: 2004101849

Manufactured in the United States of America.

5 4 3 2 1 0
f e d c b

For information, write: Bedford/St. Martin's, 75 Arlington Street, Boston, MA 02116
(617–399–4000)

ISBN-10: 0-312-67586-0
ISBN-13: 978-0-312-67586-8

Acknowledgments

Preface

The Information Age is upon us, and the advantages it offers for research and communication are evident all around. In minutes, students can access an enormous number of electronic documents on almost any subject and from a multitude of perspectives. Even traditional print sources such as books, magazines, and newspapers are being published and made available in record volumes. Because of electronic search tools, methods for finding both traditional and electronic sources have become so fast and efficient that a world of interconnected information awaits the student researcher.

However, along with the obvious advantages of this technological revolution come many challenges. Students need to learn that quality research involves more than simply gathering huge quantities of data. They need strategies for using powerful search tools, including critical-thinking skills for selecting relevant material from the bounty of available sources. And what about writing? The wide variety of available source material has made writing more challenging than ever. Students need to know how to weave together information from varied perspectives while paying attention to their paper's purpose, audience, and voice.

Writing Research Papers: A Guide to the Process helps students to understand that writing a good research paper requires planning, organizing, and making thoughtful choices about each step in the process. *Writing Research Papers* walks students through every research step, offering concrete strategies for choosing a topic, developing a working hypothesis, consulting the best sources, taking effective notes, and putting these notes together into a coherent, purposeful paper that reflects not only the quality of the research but also the writer's thoughtful interaction with his or her material. This step-by-step approach can be the key to mastering the fundamental skills of writing research papers.

Features

Although we have thoroughly revised this edition of *Writing Research Papers* to reflect the key role of technology in the research process, the seventh edition of the book retains all of the features that have made it work for so many students and instructors over the last two decades.

Straightforward, step-by-step approach. Offering comprehensive coverage without overwhelming students, *Writing Research Papers* presents the research process as a series of simple steps — from finding a topic to searching the Web to formatting the final manuscript. We thoroughly discuss each step using an easy-to-follow organization, easy-to-understand explanations, helpful illustrations, and a clear and friendly writing style.

Frequent and substantial student examples. Four sample student papers from a variety of disciplines are annotated to show both rhetorical features and various documentation styles. (Two use MLA style, one APA style, and one *Chicago* style.) Throughout the book, we refer to these papers and to the student writers' experiences in working on them. These detailed student examples provide concrete illustrations of strategies for finding a topic, developing a hypothesis, searching for and evaluating sources, taking effective notes, and writing and revising the paper. Your students will relate to these examples of first-time researchers facing — and overcoming — common stumbling blocks.

Thorough coverage of early steps of the research process. In Part One, the popular sections "Four Students Find Their Topics" and "Four Students Form and Revise Their Hypotheses" offer a uniquely detailed focus on the initial stages of research. This feature emphasizes the crucial role of the working hypothesis in the later stages of searching for and evaluating sources.

Easy-to-use design. To help students quickly find the information they need, the book includes manageably sized chapters, color tabs for each part, shaded pages for the MLA and APA documentation sections (now in separate colors), and tables of contents inside the front and back covers. Charts, bulleted lists, and uncluttered pages make key information easily accessible. The handy spiral-bound format keeps the book open while students consult it as a reference.

Thorough coverage of documentation. To assist students in this critical and complex aspect of research writing, we explain in detail how to avoid plagiarism; what constitutes common knowledge; how to cite both print and online sources using MLA, APA, *Chicago,* and other standard formats; and which disciplines follow which styles.

An extensive list of reference sources. An up-to-date appendix directs students to reliable print and online sources — both general and discipline-specific.

New to This Edition

Recognizing that first-time researchers can become easily overwhelmed by the volume of electronic search results and need extra help finding and identifying high-quality sources, we have thoroughly updated the book's coverage of searching for and working with sources in the electronic age. In addition, we have significantly sharpened the focus on key writing issues.

More Help with Searching for Sources

New chapter on developing a research strategy. To get students thinking critically about the types of sources that will best suit their purpose and audience *before* beginning an in-depth search, this chapter provides an overview of the strengths and limitations of the major types of sources and an introduction to today's library as the gateway to reliable print and electronic material. It also covers practical keyword search strategies that apply to all three major electronic search tools: library catalogs, periodical databases, and Web search engines.

Updated and expanded coverage of electronic search tools. Part Two, "Searching for Sources," has been revised to better help students find high-quality sources. Additional screen shots and more detailed, up-to-date explanations offer extra help for filtering search results and finding reliable and relevant books, periodicals, and Web sites.

More Help with Working with Sources

More thorough coverage of evaluating sources. *Writing Research Papers* treats evaluation as an ongoing process throughout the research project, not just as an isolated step. Concrete advice on evaluating sources now features prominently throughout the book as well as in Chapter 10, "Evaluating Potential Sources." The chapters on finding books, periodicals, and Web sources each include a new discussion of filtering and evaluating search results.

New section on annotated bibliographies. In response to instructor feedback, Chapter 10 now includes advice on preparing an annotated bibliography. This process gets students to think critically about their sources, helping them see connections between them.

Expanded advice on avoiding plagiarism. The focus of Chapter 13 has been extended to include a discussion of intellectual property, academic integrity, and the citation conventions of different writing communities. This expanded discussion shows students that avoiding plagiarism is not just a matter of avoiding consequences, it is a matter of practicing ethical responsibility and establishing credibility as a writer.

More Help with Writing the Paper

Improved coverage of audience and purpose. The text now defines three types of research papers, according to their purpose: a report, an analysis, and an argument. Examples throughout the text now show students making appropriate research and writing choices for these rhetorical situations.

Expanded advice on organizing, drafting, and revising. In response to instructor feedback, Part Four now includes expanded advice on developing an outline and using it to draft and revise, more on integrating sources, and a greater focus on global revision. A new, extended example of revising for support helps students understand that effective revision involves more than just tinkering with paragraphs, sentences, and word choice.

Updated and expanded documentation guidelines. Providing the latest MLA, APA, and *Chicago* style guidelines, this edition also includes more advice and models for documenting audiovisual and electronic sources. A separate chapter for APA citation now provides more detailed treatment of this style. In addition, new directories to documentation models make the MLA and APA chapters easier to use.

New Companion Web Site

This new companion Web site includes research exercises that provide extra practice in evaluating Web sites, avoiding plagiarism, integrating and documenting sources, and performing other key steps in the research process. In addition, annotated links direct students to reliable starting points for Web research, and collaborative exercises and peer-review checklists provide opportunities for group work and guidance in responding to peers' writing.

Acknowledgments

In making these revisions, we have benefited greatly from the thoughtful, constructive advice we have received from instructors across the country. In particular, we wish to thank Linda Black, St. Johns River Community College; Michael M. Chemers, Shoreline Community College; Deborah Coxwell-Teague, Florida State University; Stacey Donohue, Central Oregon Community College; Sherle Furnish, West Texas A&M University; Melody M. Hargraves, St. Johns River Community College; Susanmarie Harrington, Indiana University/Purdue University–Indianapolis; Morgan Kellock, Edmonds Community College; Donna Matsumoto, Leward Community College; Loretta Navarra, Kingsborough College; Patricia J. Nebrida, DeVry University; Kelly A. O'Connor-Salomon, Black Hills State University; Laura L. Phillips, Eastern Washington University; Alvin J. Seltzer, Bucks County Community College; James Stokes, University of Wisconsin–Stevens Point; and Anne Williams, Indiana University/Purdue University–Indianapolis.

We would also like to thank everyone at Bedford/St. Martin's for their commitment to excellence in publishing, beginning with the vision and oversight provided by Joan Feinberg, President; Denise Wydra, Editorial Director; and Karen Henry and Nancy Perry, Editors in Chief. Among those who spent many hours of close work on the manuscript, thanks go to Kathleen Benn McQueen, our copyeditor; Sandy Schechter, Permissions Editor; Emily Berleth, Manager of Publishing Services; and Nancy Benjamin, Project Manager for Books By Design. The book would have never come to fruition without the behind-the-scenes work done by Stefanie Wortman, Editorial Assistant at Bedford/St. Martin's. Finally, we would like to thank our editor Karin Halbert for her amicable guidance, her knack for brevity, and her unwavering attention to the needs of the book's audience.

Stephen Weidenborner
Domenick Caruso
Gary Parks

Contents

Part Three   Working with Sources

Part Five   Documenting Sources

Part Six   Preparing the Manuscript

Writing Research Papers

A Guide to the Process

Part One

Laying the Groundwork

1

Understanding
the Research Process

As you think about writing a research paper, you may wonder how this assignment differs from other kinds of papers you have written. The fundamental difference has to do with the major content of each. Research papers do not grow out of your personal experiences and opinions to the same extent that other types of compositions do. Instead, they require that you use your critical thinking skills to evaluate information and ideas that you uncover while learning about a topic through research.

Sometimes, virtually all the information and ideas will come from books, magazines, newspapers, and nonprint sources like the Internet, database articles, or personal interviews. In these cases, your work will consist mainly of finding the information and organizing it into a coherent *report* of your findings. More often, however, you will be encouraged to go a step further and make judgments about the information you discover — that is, to *evaluate* it. You will then present a paper that reflects your own newly informed viewpoint on the topic.

For example, if you chose to investigate the controversy over the effect of acid rain on forests and lakes, you would be expected to evaluate (as an intelligent citizen, not as an expert, of course) the arguments put forth by both sides. You might conclude that the environmentalists have made the better arguments, you might decide that the experts working for the smokestack industries have provided good reasons for doubting the accuracy of their opponents' charges, or you might feel that it is impossible to choose between the two positions, deciding instead to evaluate the merits and limitations of each position. That, too, would amount to a judgment on your part.

Producing a good research paper is not easy. However, completing this work has its reward, not only in the beneficial effect a good paper will have on your course average but also in the satisfaction you will get from having met this formidable challenge. Furthermore, as you increase your knowledge of a topic and begin thinking critically about source material, you rapidly become an *expert* on the topic — someone who knows the subject well and whose opinions other people will listen to. This means that when you write your paper and share it with your instructor or other students, you are fulfilling an important goal of research-paper writing: adding your voice to an academic conversation about a meaningful issue.

Basic Steps in the Process

Before you examine the research process in detail, it is important to grasp the following four essential operations:

1. **searching**   You must search harder than most people realize for a good topic; rarely can you find a topic merely by thinking about the matter. Once you have a topic, you must learn how to find the information you need, starting at the library or on the Internet.

2. **reading**   This operation involves more than understanding the materials you are reading. You must learn how to recognize what information is likely to be truly relevant to your research goals. You must also critically examine your sources for relevance, coverage, currency, bias, and reliability.

3. **organizing**   One of the greatest challenges of writing a research paper is keeping the vast project organized. You must learn how to keep track of information from a variety of sources while staying focused on the project's timeline and ultimate goal.

4. **writing**   For a good finished paper, you must integrate reliable information from various sources into an organized discussion that clearly supports a thesis. Your writing style should be appropriate to your paper's audience and purpose.

All of these operations demand constant exercise of good judgment as well as competence in reading and writing. In addition, neatness counts — not just from the instructor's point of view but from your own; carelessness can be costly when you are working with large amounts of information.

Mastering these skills and developing your judgment will take time and experience, so you should plan to spend a few weeks — more likely a month — completing your first full-length research assignment.

Some Essential Definitions

Be careful to note the specific ways in which the following terms are used in this book, for they are often treated much more loosely in daily conversation. You will need to understand their precise meanings if you are to benefit fully from the discussions that follow.

- **subject**   a broad area of interest that can be narrowed to a suitable topic. Subjects themselves are either too broad or too loosely de-fined to serve as topics for research papers. For example, entire books have been written on the following subjects:
  - addictive behavior
  - Russia's economic troubles
  - Jane Austen's novels
  - prehistoric animals
  - rain forests
  - cancer cures
  - early childhood education
  - illegal immigration

  To develop a workable topic for a research paper from one of these subjects, ask yourself what you would be looking for in your read-ing on the subject. What questions would you be answering?

- **topic**   a reasonably narrow, clearly defined area of interest that could be thoroughly investigated within the limits set for a given research assignment. Here are some topics that might work quite well for a paper of seven to ten pages:
  - the effect of parental attitudes on teenage alcoholism
  - the role of U.S. policies in the collapse of the Russian economy
  - the relationship between young women and their fathers in three novels by Jane Austen
  - the role of humans in the extinction of large prehistoric mammals
  - the effect of U.S. policies on the depletion of rain forests in South America
  - the role of emotions in the cure of certain cancers
  - the effectiveness of Head Start programs in preparing children for grade school
  - the effect of illegal immigration on unemployment in the South-west

- **thesis**   a general statement that announces the major conclusions you reached through a thoughtful analysis of all your sources. This state-ment appears near the beginning of your paper; the main body will then explain, illustrate, argue for, or in some sense "prove" the thesis.

- **hypothesis** a prediction, made sometime before you read the sources, as to what conclusions your research will produce. That is, a *hypothesis* is an attempt to predict what the paper's thesis will be. As you will see, this educated guess helps you find exactly the information you need, as quickly and efficiently as possible, by keeping your attention focused on several specific aspects of the topic.

A More Detailed Look at the Research Process

Now that you have these definitions clearly in mind, we can examine the research process more closely. Here is a brief summary of the steps you need to follow.

Step 1. Finding a Topic and Forming a Hypothesis

- Choose an interesting subject, if the choice is left to you.
- Read about this subject in a textbook, on a Web site, in an encyclopedia, or in another general reference work.
- Find a workable topic appropriate to your assignment and audience.
- Form a hypothesis as to what your research is likely to reveal.

Step 2. Finding Useful Sources

- Consider your audience and purpose as you develop a *research strategy* — a plan for the types of sources you will focus on and how you will track them down.
- Keep your hypothesis in mind as you look for titles and *abstracts* (summaries) of what seem to be valuable sources.
- Collect more potential sources than you will need.
- Skim these sources, keeping only those relevant to your hypothesis.

Step 3. Taking Stock of What You Have Found

- Decide whether you have a sufficient number and variety of sources, and evaluate them for relevance, coverage, currency, bias, and reliability.
- Determine whether your hypothesis is clearly focused and still seems valid.
- Construct a brief preliminary outline for the paper based on what you have seen so far.

Step 4. Reading Sources Closely and Taking Notes

- Keep your hypothesis and preliminary outline in mind to save time and avoid taking too many notes.
- Be ready to revise the hypothesis and preliminary outline in light of what your research turns up.
- Fit your notes into the preliminary outline to make sure that you have covered each subtopic fairly well.

Step 5. Arriving at the Thesis

- Analyze your findings to see how closely they support the hypothesis.
- Revise your hypothesis into a clear thesis that the body of your paper will support.

Step 6. Preparing to Write

- Write a brief abstract of your paper's projected content.
- Construct an outline to guide your discussion.
- Determine where the pieces of source information you have collected will fit into the outline.

Step 7. Writing the Paper

- Write your rough draft fairly rapidly, but as you work remember to cite your sources (in parentheses, endnotes, or footnotes). Incorporate any visuals.
- Prepare a revised draft (or drafts). Check the paper's organization, support, use of language, and placement of documentation, revising as necessary.

Step 8. Finalizing the Documentation

- Ensure that all borrowed source material (except general common knowledge) is documented, regardless of whether it is changed into your own words or quoted.
- Carefully check the content and form of parenthetical notes throughout the paper for accuracy.
- Construct the list of sources at the end of the paper (Works Cited, References, or Bibliography, depending on the required documentation style).

Step 9. Preparing the Final Version

- Proofread the paper with your audience in mind and correct any errors.
- Format the paper appropriately; check the layout of any visual material.
- Make an electronic and a paper copy for your files.

A glance at these steps might lead you to believe that you can produce a fine paper by following a simple, step-by-step prescription — moving from subject to topic to hypothesis to thesis. However, writing a good research paper is a recursive process. Although the steps provide a general guideline to help you make progress, you must be ready at every step to revise earlier decisions given information you uncover or to revisit an earlier step for new information. Remember that your hypothesis, after all, is only an educated guess at the beginning of the project, a tentative viewpoint to be tested against the available information, so you may need to refocus as you go based on your findings.

Much of the discussion so far has been rather abstract. To get a good idea of what an actual research paper looks like, read the sample student papers in Chapter 22. Note how three of the four writers state, early in the paper, the thesis they intend to "prove." (Although the writer of the third paper does not state a thesis, he does state the purpose of his paper.) As you read the body of a paper, think about the way the writer presents the ideas and information that led to the thesis. Finally, notice the parenthetical (or numbered) citations that indicate where the various pieces of supporting information were found. After you finish looking over the sample papers, return to Chapter 2, where we begin discussing each step of the process in detail.

2

Deciding on a Topic

One of the pitfalls awaiting someone doing a research paper is to think that all that is needed is a good subject, and then everything will easily fall into place. However, as you learned in Chapter 1, a subject is an area of interest that is either too broad or too loosely defined to serve as a workable topic for a research paper. For example, student Fred Hutchins, whose paper appears in Chapter 22, decided to research Cotton Mather's role in the Salem witch hunts. This was a good subject, but with only this broad area as a guide, Fred could have ended up producing a brief history of Mather's actions as judge and commentator. That, however, would have been only a short *report* because historians do not disagree to any great extent on *what* Mather did. The interesting question concerns Mather's motivations. Was he a woman hater? A thoughtless conformist? A politically motivated crowd pleaser?

Once Fred realized that the interesting question concerned why Mather played such an active role in the witch hunts, he had a goal for his research: to answer that question. His research would consist of finding various historians' theories about Mather's motivation, evaluating the information, and taking a position on the issue. That position would be his thesis.

Having a question to investigate compels you to think about possible outcomes of your research, resulting in a more efficient search process and eventually leading to a stronger thesis statement. This chapter will help you narrow a general subject into an effective topic — a focused issue that raises interesting questions for discussion.

Moving from Subject to Topic

Step 1 of the research assignment consists of deciding just what question the research will answer — what problem will be worth exploring. Your first thoughts, however, are likely to be very general, only indicating the direction of your immediate interest. "I want to write about the trouble in the Middle East." "I want to know more about dinosaurs." "I am interested in UFOs and alien abductions." "I've always been fascinated by the flower children of the 1960s." You don't yet know what to say about the subject, or even whether it will lead to a satisfactory topic, but you are moving in the right direction.

The question now becomes: "How do I know whether the subject is any good?" To help you decide, consider whether the subject meets the following criteria:

1. You like the subject well enough to spend a good many days and nights working on it.
2. The subject leads to a good topic, one that typically raises complex questions requiring either analysis or argumentation skills to address, depending on the paper's purpose.
3. The subject requires the use of media and source material expected in college-level research.

Finding the Best Topic

Although you should start thinking about finding a topic as soon as you know a research paper is required and not wait for the instructor to push you into action, never choose a topic hastily. Many people make the mistake of picking the first attractive topic that comes along, then rushing to the library (or the computer) and taking piles (or files) of notes, all before they have defined a research question or hypothesis. After days or even weeks of work, they come to realize that they have no control over the project, no clear sense of direction, and, worst of all, no time to go back and begin again. It is best to take some time to ensure that you have a good topic.

Good Topics

The best topics raise questions that have no simple answers. When a question has no single accepted answer, the experts (your sources) will disagree to some extent, which is usually just what you want. This gives you the opportunity to interpret the information and use it to support a thesis that reflects your own informed view.

Good topics should also be manageable, clear, appropriate, and engaging.

- **manageable**   Don't pick a topic that is too broad to explore thoroughly and in detail, or too narrow to find a variety of good sources on.

too broad	The contribution of organized sports to society.
improved	The benefits of sports leagues for elementary-age children.
too narrow	The role of women in the battle of Bull Run.
improved	The role of women in the U.S. Civil War.

- **clear**   Avoid using terms that are confusing or unnecessarily general.

unclear	The effect of new devices on personal connection issues.
improved	The effect of cellular phones and e-mail on relationships and communication.

- **appropriate**   Read and understand the assignment before fully committing to a topic. Check with your instructor if you have any questions about whether a topic is appropriate to the assignment.
- **engaging**   A topic works best if you feel a strong interest in it and are willing to spend a lot of time reading, thinking, and writing about it.

As you decide on a topic, it is also important to consider the paper's purpose. Your paper will be more effective if your topic is appropriate to the type of writing you are expected to do. Grouped according to purpose, most research papers fall into one of three broad categories: report, analysis, and argument.

- A *report* or data-driven paper summarizes existing knowledge on a topic for which there is little or no disagreement in the field. Report topics might include a discussion of the use of computers in education, a history of AIDS research, a summary of feminist criticism on Emily Dickinson, or a description of the primary industrial applications of aluminum. For a report, the research consists of assembling information from various sources in order to present readers with a composite picture of the topic as it currently stands. David Perez's paper "*Solenopsis invicta:* Destroyer of Ecosystems" in Chapter 22 is an example of a data-driven report.
- An *analysis* provides an in-depth examination of a topic. The purpose of an analysis is generally to provide an audience with your

opinion on a question that has no single accepted answer. Analysis usually involves separating the different aspects of a topic and examining them with structured approaches such as cause-and-effect reasoning, comparison and contrast, evaluation, or the application of a known theory or principle. The following topics, for example, lend themselves well to analysis papers: *the reasons behind Cotton Mather's involvement in the Salem witch trials* (cause and effect) or *the films of Spike Lee and Quentin Tarantino as expressions of their cultural vantage points* (comparison and contrast from an ethnic-studies viewpoint).

- An *argument* (sometimes called a *persuasive paper*) takes a position on a controversial issue and attempts to persuade readers to accept the writer's position. Controversial topics that might lead to an argument include *the success of privatizing prisons, the necessity of the recent war against Iraq,* and *the effect of new immigrants on the U.S. economy.*

Reports, which can be somewhat encyclopedic in nature, are generally not assigned as frequently as analyses or arguments, although for some classes or situations they may be required. For example, you may be asked to write a type of report called a *literature review* — a summary of scholarly source material on a particular topic. Analysis and argument are more common research-writing assignments because they require you to make judgments about the information that you collect. Make sure you understand the instructor's assignment and expectations for the paper's purpose before committing to a topic.

Topics to Avoid

It is impossible to create a hard and fast list of topics to avoid. Nearly every subject, if approached from the right angle, can make an effective topic. Here are a few guidelines, however, for avoiding certain types of topics that would be difficult to turn into a good research paper.

Avoid Topics That Would Result in a Report Essay, Unless Your Assignment Calls for One. The question "Why is the sky blue?" would not make a good topic for most assignments because it has been answered to everyone's satisfaction. Any general science book or encyclopedia provides the same general explanation. The same holds true for seemingly more complex questions such as "How does vitamin C help the body fight disease?" "Why did the popes leave Rome for southern France in the 1300s?" or even "Why did Guiteau shoot President Garfield?" (Perhaps no one really knows the answer to the last question, but historians — the experts — agree on one view of the event.)

When you start to form a topic, it may be natural to slip into a "report" mode. However, if your assignment requires analysis or argument (usually the case), you should avoid research questions with a single accepted answer.

Avoid Topics That Rely on Personal Opinion, Personal Belief, or Unverifiable Observation. Typically, the following research questions would not lead to workable topics:

"Is poetry a higher art form than the novel?"

"Was Muhammad Ali the greatest boxer ever?"

"Did a divine entity create life as we know it?"

"Is financial success worthwhile?"

We are not saying that these issues are not important. Some of them may be more important to more people than any topic you will write about. However, such questions can only be resolved by each individual in the light of his or her personal values.

Similarly, beware of topics involving the paranormal (UFOs and ESP, for example). The problem here is that almost all the sources consist of personal accounts of occult phenomena or weird experiences. That is not to say that good topics cannot be found in these subject areas. However, you must choose a research topic carefully to avoid simply reporting the fanciful opinions and accounts of the kind frequently published in popular magazines. The subject *UFOs* could lead to a reasonable topic such as *the Air Force's response to reports of UFO sightings.* (Question: "Are they hiding something, perhaps to avoid public panic or to keep new weapons secret?") The subject *ESP* could lead to the topic *scientific techniques for investigating ESP.* (Question: "Have scientists found any reason to consider parapsychology a valid field of study?")

Doing Background Reading or Preliminary Research

Until you feel certain that you have a good topic, take time to do some background reading in the subject area. Look up your subject or topic in such general reference works as these:

- encyclopedias
- biographical dictionaries

- surveys, textbooks, or general Web sites on wide areas such as Eastern religions, Native Americans, business administration, or English literature

For example, if your subject is *astronomy* and your idea for a topic is *the beginning of the universe,* you could do the following:

- Look up "universe" in the *Encyclopedia Americana* or an encyclopedia of science.
- Read the section on astronomy in an atlas such as *Earth and Man.*
- Read ahead, or reread, the section on astronomy in your textbook if you are writing the paper for an earth science course.
- Find a good Web site on astronomy, such as the astronomy page on the Science@NASA Web site at <http://science.msfc.nasa.gov/Astronomy.htm>.

The purpose behind preliminary research, or background reading, is to make sure you have the best topic within your subject area. A number of possibilities are likely to appear during your background reading. The student who wrote about Cotton Mather discovered several reasonable topics in the *Encyclopedia Americana,* as we shall see in Chapter 3.

Even if your original idea for a topic was a fine one, do not skip this preliminary step. It is important to refresh your knowledge of the subject to make you aware of the many facts and ideas your research will uncover.

Tips for Effective Background Reading

- *Do not read entire books* during preliminary research. For instance, if your subject is *Martin Luther King Jr.,* do not begin by reading a full-length biography. Because you have not yet settled on a topic, most of the book will not be directly relevant to whatever topic you eventually choose. Even if you have a definite topic in mind, such as *King's relationship with militant black leaders,* you should first review King's career as a civil rights activist in an encyclopedia or a biographical dictionary.
- *Look for a list of sources for further reading* at the end of encyclopedia articles and other reference works. Jot down these titles for future reference. They may be useful as sources for your paper.
- *Take notes you can refer to later* if you need to revise your topic or hypothesis. In taking these notes, avoid recording detailed factual information. Concentrate instead on major ideas and possible topics. You do not want your search for a topic to become lost in a flood of facts.

Brainstorming to Find a Topic

Another approach to finding a strong topic is an exercise called brainstorming. If you are already fairly familiar with your subject area, a little brainstorming may turn up several good possibilities for research. *Brainstorming* consists of wide-open, no-holds-barred thinking about some subject, in which your mind is free to generate many ideas, some good, some not so good. Because you are looking for a problem to investigate, these ideas may well come to you as questions. You may want to find a partner for this exercise; brainstorming with someone else can be especially helpful.

Tips for Effective Brainstorming

1. Record every thought, large or small, either in shorthand notes or, better yet, on an audiotape. Do not reject any idea, even if it sounds irrelevant or silly or otherwise useless.

2. Stop after ten or fifteen minutes and review your notes or the tape. Decide which ideas seem most promising.

3. Put all the material aside overnight and review it again in a fresh light the next day.

Let's look at an example of what one student produced when she unleashed her mind on what was for her a fairly familiar subject, *dinosaurs.*

What exactly was a dinosaur? How do we know what it was, aside from the bones? When did people first find dinosaur bones? Where did dinosaurs live? What did they eat? Did any other creatures prey on them? What caused dinosaurs to die out? How long were they around? Did they evolve from earlier life forms? From sharks? From little lizards? Are crocodiles really modern dinosaurs? Are there any other dinosaurs around now, possibly in some unexplored jungle or on a deserted island? Someone said birds evolved from dinosaurs — are they right? What caused the extinction of dinosaurs? Did they just become too big? But what about the smaller ones? Did they run out of food? If so, how could that happen? Did they become unfit for survival? How? Were other creatures smarter than they were? How could we know how smart they were? Their brains were probably larger than ours. How do we know about these long-gone beasts? Or don't we know? Is it all guesswork? Do we find each skeleton all in one spot, or do we assemble possible skeletons from a mixed heap of bones? How come no animals are that big today (except whales)? Why are today's lizards and other reptiles no larger than alligators?

Obviously, this student had to know something about this subject or she couldn't have produced so much specific material. Notice that she returned to some points but that other ideas led to dead ends.

Did you see several themes recurring throughout the notes?

- Why did dinosaurs become extinct? Topic: *cause of extinction.*
- What exactly was (or is) a dinosaur? Topic: *their place in evolution.*
- How do we know what we say we know? Topic: *the basis of our knowledge of prehistoric creatures.*

Any of the three topics would do just fine because these questions have no simple, uncontroversial answers.

Four Students Find Their Topics

We asked the writers of the four papers in Chapter 22 to describe how they got started. Their approaches were not identical, but all four led to worthwhile research projects. The only thing they had in common was a consultation with their teachers.

Fred Hutchins

While in high school, Fred Hutchins had seen a television program about the Salem witch hunt of 1692. The half-hour program was, of necessity, superficial, and it managed to provide little more than an overview of the witchcraft hysteria and trials. Nonetheless, the program sparked Fred's interest in Cotton Mather, a powerful Puritan minister involved in the witch trials.

Several years later, Fred enrolled in a history course called Witchcraft in America that included a unit on the Salem witch hunts. From the first day of class, Fred mulled over the possibility of doing research on Cotton Mather. When his instructor asked for possible topics for research papers, Fred saw an opportunity to learn more about Mather.

In an after-class discussion, the instructor asked Fred what he particularly wanted to learn about Cotton Mather. Fred realized that "Cotton Mather" was far too broad to be considered a workable topic, so he narrowed that down to "Cotton Mather and the Salem witch trials." The instructor said that although this topic still seemed too broad, it did provide Fred with a starting point for his background reading.

The instructor then offered Fred some advice: "I think you need to do some reading about Mather that uncovers a controversy or some other angle that you can dig into — maybe a specific question about Mather's character that you'd like to answer for yourself." The instructor suggested that Fred begin his background reading with the *Encyclopedia Americana.* Here is the encyclopedia's Cotton Mather entry, reproduced in its entirety. Marginal notes point out how Fred used the article to help him find an interesting and workable topic.

Fred notes that Mather was a theologian as well as a minister. He wonders about the connections between Mather's religious beliefs and his involvement in the witchcraft hysteria.

MATHER, math́ ər Cotton (1663–1728), American clergyman, theologian, and author. The eldest son of Increase Mather and the grandson of Richard Mather, he was born in Boston, Mass., on Feb. 12, 1663. He graduated from Harvard in 1678, received his M.A. in 1681, and in 1685 joined his father at the Second Church in Boston, where he served until his death.

Fred realizes this paragraph deals with matters about which he knows little. He doesn't expect this paragraph will be useful.

Mather was active in the rebellion in 1689 against Sir Edmund Andros, royal governor of Massachusetts, and wrote the manifesto of the insurgents. He vigorously defended the new Massachusetts charter of 1691 and supported Sir William Phipps, appointed governor by King William III at the request of Increase Mather.

Fred reads carefully here because the material refers to the subject of his interest. He also jots down "spectral evidence" because he wants to learn what it means. Fred notes Mather's humane attitude toward accused witches and considers exploring the reasons why Mather took this position. After reading about Mather's "popular reputation," Fred notes how this seems to contradict evidence of Mather's humane attitude.

During the witchcraft excitement of 1692, Cotton Mather wrote the ministers' statement exhorting the judges to be cautious in their use of "spectral evidence" against the accused, and he believed that "witches" might better be treated by prayer and fasting than by punitive legal action. In spite of this, Mather's popular reputation is that of a fomenter of the witchcraft hysteria who rejoiced in the trials and the executions. He was ardently interested in what he believed to be witchcraft, and his writing and preaching may have stimulated the hysterical fear of "witches" revealed at Salem, Mass., in 1692. In writing about the trials he defended the judges and their procedure more than seems consistent with his earlier warnings against "spectral evidence." He was no doubt unwise in helping to keep the witchcraft excitement alive, but the idea that he was a ruthless tormentor of the innocent is not justified by the evidence. If the court had paid more attention to his advice some lives might have been saved. The witchcraft trials ended before he was 30; most of the achievements that made him the most famous of American Puritans came later.

Fred notes Mather's defense of the witchcraft judges: Was Mather confused about how he regarded witches?

Renowned as a preacher, man of letters, scientist, and scholar in many fields, he read widely and wrote more than 450 books. The most celebrated is the *Magnalia Christi Americana* (1702), an "ecclesiastical" history of New England and the most important literary and scholarly work produced in the American colonies during their first century. It shows an amazing range of erudition and great stylistic skill.

Fred is impressed by Mather's accomplishments. Was it unusual for a person of such learning to believe in witches?

Mather's interest in science is revealed principally in other books, notably *The Christian Philosopher* (1721). He admired Sir Isaac Newton, advocated inoculation for smallpox when it was generally regarded as a dangerous and godless practice, and wrote one of the earliest known descriptions of plant hybridization. He was one of the few American colonists elected to the Royal Society of London and probably was better known abroad than any of his countrymen before Jonathan Edwards and Benjamin Franklin.

From the mixture of characteristics given in this paragraph, Fred concludes that Mather was a complicated person. Is it possible that his fascination with witches had something to do with his erratic personality?

Mather was vain, ambitious, hot-tempered, and sometimes a pedant, but had genuine piety and worked tirelessly for moral reform. His tolerance increased with age, and his later thinking moved somewhat away from the strict Puritan orthodoxy of the seventeenth century toward the rationalistic and deistic ideas of the eighteenth. He died in Boston on Feb. 13, 1728.

KENNETH B. MURDOCK
Author of "Literature and Theology in Colonial New England"

Bibliography

Fred now turns to the bibliography that followed the article to get a head start on his search for sources.

Breitweiser, Mitchell R., *Cotton Mather and Benjamin Franklin* (Cambridge 1985).

Holmes, Thomas J., *Cotton Mather: A Bibliography of His Works*, 3 vols. (1940; reprint, Crofton Pub. 1974).

Levin, David, *Cotton Mather: The Young Life of the Lord's Remembrancer* (Harvard Univ. Press 1978).

Middelkauf, Robert, *The Mathers: Three Generations of Puritan Intellectuals, 1596–1728* (Oxford 1971).

Silverman, Kenneth, *The Life and Times of Cotton Mather* (Harper 1984).

Wendell, Barrett, *Cotton Mather: The Puritan Priest* (1981; reprint, Arden Library 1978).

Wood, James P., *The Admirable Cotton Mather* (Seabury 1971).

After finishing the article, Fred saw that he had several good potential topics:

- a possible connection between Mather's religious beliefs and his attitude toward witches
- Mather's humane stance toward accused witches
- the origin of Mather's popular reputation as a bloodthirsty witch hunter
- Mather's intense interest in witchcraft and the possibility that this interest may have fanned the hysteria
- Mather's possibly confused attitude toward witches
- Mather's erratic personality as a source of his fascination with witches
- Mather's later change of view toward the outbreak of hysteria

In the end, Fred decided that the question he had asked himself several times — "What did Cotton Mather believe about witches and witchcraft?" — held the most interest for him. Looking ahead to further reading, Fred submitted *what the Salem witches actually meant to Cotton Mather* as his topic.

Note the short list of titles under the heading "Bibliography" at the end of the encyclopedia article. Always be sure to note this information during background reading because it can give you some good leads on finding potential sources. Fred used several of the books on this particular list for his paper on Cotton Mather.

Shirley Macalbe

Shirley Macalbe found her topic during a sociology class discussion of immigration. Although the discussion revolved around the great waves of immigration during the early part of the twentieth century, several students commented on the large influx of foreigners into the United States during recent years. Some students described the changing characters of their neighborhoods. Others questioned the ability of the country to absorb so many new people. A few students defended the right of the newcomers to be in the United States, arguing that everybody in the room had immigrant roots of one sort or another.

The instructor informed the class that the recent upsurge in immigration was indeed a controversial issue in the United States today. She also said that similar controversies about the wisdom of allowing great numbers of people to immigrate to America had arisen during earlier periods in the nation's history.

Shirley, who had not had much luck thinking about a topic for the required research paper, found herself interested in the spirited discussion of the new immigrants. She wanted to draw a topic for her research paper from the controversy, but she wondered whether the subject was too current for her to find enough authoritative sources. Consulting with her instructor after class, she learned that experts were already studying the newcomers' impact on the country and their prospects for success. Satisfied that the project could prove fruitful, she settled on the topic *are the new immigrants an asset or a burden?*

Susanna Andrews

Finding a topic consumed less time in Susanna Andrews's case. While taking a course in American literature, she had been excited by Emily Dickinson's rather mystical poetry. In thinking about a possible topic for her paper, Susanna remembered reading in the introduction to her textbook that Dickinson "did not write for publication and was easily discouraged from it." Only eight of her nearly eighteen hundred poems appeared in print during her lifetime. This point had also been made (noting *six* instead of *eight*) in *The Oxford Companion to American Literature,* a standard background resource that Susanna consulted.

In lectures, her instructor had painted a fascinating picture of this remarkable woman, and Susanna had no trouble finding an account of

Dickinson's life in the biographical dictionary *Notable American Women*. Once Susanna thought she knew a fair amount about her subject, she reviewed her notes and discovered that one idea for a topic persisted in her thoughts about the poet and her work: *her failure to publish her poetry*.

Susanna naturally wondered why such a great poet had published so few of her works. Consulting her instructor, she learned that the question had not been decisively resolved, so Susanna confidently chose as her topic *Emily Dickinson's reluctance to publish her poems*.

David Perez

David Perez was taking a course called Current Issues in Ecology, for which the instructor assigned several "research essays," giving students a rather limited set of subjects from which to choose. The papers were expected to run from four to seven pages. David's choice, *the disruptive effects of a transplanted species on its new environment*, left just one point undefined — which species to investigate.

While reading his textbook, David had found ants, especially army ants, very interesting. His instructor pointed out that army ants cannot be considered "transplanted" when they march across the jungle floor, destroying everything in their path. But the instructor thought that, nevertheless, ants were a good species to examine for this project. Reading an encyclopedia on CD-ROM in the library led David to a ferocious ant species that was likely to have received a good deal of attention for the way it disrupted the ecosystem to which it had been accidentally transplanted.

As you can see, no hypothesis was needed because the scope of the research had been so clearly defined by the instructor's wording of the subject. David's topic was *the harmful effects of [his species of ant] being introduced to a foreign environment*. (The guiding word for his research would be *harmful*.)

Notice that if David had begun with a broader subject — for example, *introducing species to new environments* — he would have had to consider various possible results, good and bad, of such transplantings. Some species become extinct in their new habitat, some destroy parts of it, some improve conditions, and some make an interesting adaptation. David's instructor had cut through all that background research and produced a list of subjects that were easily converted to topics.

This assignment was certainly easier to research than those completed by the other students whose work we have been following. We include this kind of research assignment because it is different, although not unusual, and because it illustrates the APA style of documentation (described in Chapter 19).

3

Moving from Topic to Hypothesis

We have been discussing the choice of a topic as though you had to complete this step before moving on to the next one: forming a hypothesis. In practice, however, you should be thinking about a hypothesis while you are looking for your topic. This is only natural when you consider that *the topic raises unanswered questions and the hypothesis predicts possible answers*. For example,

topic	What the witches meant to Cotton Mather.
hypothesis	Cotton Mather accepted the existence of witches because such a belief was deeply embedded in the culture of his time.
topic	New immigrants: Are they an asset or a burden?
hypothesis	If we look at the history of U.S. immigration, we can believe that these people will be just as successful as earlier immigrants.

Research can be made easier if you form a hypothesis as early as possible because the topic alone will not be strong enough to guide you through this complex process. The main problem is that the topic by itself offers little help when you are trying to decide whether a potential source is useful. Your research will uncover a great deal of information that touches on your topic in some way or other, but unless you have some idea of where you are going with the topic, it will be hard to tell which ideas and facts will play a definite role in the paper. Your notes will begin to look like a very long grocery list. If you tried to write a paper based on such loosely related materials, the result would lack focus and direction.

It would be impossible to form a thesis that could make sense of all the information. Such a paper would do little more than show you had spent a lot of time doing research.

Benefits of a Hypothesis

Because the hypothesis is a prediction of your eventual thesis, you can always modify the hypothesis as you read your sources and learn more about the topic. In fact, you should plan to review the hypothesis periodically throughout the research. Although the hypothesis may prove to be more or less inaccurate when you have completed all the research, the following are good reasons for starting out with a hypothesis.

First, the hypothesis points you in the right direction. It indicates the specific questions you need answers for. As you look for information that either supports or refutes your hypothesis, you move closer to the well-supported assertion that will become your thesis.

Second, the hypothesis tests the thoroughness of your research. If your conclusions are to be considered reasonable, you must consult a variety of sources representing different points of view. Seek controversy; don't avoid it. Do not try to defend your original hypothesis by using only those sources that support it. Your mission is to present readers with a comprehensive view, giving them enough information to evaluate your conclusions intelligently.

If you are investigating the theory that intelligence (IQ) is measurable and inherited, for example, you cannot restrict your search to *The Bell Curve,* by Richard J. Herrnstein and Charles Murray, plus the writings of E. O. Wilson, Arthur Jensen, and other advocates of this theory. You need to find experts such as Steven Rose, Howard Gardner, and Stephen Jay Gould, who are less convinced of, if not downright opposed to, this theory.

Of course, you may interpret information differently than other writers, depending on your own beliefs, experiences, and style of thinking. Based on these factors, your topic might result in a variety of possible thesis sentences by the time the paper is finished:

argument for IQ tests	Intelligence is an inherited trait that is measurable with standard tests; it is also one of the main determinants of social success.
argument against IQ tests	IQ tests are inaccurate and useless when it comes to measuring true abilities.
analysis of IQ tests	Certain types of abilities, such as computational and linguistic skill, can be measured more easily than other types. Therefore, these more measurable types are often called "intelligence."

Although each thesis expresses a different finding, each should reflect (and the paper's development should clearly show) that the writer weighed the information and became familiar with all sides of the question.

Finally, the hypothesis helps ensure that the paper fulfills its purpose. If you have been assigned to write an argument, but your hypothesis is a statement of fact that raises no debate, you may be headed toward turning in a report instead of the type of paper required. Try adding controversy or analysis to a merely informative hypothesis.

report hypothesis	Advertising helps to shape the behaviors of Americans.
argument hypothesis	Because advertising has the power to shape behaviors, courses on advertising awareness should be made mandatory in high school.
report hypothesis	Modern health care can be extremely expensive because of the cost of medical equipment.
analysis hypothesis	Health-care costs today are so high largely because of the development of expensive medical equipment that benefits only 2 percent of patients.

Keep in mind that you have a limited amount of time to spend finding sources, reading them, and taking notes. You will need a hypothesis to help you decide which ideas and facts in each source will be most useful in your effort to cover the topic thoroughly, intelligently, and in a way consistent with your paper's purpose.

Arriving at a Hypothesis by Brainstorming

Brainstorming can be as useful for arriving at a hypothesis as it can for deciding on a topic. Here are two examples.

Example 1: Dinosaurs' Extinction

The student who had brainstormed about dinosaurs was able, after a little background reading, to reject several potential topics. She discarded *the basis of our knowledge* and *what dinosaurs really were* because she was not very interested in either topic, but the extinction problem seemed likely to lead to some exciting ideas, some of which had been mentioned in her background reading.

After she had settled on *causes for dinosaurs' extinction*, another brainstorming session helped her form a hypothesis. Here are her notes.

Did the evolution of smaller, smarter animals somehow lead to the extinction of the slow-witted dinosaurs? Were these new creatures mammals? Or did major climatic changes bring about the extinction by eliminating the trop-ical swamplands in which the dinosaurs thrived? How fast might such changes take place? Could a meteor striking the Earth cause such a change? Or did deadly radiation from an exploding nearby star do them in? In either case, wouldn't some have survived? Or did dinosaurs become so large they could not find enough food in their environment? Were they the victims of a deadly virus? Or a fatal genetic mutation?

All these ideas made sense; her background reference materials did not take a stand on the question, and without reading all the sources, she could not judge the relative merits of the theories. She decided, therefore, to go with the newest idea: "Radiation from an exploded star caused the Great Extinction." This became her hypothesis.

(Her hypothesis took another turn, however. After reading all her sources, she decided that equal support had to be given to the theory that a meteor had hit the earth 65 million years ago, drastically cooling the atmosphere and killing off the dinosaurs.)

Example 2: Alcoholism Therapies

After some background reading, another student narrowed the sub-ject *alcoholism* to the topic *treatment of alcohol addiction.* A bit of brainstorm-ing at that point produced the following notes:

> How well do support therapies such as Alcoholics Anonymous work in their efforts to treat alcoholism? Does the addict have to be religiously in-clined for such therapies to work? How successful are aversion therapies that use chemicals to make liquor repellent? Doesn't the effect wear off? How effective are cognitive therapies that try to get alcoholics to stop drinking by showing them films of their own drunken behavior? Is psychotherapy able to treat alcoholism by helping the patients understand the unconscious reasons for their drinking? How would knowing why you drink help you stop?

Again, we find someone faced with several possible answers to his research question. However, this student could see no grounds for choos-ing any one of them while still in the preliminary research stage. Also, he had personal reasons for doubting whether any method offered success-ful treatment. So he took a neutral position that expressed his intuition: "Of the four most common alcoholism therapies, none seems to have con-vinced its critics that it offers a strong likelihood of success."

The student did not feel committed to this pessimistic view; he hoped that his sources would show him good reason to believe that one of the approaches was better than the others. Considerable research into this problem, however, did not fulfill this hope. Eventually, his thesis read:

"The success of a particular alcoholism therapy depends almost entirely on the personality of the individual addict."

By the way, other students who chose the same topic of alcoholism therapies arrived at somewhat different conclusions (theses). Your thesis will depend on what sources you find and what you, as an individual reader, discover in them.

Four Students Form and Revise Their Hypotheses

What about the writers of our sample research papers? They moved from topic to hypothesis in different ways.

Fred Hutchins: Developing a Hypothesis through Skimming Sources

Although Fred Hutchins was happy with his topic, *what the witches meant to Cotton Mather,* he could not see a reasonable hypothesis in the encyclopedia article or his textbook. So he took to skimming a few of his sources, looking for comments about this question.

The first few writers tended to agree that Mather's belief in witches was not at all unusual, considering the times in which he lived. In late-seventeenth-century America, almost everyone, intellectuals included, believed in witches. True, Mather's interest in witches was particularly intense because he liked to delve into subjects that challenged his intellect and imagination. This led Fred to the following hypothesis: "Cotton Mather accepted the existence of witches because such a belief was deeply embedded in the culture of his time."

Shirley Macalbe: Developing a Hypothesis through Interviewing

Shirley Macalbe's topic, *the new immigrants: asset or burden?*, grew out of a class discussion in which students expressed strong opinions about the impact the newest wave of immigrants was having on their city and on the United States as a whole. Because it had been her fellow students who had aroused her interest in the subject, Shirley decided to interview a number of them, with the idea of gathering impressions related to her topic. She thought the interviews might also help her develop a hypothesis to test against the sources she would find in the library.

After analyzing the results of her interviews, Shirley leaned slightly toward the hypothesis "the immigrants were becoming a burden to the country." Of course, she knew that the students' opinions might not hold up in the face of expert research, opinion, and theory.

Once she began reading sources, Shirley found that her interviewees had touched on several issues that the experts also discussed in some detail. However, the experts gave less weight to the students' greatest concerns and provided insights into other issues that seemed more likely to determine the answer to Shirley's question, "Are immigrants an asset or a burden?" She moved fairly soon to a revised hypothesis: "If we look at the history of U.S. immigration, we can believe that these people will be just as successful as earlier immigrants."

Susanna Andrews: Developing a Hypothesis through Brainstorming

Susanna thought she had a good topic, *Emily Dickinson's reluctance to publish her poems,* but her background reading offered only a vague suggestion that the poet's not publishing her poems grew out of her eccentric character. If that was the only answer to the question, Susanna's topic was too weak to pursue. She then brainstormed to see whether she had good reason to continue. Developing a better hypothesis would indicate that the topic was worth the effort. Here are a few notes from her brainstorming session:

> Why didn't Dickinson publish most of her poems? Why would any poet do that? Did she think they weren't good enough? Didn't she know how great her poems were? Or did she write them for her own pleasure only? Was she too shy to let other people see her thoughts? Who did she let read them? Her family, her friends, or other writers? What did these readers say? Did she ever *try* to have the poems published? Why did she write poetry anyway? What did writing mean to her? What might publication have done for her, or her poems? How did the poems eventually get published?

These notes did not immediately yield a satisfying hypothesis, but as Susanna reviewed her lecture notes, she recalled her professor talking about Dickinson's idealistic attitude toward the art of poetry and toward herself as an artist. When Susanna read some of the poems, these lines caught her eye: "The Soul selects her own Society / Then — shuts the Door — . . . ." Remembering her background reading notes, which said the poet was extremely shy, Susanna decided on the hypothesis "Emily Dickinson chose not to publish most of her poems because she was a shy, reclusive person, more interested in her art than in winning public praise." This hypothesis forced Susanna when reading literary criticism to focus on those comments and facts that shed light on the poet's character and her deep concerns regarding publication.

David Perez: Using Data-Driven Research as a Hypothesis

David Perez, the student who wrote about ants, had no problem finding a hypothesis because of the nature of his assignment. Being so sharply focused, his assigned topic did the work of a hypothesis.

In short, as you can see from reading the full papers in Chapter 22, each student's hypothesis was only a beginning. In each case, research into specific sources disclosed additional information and persuasive reasons for coming to a somewhat different conclusion (thesis). Nevertheless, the students' hypotheses served them well as guides through the difficult steps of finding sources and extracting useful information from them.

Reviewing Part One

The following questions and exercises will help you reinforce and practice the skills covered in Part One. For additional practice, visit <bedfordstmartins.com/writingresearch>.

Questions

1. Explain the difference between a subject and a topic, as the terms are used in this book.
   - What is your primary concern when choosing a subject?
   - What must be your first concern when looking for a topic?

2. Which of the following items seem likely to work well as topics for research papers? Explain why you reject each item that seems to have poor potential. (Some are too broad for a paper seven to ten pages long, others would require no more than reading an encyclopedia to complete a full investigation, and others are too deeply involved with personal values or deal with areas about which there is no concrete knowledge.)
   - working women in the United States today
   - the way FM radio signals are sent and received
   - the effect of robot machines on workers in heavy industries
   - the invention of gunpowder in China
   - treatments for breast cancer
   - the role of the pharmaceutical industry in AIDS research
   - the history of the Congo since independence
   - programs for prevention of child abuse
   - the role of parents in teenage alcoholism
   - the use of computers in small businesses today
   - the effectiveness of capital punishment in reducing violent crime
   - the solution to Russia's economic woes
   - the effect of illegal immigration on the economy of the Southwest
   - the effect of high salaries on the quality of major-league baseball
   - the ability of some people to see the future in their dreams

3. What is the value of brainstorming? At which point(s) in the research process is this activity likely to help you?

4. What is the purpose of background reading? If you know your topic from the start, should you skip this step?

5. Why is it a good idea to look for a controversy of some sort when trying to think of a topic?

6. Why is it important to know the purpose of your paper when forming a hypothesis?

7. Why do you need to form a hypothesis if you have an excellent topic? How does a hypothesis help at various stages of research?

Exercises

1. Read the following article on Emma Goldman, which comes from *Feminist Writers,* an excellent background resource available online through the Gale Group *Biography Resource Center* database. Take notes, much like those described in the margins of the Cotton Mather article earlier in this chapter, identifying several potential topics suitable for a seven- to ten-page research paper. For each topic, think of a reasonable hypothesis.

> **Emma Goldman**
> **Birth:** June 27, 1869 in Kovno, Lithuania
> **Death:** May 14, 1940 in Toronto, Ontario, Canada
> **Nationality:** Russian
> **Occupation:** Writer
>
> **BIOGRAPHICAL ESSAY**
> Called "Red Emma" and a "most dangerous woman," spirited and rebellious Emma Goldman stood for freedom and the individual. Impacted by the events of the Haymarket bombing in Chicago and the martyrdom of immigrant radicals shortly after her arrival in America from Russia in 1886, Goldman became a vocal anarchist. Throughout her thirty-year residency in the United States, she crossed the country, energetically addressing issues of concern — especially those addressing women's rights. Despite police interference and occasional arrest, Goldman attracted large audiences as she advocated birth control, elevated the position of the "working girl," and criticized the deplorable economic situation that, she believed, forced many young women into prostitution.
>
> Goldman's birth in Russia was neither welcomed nor happy. Her mother, trapped in an arranged marriage shortly after being widowed, feared pregnancy; with two daughters from her first marriage, she did not want the additional strain of more children. Goldman's father, disappointed by the birth of a girl, would physically and verbally abuse Emma throughout her growing years. A sad and isolated child, Goldman sought the individual within herself; she would emerge from her tragic beginnings to fight repression and encourage women to stop being victims of their own female circumstances.

During her childhood, Goldman secretly read many novels and radical political books. She idolized revolutionary women and Russian nihilists and believed that she, too, could stop the injustices in her native country. Unable to attend medical school and facing an arranged marriage herself, Goldman fled Russia for the United States, where her radical ideology would crystallize.

Her years spent in her adopted country would be newsworthy ones: arrested for agitation in 1893, accused of involvement in President McKinley's assassination, forced underground and deported, Goldman became almost notorious. Goldman would express her anarchist viewpoints in *Mother Earth,* a journal she founded in 1903 and edited with her lover, the anarchist Alexander Berkman. The journal featured established authors such as Ibsen and Whitman and introduced new artists and literary talents as well. Publication would cease in 1917 when its editorial board — Goldman and Berkman — was arrested for opposing the conscription of young men during World War I. After serving her two-year sentence Goldman would be exiled; although she longed to return to the United States she would only be permitted a three-month stay in 1934 for a lecture tour. Goldman's anarchist stance was misunderstood by many; in *My Disillusionment with Russia* she claimed that her vision of anarchy was constructive rather than destructive, as she was so perceived.

Anarchy without violence and the drive to achieve individual rights for women were related ideologies, according to Goldman, who pursued both vigorously. Within her writings she maintained that women needed to loosen the bonds which held them psychologically. Four feminist essays in *Anarchism and Other Essays* — "Marriage and Love," "Woman Suffrage," "The Traffic in Women," and "The Tragedy of Woman's Emancipation" — stressed this theme, describing the constant victimization that women endured. Goldman wrote in a direct style, confrontational rather than mollifying, and she ended each essay with a brief but emotionally focused finale.

Although twice married, Goldman denounced the institution of marriage as destructive to woman's identity. In an interview for the *St. Louis Post Dispatch* she stated that when married women lost their names they became the "servant, the mistress, and the slave of both husband and children." Instead of a married state, Goldman promoted free love. To her, free love referred not to indiscriminate sex but to mutuality in a relationship. Her essay "Marriage and Love" related that women should not look to marriage as an ultimate goal but should seek free love in liberating themselves and finding their individuality. Because she felt that love was "the strongest and deepest element in all life," Goldman believed that a relationship should not be one of dependency, but rather of separate and equal existence.

Goldman realized that free love required that women have access to birth control to prevent pregnancy, thus avoid the dangers of abortion. Skilled as both a nurse and midwife, she had seen firsthand how women's health was endangered by frequent pregnancies. Goldman vehemently crusaded on behalf of women's right to dictate what happened to their own bodies, writing the pamphlet *Why and How the Poor Should Not Have So Many Children.* She was jailed for two weeks after distributing contraception information alongside birth-control advocate Margaret Sanger in 1915. The uncompromising efforts of both Goldman and Sanger would pave the way for the free access by women to information on contraception methods, as well as the nationwide formation of birth control clinics. In her *The Traffic in Women and Other Essays on Feminism,* Goldman took on the issue of prostitution, stating that a correlation existed between a woman's substandard wages and her need to exchange her sexual favors for money. In fact, argued Goldman, economic necessity was not only the motive behind prostitution; it was the basis of marriage. Contending that women had not yet fully realized their oppressed condition, she noted that they erroneously imagined that full rights would be gained by winning the vote.

The essay "Woman Suffrage" exemplified Goldman's belief that even with the power to vote, women would still be bound to oppression and the home, where the "life-energy of woman" was sapped. Concerned with the plight of women workers, Goldman did not dispute that women should be eligible to vote but she did not agree that it gave women true emancipation. "The Tragedy of Woman's Emancipation" portrayed women's right to vote as superficial because, while it gave women equal opportunity to compete professionally with men, they were ill-equipped for the task because they had not been trained to be competitive. Goldman also disagreed with several of her prominent feminist contemporaries who had a puritanical view of sex, encouraged chastity, and banished men from their existence. Goldman dismissed this "New Woman" and although she agreed that a woman should not be treated as a sex commodity she believed that women should not repress their healthy sexual instincts, which had too few outlets in civilized society.

Emma Goldman was a woman of restless ambition who attempted to meld the forces of the free individual with a cooperative spirit. A compelling orator, she delivered her powerful message to audiences around the world. Yet, unhappily, no recordings of Goldman's spirited speeches have survived. Her legacy remains in essays, in her autobiography *Living My Life,* in memoirs, and in letters that provide modern readers with a clear picture of the woman who sought justice in a unified world and demanded personal liberty for men and women equally.

FURTHER READINGS
Media Adaptations
Emma Goldman (film), Toronto, Avco Embassy, 1975.

Bibliography
Rebel in Paradise: A Biography of Emma Goldman by Richard Drinnon, Chicago, University of Chicago Press, 1961.

Manuscript Collections

Labadie Collection, University of Michigan Library; New York Public Library; Yale University Library; University of Illinois Library, Chicago Circle; Schlesinger Library, Radcliffe College; International Institute for Social History, Amsterdam; Emma Goldman Web site at http://sunsite.berkeley.edu/Goldman/.

Critical Studies

"What Is There in Anarchy for Woman?" (interview), in *St. Louis Post Dispatch Sunday Magazine,* 24 October 1897

Emma Goldman: A Challenging Rebel by Joseph Ishill, Berkeley Heights, New Jersey, Oriole Press, 1957.

Rebel in Paradise: A Biography of Emma Goldman by Richard Drinnon, Chicago, University of Chicago Press, 1961.

To the Barricades: The Anarchist Life of Emma Goldman by Alix Kates Shulman, New York, Crowell, 1971.

Love, Anarchy, and Emma Goldman by Candace Falk, New York, Holt, 1984, revised, New Brunswick, New Jersey, Rutgers University Press, 1990.

Emma Goldman: An Intimate Life by Alice Wexler, New York, Pantheon, 1984, as *Emma Goldman in America,* Boston, Beacon Press, 1984.

Emma Goldman by Martha Solomon, Boston, Twayne, n.d.

Emma Goldman: American Individualist by John Chalberg, New York, HarperCollins, 1991.

Emma Goldman and the American Left: Nowhere at Home by Marian J. Morton, New York, Toronto, and London, Twayne, 1992.

Emma Goldman: Sexuality and the Impurity of the State by Bonnie Haaland, Montreal, Black Rose Books, 1993.

2. Choose a subject area from the following list, and then do enough background reading to find two or three potential topics for a seven- to ten-page research paper.

- alcoholism
- endangered species
- China-U.S. trade relations
- environmental controls on large industries
- safety and the auto industry
- group therapy for emotional problems
- problems in the U.S. prison system
- Mexican immigration to the United States
- religious movements in the United States since the 1960s
- artificial intelligence
- genetic experimentation
- the role of government in medical care

- preschool education
- toxic-waste disposal
- the new global economy
- U.S. government treatment of Native Americans
- ethnic conflicts in the former Yugoslavia
- legalized gambling
- South American rain forests
- the ozone layer and ultraviolet radiation
- U.S. immigration policy for Caribbean peoples
- the Arab-Israeli prospects for peace
- the U.S. economic boom of the 1990s
- affirmative action programs
- the U.S. embargo of Cuba
- IQ studies
- the war on drugs
- the use of special effects in movie making
- government involvement in issues concerning parents' rights
- the use of force by police in minority neighborhoods
- the tobacco industry
- the USA Patriot Act
- problems with capital punishment
- Harry Truman, controversial president
- Helen Keller, social activist of the early 1900s
- Malcolm X, militant African American leader of the 1960s
- Martin Luther King Jr., civil rights leader of the 1960s
- Eleanor Roosevelt, world leader in humanitarian issues

3. Start your own research paper now, following these steps:

   Step 1: Choose a subject — one of those listed in question 2 or any other that meets the requirements of this course.

   Step 2: Go to three or more background sources and find two to five potentially workable topics. (Record the titles of the sources, and take some notes as you read through them.)

   Step 3: Choose the topic that seems most interesting or most workable.

   Step 4: Try to form a hypothesis.

Part Two

Searching for Sources

4

Developing
a Research Strategy

After choosing a research topic and forming a hypothesis, you are ready to take the next step: identifying the kinds of sources that you will need and planning how to find them. This plan, or *research strategy*, will help you gather useful sources efficiently. A few promising sources may have already surfaced in your background reading and preliminary searches, but now you need to search on a wider scale and in a more informed way. This process will be easier if you first understand the various types of sources available, their strengths and limitations, and typical ways of finding and retrieving them. Because libraries hold many of these sources, particularly the ones that are the most useful to academic research, you must become familiar with the key role of libraries and librarians in the search process. Of course, your search may extend beyond the walls of libraries into specialized archives, television or radio programs, Internet sources, and field research such as interviews or surveys. This wealth of information is a great advantage of the Information Age, but it also requires that you develop general skills in searching for and evaluating information, skills that you can take with you anywhere. This chapter focuses on helping you develop these skills.

Types of Sources

The variety of information available today and the various ways to publish it (in print, electronically, on video, and so on) create an array of offerings that can seem bewildering in the early stages of research. It is sometimes tempting to explore only one or two types of sources, searching entirely on Web sites, for example, or relying too much on one or two books. In some cases, your assignment may specify the types of sources you can use. You may be required to focus on books and scholarly articles, or the assignment may restrict the use of Internet information. However, for most projects, it is best to consider using a variety of source types if your assignment allows it. Because different types of sources offer different advantages and disadvantages, using a diverse mix will help you explore your hypothesis more thoroughly and, ultimately, support your paper's thesis more effectively. Moreover, you will learn lifelong skills in searching through these media and incorporating the information into your thoughts and writing.

This section will help familiarize you with the most commonly used types of sources for a research paper and the strengths and limitations of each. Chapters 5 through 8 cover these sources in more detail, offering specific strategies for incorporating them into your search.

Books

Books in their current, mass-produced form have been around for over five hundred years, and they remain one of the most effective methods for transmitting complex ideas and detailed findings. Although electronic books exist, most books used for research projects appear in print.

Strengths. A book typically offers both broad coverage of its topic and a depth of detail unmatched in other sources. Because books are published selectively and their content is generally reviewed and edited for quality, they may require less critical evaluation for authority and credibility than other sources. In particular, scholarly book publishers, such as university presses, publish carefully documented work written by experts in the field. Books are portable and can be used in a variety of settings. Because they are referenced in library catalogs, relevant book sources are easy to identify, and a librarian can readily assist you.

Limitations. Books may not be as current as other sources. Because books can offer extensive information, it may be tempting to rely too much on the work of one or two authors; even if you find a comprehensive book, seek out other viewpoints. It is usually more difficult to search for specific details within a printed book than within shorter sources or within electronic media. Availability may be a problem; your library may not hold a book you want to use, or the book may be checked out. If you find yourself in this situation, consider requesting an interlibrary loan (see page 62).

Periodicals

Periodicals are publications that appear at regular intervals, such as magazines, professional journals, and newspapers. Print-based periodicals have been around for hundreds of years. Recently, increasing numbers of periodicals and periodical articles have become available online, especially in databases, and you will likely use these electronic versions in your research.

Strengths. If you have access to an online database that includes full-text articles or a library with large periodical holdings, articles are readily available and librarians can often assist you in your search. Currency is a great advantage of using periodicals, because they can be published much more quickly than books. You can easily find articles on events that happened last month, or even yesterday. Professional journals as well as some popular magazines and newspapers (*Atlantic Monthly, Scientific American,* and the *New York Times,* for example) offer credible, well-researched articles. Depending on the publication, both popular and scholarly articles may focus on a narrow topic in excellent detail. For example, a book about the world's food supply might include a chapter about innovations in agricultural production but only a paragraph or two about "farming" the ocean floor. However, you can probably find several recent periodical articles on ocean farming that cover the topic in much greater detail and depth.

Limitations. Topics covered in popular magazines may be influenced by advertising or may cater to the views of their primary audience. Because they are written for general rather than academic audiences, some popular magazine and newspaper articles may lack depth and background information. However, professional journals often use jargon or refer to background information, such as established studies, that are unfamiliar to researchers outside the field. Also, professional journals, many of which are still print based or offered on databases only for subscription, may be difficult to acquire if your library does not have an extensive periodical collection or provide access to full-text databases containing the publications you need.

Internet Sources

The Internet, a worldwide network of computers, has been in use for over thirty years. It is only within the last decade, however, that its use and popularity have increased greatly, and it has become an important media source for research writers. Today a vast amount of material is available online through a variety of Internet media such as e-mail, newsgroups, and, of course, the World Wide Web. This wealth of accessible information offers both benefits and unique challenges to researchers.

Strengths. Many researchers have easy access to the Internet either in a library or in their homes. Powerful search engines such as Google and Yahoo! retrieve links to a great amount of information very quickly.

General Web sites on almost any topic provide background information and can lead you to other sources that offer more specific material. Along with a growing amount of credible, well-researched information, the Internet contains a significant amount of anecdotal, first-person experiences. Although this anecdotal material may not provide full evidence for your paper's claims, first-person examples can help illustrate general concepts. Because it is easy to publish on the Web, well-developed alternative views on a variety of subjects can be found.

Limitations. The sheer amount of information available on the Internet can be challenging for many researchers. You may wonder what to do with the vast list of hits retrieved from a search or how to stay focused amid so many links. Information published on the Internet varies widely in terms of credibility. Search engines do not distinguish between peer-reviewed, edited material and that published by nonexperts. Therefore, you need to spend more time evaluating the credibility of these sources. Access to Web sources can be another limitation — some researchers do not have home access or proximity to a networked library.

Audiovisual Material

With the growth of the Internet and the continued predominance of books and periodicals in library holdings, it is easy to overlook nontext materials such as videotapes, DVDs, television or radio programs, photographs, and audio recordings. These types of sources, which are well-represented in many libraries, offer excellent material for many research projects.

Strengths. A great variety of audiovisual material is available — from hard news and documentaries to talk shows and films. Video or audio documentaries can provide excellent background information and may quickly help you establish the basics needed to dig more deeply into a topic. Visual images and sounds can carry information not easily transmitted in words, helping you understand situations in a more comprehensive way. For example, video of the collapse of the World Trade Center towers in New York City provides information about the horrific magnitude of the event that writing cannot convey. An audio interview allows you to hear voice inflection and intonation.

Limitations. Audiovisual sources require careful note-taking skills. If you cannot record the television or radio program, you may not be able to take down all the information you need. Because of limitations in programming or recording time, many audiovisual sources lack depth of detail when compared to print sources. Aside from public programming such as the Public Broadcasting System and National Public Radio, television and radio companies may be biased (even more than other media) toward corporate ownership, advertisers' perceptions, and audience ratings.

Field Research

Sometimes the best way to collect information on a topic is to do so directly, through field research. Field research includes interviews, surveys, direct observation of a situation, and other methods in which you become an active primary researcher.

Strengths. Interviews with experts can be a source of helpful background material, opinions, and in-depth information that you can use to support your thesis. Field research might also provide concrete details that bring your topic to life, conveying the actual experiences and perceptions of people affected by issues you are researching. Interviews with local people or observation of local events might help establish the relevance and immediacy of your topic for your audience. Because you design it yourself, field research can be customized to provide information you need but cannot find in other sources. Field research also allows you to make adjustments as you go; for example, you can ask for clarification of a point during an interview. Information you collect through direct observation needs less critical evaluation for bias because it has not been interpreted and presented by others.

Limitations. Unless you have extensive time to conduct field research, your findings may be limited in scope. Even brief interviews or simple surveys may take a surprising amount of time to carry out. If field research is not designed correctly, the information collected may be inconclusive or inaccurate. Check with your instructor to ensure you are using methods appropriate to your project's topic.

Personal Experience

Although research projects do not often focus primarily on your own experience, in some cases, depending on your instructor's guidelines, you may consider using personal experience as a source. If you have a personal connection to your topic, you may have firsthand experience that can be used to supplement researched information.

Strengths. Personal experience can add tangible detail to a project and introduce variety into the paper's discussion. For many writers, the inclusion of personal experience helps give the paper a clearer purpose. Likewise, some audiences may relate more strongly to a paper containing personal examples.

Limitations. Because research papers are conventionally written in an academic style, your instructor may limit the use of personal experience, which can give your paper an informal tone. Check with your instructor before using personal experience as a source; he or she may want you to write formal prose, a skill that will benefit you throughout college and beyond. The use of personal experience also presents the challenge of shifting between the first-person point of view (*I* or *we*) and the third-person point of view (*he, she, it, one,* or *they*). Firsthand experience is limited in scope, and you must be careful not to use it as proof of general ideas or conclusions.

The Role of Libraries and Librarians

Once you understand the types of sources that can be used for research writing, the next step is to become familiar with your library. Because libraries offer a wealth of print and nonprint sources, the closest good library is the best place to start identifying useful sources for your paper. Libraries still offer the collections traditionally associated with them: books and periodical holdings, special collections, print-based reference works, and audiovisual material. Libraries now also offer access to a significant amount of electronic media, such as full-text databases, electronic bibliographies, local databases, and access to Web sites. See Table 4-1 for an overview of the types of sources you will find in most libraries.

The reference section, which contains encyclopedias, bibliographies, biographies, statistical information, atlases, yearbooks, and discipline-specific resources that can help you establish basic background information on your topic, is one particularly useful area of the library. Reference sources cannot be checked out, so they are almost always available to you in the library. These sources are discussed in more detail in Chapters 5 and 6.

One of the most valuable sources of information in a library is the reference librarian. It is a good idea to introduce yourself to this person early in your research and to describe your project briefly. Librarians are professionals in information management. They are trained not only to manage libraries but also to keep current on all existing sources. Typically, reference librarians are the resident experts, for example, on online sources and search tools. Their job is to help people with research projects on any subject. They can tell you about any special resources your library offers and can often help you solve problems quickly that might take hours to solve on your own. The research librarian may even have assisted someone else working on a topic related to yours and may be able to give suggestions leading to valuable sources you might otherwise miss.

Keep in mind that although most librarians are quite willing to assist you with your research, they are not obliged to do the research for you.

Table 4-1   Types of Library Sources

Type of Source	Location	Search Tools
Books		
• Scholarly books • Biographies • Reference books (general and specialized encyclopedias, bibliographies, indexes, almanacs, atlases) • Trade books	• Stacks • Reference section	• Online library catalog
Periodicals		
• Scholarly and professional journals • Popular magazines • Newspapers	• Periodical collections • Microform collections • Full-text databases (LexisNexis, EBSCOhost, ProQuest)	• Periodical indexes and databases (to find specific articles) • Online library catalog (to locate periodicals the library owns)
Unpublished Sources		
• Manuscripts • Letters • Business and personal diaries	• Special collections	• Online library catalog • Reference librarian
Audiovisual and Multimedia Sources		
• Sound recordings • Video recordings • Visual images • CD-ROMs	• Media collections	• Online library catalog • Special Web collections

Searching for Sources

Do not go to the librarian and announce, "I have a paper to do for my American history course, but I don't know what to write about. Can you help me find some books?" The librarian has not attended your classes or read your textbooks and is therefore in no position to provide you with a topic. If you are having trouble finding a topic, see your instructor, not your librarian.

The Library's Home Page

Most libraries offer an electronic home page with links to the library catalog and other electronic resources (see Figure 4-1). Typically, computers in the library will display the home page when you begin a search session. If your library's home page is on the Web, you can probably

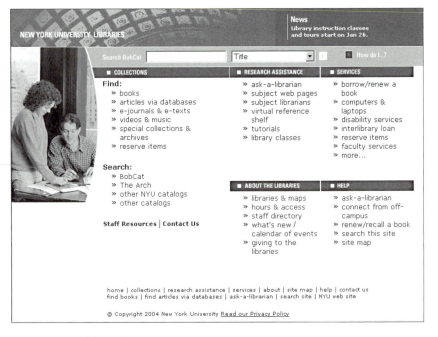

Figure 4-1   A library home page.

search the catalog and other electronic resources from computers outside the library.

Of course, libraries may also offer print-based resources to help you locate material. In many libraries, for example, bound periodical indexes such as the *Humanities Index* or the *Social Sciences Index* are important tools for finding periodical articles. See Chapter 6 for more information on these and other indexes.

The Data Record

As you begin to search for sources, you will notice clear contrasts in the function and appearance of each major electronic search tool — online library catalogs, electronic periodical databases, and Web search engines. Some of the unique aspects of these resources will be covered in Chapters 5 through 7. However, most search resources organize and store their reference information in similar ways. They all house a collection of *data records* — files of basic information about individual sources. A data record may be called a *citation*, a *listing*, or a *catalog entry*, depending on the search tool you are using. Understanding the data record and how to use it will help you develop critical-thinking and resource-navigation skills that you can use in a variety of research situations.

The data record, whether for a book, an article, a videotape, or another source, assembles various categories, or *fields,* of information about the source into one document. Here are some of the common fields of information you will encounter:

- **title**   The title of the work.
- **author**   The person or persons who wrote the work, or the institutions or corporations that sponsored or published the source. Editors may be listed in this field, too.
- **subject**   The main ideas or concepts of the work. Although a source may be described by only one subject heading, it is typical for a few subject headings to be listed. This field may be referred to as *headings* in some search tools.
- **date**   The date of publication.
- **abstract**   A short summary of the source. Abstracts highlight the source's main points, its methods of developing the points, important people, organizations, or events mentioned in the source, the methodology of any research used, and so on.

Other data fields you may see, depending on the type of source the record is for and the search tool you are using, are *publication* (the name of the periodical in which an article appears), *publisher, person* (people whose names appear in the work), *location, call number,* and *article type.*

To help you locate a source's data record, most electronic search tools provide a basic search template on their initial screen. A *search template* is a form consisting of one or more boxes in which you enter words or phrases to search for; most basic templates look something like this:

Search for [   ] in [Title ▼]

[Submit Search]

This template includes a drop-down menu so that you can select the data fields you wish to search. For example, in a bibliography of works on the Puritans, Fred Hutchins found a listing for an authoritative book about Cotton Mather that he wanted to locate. Because he knew the book's exact title, he typed it into the library catalog's search template and selected the "title" field from the drop-down menu. His search produced the data record shown in Figure 4-2.

Searching for Sources

Phrase Search		
	Previous	Next

Keyword Search	
	Record Display in BobCat
	Record 7 of **36** for Search:

Search Controls

1 11 21 31

RESULT LIST		○ Save this record			MARC21 Display Location/Call Number

HISTORY	**Author**	Silverman, Kenneth.
	Title	The life and times of Cotton Mather / Kenneth Silverman.
RECALL ITEM	**Edition**	1st ed.
	Publisher	New York : Harper & Row, c1984.
	Description	x, 479 p., [8] p. of plates : ill. ; 25 cm.
Help	**Notes**	Includes bibliographical references and index.
	Subject (LCSH)	Mather, Cotton, 1663-1728.
Patron Functions		Massachusetts -- History -- Colonial period, ca. 1600-1775.
		Puritans -- Massachusetts -- Biography.
LOGOFF	**ISBN**	0060152311

Location	Call Number	Status
NYU Bobst	F67.M43 S57 1984	Available
NYU Bobst	F67.M43 S57 1984	Available
NYU Bobst	F67.M43 S57 1984	Available
NSSR NewSchool	F67.M43 S57 1984	Available
NYHS NYHistSoc	F67.M43 S57 1984 Non-circulating	Available

Figure 4-2   A data record for a book.

Searching for Sources

Search Strategies

Electronic referencing provides many advantages in the speed and efficiency of searches. Using electronic search tools, you may be able to locate dozens of useful sources in a matter of minutes and retrieve full-text articles without visiting library shelves. It also creates challenges. You must learn how to construct searches properly, using a variety of sophisticated resources, and then select promising sources from lists of search matches (or *hits*). This section offers general information that will help you develop these skills.

Subject Searches

The *subject* field (referred to as *headings* in some search tools) is a particularly important category of information. Subjects are terms used to describe what the source is about. For example, Fred's source on Cotton Mather (see Figure 4-2) is categorized under three subject headings: *Mather, Cotton, 1663–1728; Massachusetts — History — Colonial period, ca. 1600–1775; and Puritans — Massachusetts — Biography*.

Your search will be much more effective if you know the subject terms related to your project and how to use them. Using a standard set of subject headings (for books, this is often the Library of Congress Subject

Headings), librarians or other information experts categorize a source under one or more subject headings when creating its data record. Keep in mind that catalogers' terminology may differ from your own in describing a subject. Also, different indexing systems may use different subject terms for the same material. The periodical index you select may not use the same classification system as your library's book catalog to describe the same topic. If you are not having any luck with the subject terms you are searching with, consult the list of subject headings used by the search tool you are using. Some search resources allow you to browse subject headings. Your online library catalog, for example, may have a link to its subject directory.

Keyword Searches

Keyword searches locate all instances of a word or phrase in the data fields being searched, whether it is an author's name, a title, a subject term, or, in some cases, an expression in an abstract or in the full text of an article. Sometimes keyword searches yield many more hits than could possibly be useful; all of the sources that happen to contain one of your keywords are listed, even when the sources are unrelated to your subject. An advantage of keyword searches, however, is that you can search for sources even if you are unsure about the exact wording of a title or the author's full name; you can also use keywords to find instances of specific words or phrases within the full text of periodical articles or Web sites.

Limiting a Search

In the early stages of Internet research, it is common to turn up an unmanageable number of sources. For example, if you access a large periodical database and enter *genetic engineering* into its basic search template without specifying a certain data field to search, your search will almost certainly produce too many matches because this term is commonly used in a variety of discussions. A ProQuest periodical database search for this term, for example, yields over 7,000 hits. At this point in your search, you must take steps to limit the results.

Limit the Number of Fields Being Searched. If the search template offers a drop-down menu allowing you to specify the search field (*title, subject,* or *abstract,* for example), choose a field to search within. You can also select the *advanced search template,* if available, and use combinations of drop-down boxes, filtering tabs, and check-boxes to limit the search. For example, you may be able to limit the search by date to find only sources recently published on your topic (a good idea for topics that are rapidly changing, such as genetic farming). On some periodical databases, you can restrict search results to full-text articles or scholarly journals only. Advanced search templates for books, periodicals, and Web sources are covered in more detail in Chapters 5, 6, and 7.

Narrow Your Search Terms. Examine your hypothesis to make sure that you are focusing on the information you need. For example, if your hypothesis is "Genetic farming can lead to increased agricultural production," try searching for *genetic farming* instead of the more general term *genetic engineering*. Using terms from a preliminary outline, browsing a subject directory related to your topic, or simple brainstorming can also yield more specific terms for your search. If your outline includes a discussion of genetically altered corn, try using that phrase in your search.

Select a More Focused or More Appropriate Search Resource. An Internet search might yield far too many irrelevant sources for your project. The same search in your library's book catalog may identify only two or three books, but those books are more likely to be relevant, reliable sources — and they may even lead you to other useful sources. Some large search resources are themselves collections of smaller databases that allow you to conduct more focused searches. For example, some library catalogs search all branches or collections within the parent library system. You may be able to un-select libraries that you cannot use or select specialized libraries (law or medical libraries, for example) with discipline-specific collections related to your project.

Use Boolean Connectors: AND, NOT, and OR. Most search tools support Boolean logic (consult the resource's help feature or search-tips page to make sure). *Boolean logic* refers to the use of connectors such as *AND, NOT,* and *OR* to create combinations of search terms and search fields.

AND and *NOT* connectors in particular are useful for limiting a search. The *AND* connector retrieves only those results containing both terms. For example, a search for *genetic farming AND corn* would yield only sources in which both terms, *genetic farming* and *corn,* appear in the data fields being searched. Articles that discuss genetic farming but do not mention corn (and vice versa) would not appear in the results list. If you are searching for information on genetics and retrieving too many references to cloning, you might try the combination *genetic NOT cloning.* This would narrow your results by excluding sources about genetics that mention cloning. A combination such as *genetic AND corn NOT cloning* would yield articles containing both *genetic* and *corn,* leaving out sources that also contain the term *cloning.*

Boolean searches can be conducted in several ways. You can usually type Boolean expressions directly into a basic search template (most search resources no longer require you to type connectors in all capital letters).

Some search tools, however, use symbols as operators (+ and – in place of the words *AND* and *NOT,* for example). Some search templates treat two or more words side by side as an *AND* search, whereas others conduct an *OR* search. Still others search for side-by-side words (even without quotation marks) as a phrase. Check the search tool's help feature or search tips page to be sure.

It is often more effective to use an advanced search template for Boolean connectors. Advanced search pages typically allow you to select connectors between rows of search boxes. For an example of this kind of search, see pages 57–58.

Expanding a Search

If you find that your search results are too limited, try the following techniques for expanding your search.

Eliminate Restrictive Phrasing. Often, search results are limited because the basic search template interprets the terms you enter as an exact phrase. Many search tools will treat the keywords *stop sign laws* as an exact phrase even if you type them without quotation marks. You may have to change the search to *stop signs AND laws.*

Identify More General Terms or Synonyms. For example, if a search for *stop signs AND laws* yields too few sources, try the more general keywords *traffic signs AND laws* or *traffic laws.* Sources that you find using more general search terms may contain references to your specific topic (for example, a book about traffic signs would probably mention stop signs), or they may provide useful background information for your project. Also, try to think of synonyms for your topic. For example, if *longevity* brings too few results, try *aging.*

Add More Fields to Your Search. Just as limiting the fields being searched can restrict your results, adding fields can expand your search. Often the simplest way to do this is to select "all fields" on the search template. When searching a periodical database, ensure that the "full text" or "article text" field is selected.

Use a More Comprehensive Search Tool. Sometimes search terms that produce limited results in one search resource can be used in another with excellent results. For example, if *stop signs AND laws* as a search phrase yields no library catalog matches, try the same search in a periodical database. If a search for *cancer AND home care* produces no results in the specialized periodical database Alt HealthWatch, try it in a more comprehensive database such as Academic Search Elite.

Use Boolean *OR* Connectors. If the information you are looking for is likely to be referenced under two or more terms, you can quickly return a larger list of results by connecting the terms with the Boolean *OR* connector. For example, a search for *robotics OR artificial intelligence* would bring up sources containing one term or the other (or both). *African American OR Negro OR Blacks AND segregation* would help you find sources that deal with segregation of African Americans, no matter what term the writers used to identify the group.

Use Wildcard Symbols. Many search tools allow you to use wildcard symbols in place of letters that might vary in your search term. To search for all variants of a word that can take on several endings, enter the word's root followed by an asterisk. (See Table 4-2.) Some search pages allow you to replace a single character with a wildcard symbol. This type of wildcard, often a question mark or an exclamation point, can be placed either within or at the end of a word. For example, the help page of the Pro-Quest periodical database illustrates the wildcard searches shown in Table 4-3.

Wildcard symbols can vary among search tools, so you should consult the resource's help or search tips page.

Cross-Referencing: Using Sources to Find Other Sources

While the beginning stages of research can sometimes seem slow, once you begin to identify good sources they can lead to more good sources,

Table 4-2   Searching with Truncated Terms

Truncated Term	Retrieves Results For
agri*	agriculture
	agricultural
	agribusiness
industr*	industrial
	industrialization
	industry

Table 4-3   Searching with Wildcards

Wildcard Term	Retrieves Results For
wom?n	woman
	women
educat??	educated
	education
	educator

accelerating the pace of your findings. For example, when the library catalog directs you to the stacks to locate a promising book, don't forget to browse the shelves around the book for other useful texts. You may find other books about your topic; books that are on a similar, related topic; or books that provide useful background information.

Documentation and bibliographies within sources can also lead you to other sources. Authors of scholarly books and articles, as well as some Web sites, often provide detailed documentation for the sources they used, making it easy for you to track down additional material through simple author and title searches. If a promising citation includes a page number, you will be able to find specific information within a larger work very quickly.

Electronic data records, which can provide links within their various fields of information, make cross-referencing easy. Links in library catalogs, periodical databases, and Web search engines are a powerful way for you to find useful related sources. For example, clicking on an author's name in a library catalog entry will lead you to other works by that author. Subject links in many electronic search tools direct you to other sources listed under that particular subject heading. Many online periodicals and Web pages include a "related articles" or "related pages" link.

These links typically operate only within the search tool you are using. For example, links on a library catalog record will lead only to sources within that catalog. You can overcome this limitation, however, by creating your own links from one resource to another. For example, if a keyword search has been successful in a periodical database, try it in a different database, on the Internet, or in a library catalog. If you have found a useful subject term for your topic on an electronic data record, look up the same subject term in a print-based periodical index.

Conducting a Preliminary Evaluation

Technical skills like those discussed in this chapter will help you find many sources, but it is up to you to determine whether these sources are useful for your research project. A preliminary screening of sources for credibility and relevance should be an important part of your research strategy. Chapter 10 discusses the detailed evaluation process that you will conduct after building a working bibliography; however, ongoing evaluation throughout the search process will save you time later when reviewing potential sources.

Focus your search on types of sources that are more likely to be credible. Because Web sites, in general, undergo a less rigorous editorial review process than other sources, look for books or periodicals first if you have limited time to find quality sources. Scholarly books and journals in particular typically include sound research; expert viewpoints;

and accurate, edited details. You can filter a search on some periodical databases, for example, to return only those articles published in scholarly journals, or you can skim the list of results for the names of respected journals. Try to determine whether the authors of the sources you are turning up are experts in their field. Not all of your paper's sources need to be written by top experts, but in most cases a core understanding of your subject requires some expert knowledge. Look for authors who are frequently cited in bibliographies on your topic. Check to see whether an author has an advanced degree, if relevant. Conducting a quick author search, clicking the author link on a data record, or entering the author's name into a Web search engine can indicate what else he or she has written. Using an advanced search template, you can combine a subject search with an author search to determine what other works a person has written within a specific subject area. If an author seems to be a major voice in the discussions around your topic, the source is likely to be more credible.

Finally, use other data-record information to your advantage. Check the date of a source to see if it is current. Skim abstracts for the main point of a source, its methodology or approach, major findings, scope, and other factors that would help establish its usefulness. Although you should try to stay focused on information you need, remember that useful source material does not have to be written on exactly the same topic as your own. On closer inspection, a source that looked irrelevant at first glance may actually provide background information, material on a similar situation, or bits of information from which you can build relevant points.

Searching for Sources

5

Finding Books

For most research projects, the depth and context provided by books is invaluable. Books typically represent the sustained work of experts in the field, and they are generally reviewed and edited for accuracy. Although a research project usually cannot rest on the work of one or two books alone, the use of books in conjunction with other appropriate sources will strengthen almost any project.

Using the Library Catalog

One of the central resources in any library, and a prominent link on the library's home page, is the library catalog. This resource has evolved from the *card catalog*, a system containing a vast number of cards cross-referencing books by title, author, subject, and call number. Today almost all libraries have computerized this information, so card catalogs are rare. Electronic systems afford greater flexibility than card catalogs. They offer quicker and more sophisticated searches, with links that make it easy to browse for more information. They make it possible to search the library's holdings not only from on-site computer terminals but often from off-site computers via the Internet as well. They can also show whether a source is available, and they make it possible to print out a data record rather than copy it by hand.

When searching a library catalog for the first time, it is a good idea to look for the online help feature (this might be a link titled "How to Use the Catalog"). You may also find directions posted near the computer terminals or made available as pamphlets at the library's information desk. If no instructions are readily visible, ask a librarian for help.

53

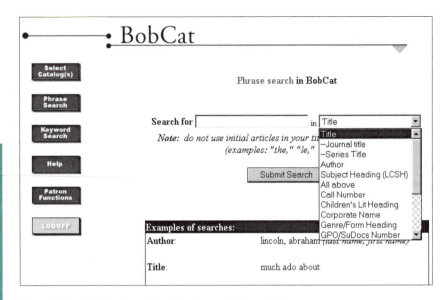

Figure 5-1   A library catalog's basic search template.

Many catalog search pages offer both a basic and an advanced search option. Figure 5-1 shows a basic search template with a drop-down menu allowing you to select which fields to search. Most library catalogs, like this one, are searchable by author, title, subject, call number, or keyword. This particular catalog also includes a *journal title* field. Searching by journal title will tell you whether the library holds a certain journal, but it will not search for articles within the journal. Use a periodical database to find specific articles (see Chapter 6).

Conducting a Subject Search for Books

When you are beginning to compile a list of potential sources and do not yet know of any specific authors or titles, it seems natural to start with a subject search. Because indexers work carefully to ensure that all related books on a specific topic are assigned the same subject heading, subject searches are often the best way to find a group of relevant books on a topic. (While keyword searches can be particularly useful for locating periodical articles and Web sites, keywords present several unique limitations in searching for books. See page 57 for more on these limitations.)

Sometimes subject terms are easy to figure out. To find literary analyses of Emily Dickinson's poetry, you would conduct a subject search for *Dickinson, Emily* (an author search, in contrast, would find books written *by* Dickinson). If you start your search with just a topic (or subject), however, be forewarned that even though the library has compiled a subject catalog, it will not include every subject you might think of. You may need to take some of the following steps to figure out the subject terms for your topic:

- Think of synonyms.
- Use the *browse subjects* function on the library catalog.
- Consult print-based subject directories.
- Use subject terms successfully employed in other searches.
- Follow subject links in data records.
- Ask a librarian for help.

For example, if a subject search for *media education* yields no results, you could try the synonym *media literacy*, which happens to be a Library of Congress subject heading. You might also come across this term by browsing the catalog's list of subjects. Most catalogs will place you in the list of subjects alphabetically, at the point closest to your search term. Figure 5-2, for example, shows the results of a subject search for *media education*. Although no matches were found for that term, the alphabetical list of subject headings provides the perfect opportunity to browse subtopics under *media*. By scrolling up and down the list, you would find *media literacy*, a subject for which four books are listed. You could also discover this subject term by looking up *media* in the appropriate print-based directory (for books, this is often *Library of Congress Subject Headings*) and then scanning the headings that begin with that word.

Another useful technique is to look at the subject headings listed in the source records you find in other searches. As you learned in Chapter 4, the hyperlinked areas of a data record allow you to click and check for other source listings. For example, Fred Hutchins retrieved the data record shown later in this chapter (see Figure 5-5) by conducting a subject search for *Mather, Cotton*. Then, by clicking on one of the record's additional subject headings, *Puritans — Massachusetts*, he was able to find additional books related to his topic.

Conducting a Keyword Search for Books

If a subject search does not produce results, the next best option is usually a keyword search. Some catalogs automatically search all data record fields for a keyword; others allow you to search for keywords in specific fields. For example, a keyword search for *Salem AND witch* in the

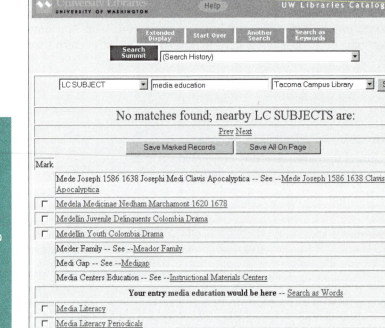

Figure 5-2   A library catalog subject search.

subject field allowed Fred Hutchins to find records for all sources under either of the following subject headings:

> Witchcraft — Massachusetts — Salem — History
>
> Trials (Witchcraft) — Massachusetts — Salem

Keyword searches in the title field are useful when you are looking for a specific book but do not know the exact title.

A keyword search in a library catalog is an effective tool, but it is not as comprehensive as keyword searches that you may be accustomed to in periodical databases or on the Web (see Chapters 6 and 7). First, you cannot electronically search the full text of print books. Second, you usually cannot search abstracts (brief summaries of source content), either — these are commonly included on data records for periodicals but not often for books. Finally, keyword searches turn up many sources irrelevant to your topic. For example, a keyword search for *Mather, Cotton* in all fields retrieves a book titled *Japanese Landscapes: Where Land & Culture Merge,* written by a twentieth-century author who happens to share his name with the Puritan minister.

Conducting an Author or a Title Search for Books

If you know the specific author or title of a book, you can enter it into the template and select the appropriate search field. When searching by title, omit articles such as *a, an,* and *the.* When searching by author, type the last name first. For example, in her search for books on Emily Dickinson, Susanna Andrews found a book titled *The Life of Emily Dickinson* to be particularly helpful. Wondering whether the author, Richard B. Sewall, had written other books that might be useful to her project, Susanna entered *Sewall, Richard* into her school library's basic search template and selected the "search by author" field. Her search revealed that Sewall had also edited a book titled *Emily Dickinson: A Collection of Critical Essays,* but when she accessed its data record she found that the book was checked out. Susanna then used the Web to log onto her local public library's online catalog, conducted a *title search* for the book she wanted, and found that it was available and waiting for her in the stacks.

Using an Advanced Search Template for Books

For many libraries and topics, a simple search of the library catalog will suffice. However, if you are researching in a large library or investigating a topic for which numerous books have been written, you may need to use an *advanced search template* (sometimes called an *expanded search* or a *guided keyword search*). Most catalogs offer this feature, allowing you to construct complex searches containing more than one row of information. By setting data fields to be searched for each row, as well as Boolean connectors between the rows (*AND, OR,* and *NOT*), you can construct complex searches to look for exactly the information you need. For example, to find books on genetic engineering in agriculture, you might construct your search like the one shown in Figure 5-3. This would find all books listed under the subject *agriculture* and containing the term *genetic engineering* in the title. This search produced eight results amid the millions of volumes held at the Library of Congress.

This type of search may also be combined with other limiters such as a specific date range or particular library locations. If the search described for *agricultural AND genetic engineering* had produced an unmanageable number of listings, you might have clicked on the "Set Search Limits" buttons on the lower right-hand side of the screen. By limiting your search to sources written in the last few years (especially for topics such

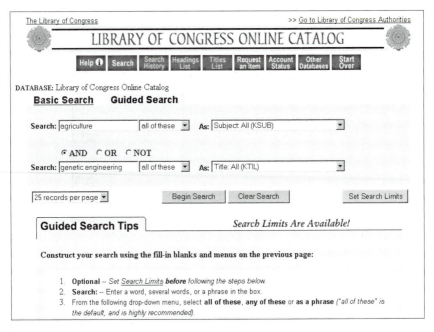

Figure 5-3   A library catalog advanced (guided) search template.

as genetic engineering, for which currency is an important evaluation criteria), you would quickly reduce search results to the most useful sources.

Searching Text-Driven Catalogs

Most library catalogs are graphical point-and-click pages navigated with a mouse, but you might occasionally encounter a text-driven catalog navigated by keyboard entries. Some libraries — especially small, specialized ones — may not yet offer a graphical gateway into the catalog. Even some large libraries may still have terminals that use text-driven menus. Also, when accessing the catalog from the Internet, you may find the library's graphical search pages to be hard to use for a number of reasons. The Internet-access catalog page often offers a text-driven menu as an option; it may be called a *telnet* menu.

Text-driven catalogs allow the same kinds of searches as graphical catalogs, but the navigation and selection is done with keyboard entries, not a mouse, using arrow keys, numerical or alphabetic menus, and so on. The text-driven catalog for the Seattle Public Library (Figure 5-4) offers a menu with a blinking cursor highlighting the place to enter your selection. To conduct an author search, for example, you would type *5* and press the "Enter" key.

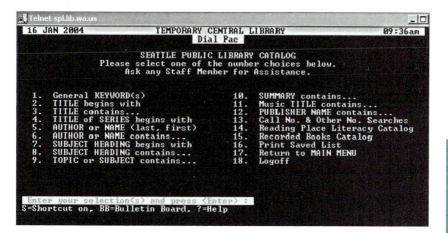

Figure 5-4   A telnet library catalog.

Evaluating Results of a Library Catalog Search

Once you have a list of hits from a library catalog search, you will need to decide which sources to retrieve from the stacks. Scan the results for relevant titles, prominent authors, and recent publication dates, clicking the promising sources to see their data records.

In addition to the author, title, and publication date, book records contain other fields that can help you determine whether a source is likely to be useful for your project. Fred Hutchins, for example, scanned the data record shown in Figure 5-5 and determined that *The Mathers: Three Generations of Puritan Intellectuals, 1596–1728* was worth tracking down. The book seemed likely to be *relevant* (its title and subject headings were related to his topic) and *reliable* (it is published by a university press and includes a bibliography). Fred also reasoned that at 440 pages, the book would probably cover his topic in good depth.

Using the Library's Reference Section

In addition to the electronic catalog, libraries also offer print resources to help you search for books. Bibliographies and indexes are two such tools that you will find in your library's reference section.

Bibliographies list books (as well as articles and other publications) on specific subjects. General bibliographies, such as *The Humanities: A Selective Guide to Information Sources,* cover a wide range of subjects, whereas selective bibliographies focus on narrower topics. To find suitable

Searching for Sources

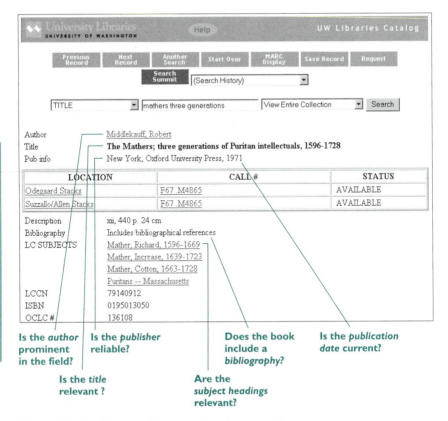

Figure 5-5   Evaluating a library catalog data record.

bibliographies for your research, try entering *bibliography* plus a keyword related to your topic into your library's electronic catalog.

Although most *indexes* direct you to articles in periodicals (see Chapter 6), the *Essay and General Literature Index* lists articles in anthologies and other book-length collections of shorter works. This *Index* can help you locate relevant articles in books that might not be referenced under the exact subject headings that you have identified for your topic.

When looking for background information early in a project or when seeking statistical or biographical data, consult general and specialized encyclopedias, dictionaries, biographical sources, almanacs, atlases, yearbooks, statistical compilations, and a variety of discipline-specific sources. These sources are referenced in the library catalog and are usually located in the reference section. Check under your topic's call number in the reference section as well as in the regular stacks. The following are some examples of common reference books:

- *The New Encyclopaedia Britannica*
- *Encylopedia of Architecture*
- *The Film Encyclopedia*
- *The Oxford English Dictionary*
- *Webster's New Biographical Dictionary*
- *The World Factbook*
- *Statistical Abstract of the United States*
- *Essay and General Literature Index*
- *Readers' Guide to Periodical Literature*
- *The National Atlas of the United States of America*

Unlike most books held in a library, reference books cannot be checked out — they must be used in the library.

Locating Books

Once you have decided which books you want to examine, locating those books within the library is relatively easy. As Susanna found out, the online catalog usually indicates whether the book is available or has been checked out.

Stacks

If the book is available, you will want to retrieve it from the *stacks* — the shelves where the books are kept. Most libraries allow you to enter the stacks, but some do not. To get books in libraries where the stacks are closed to you, you must fill out a call slip and give it to a library employee, who will find the book for you. On the call slip, you supply the author, title, and call number you found in the catalog entry for the book.

Call Numbers

In the stacks, books are shelved according to the call numbers you found with each book's name. Your library will use one of two major classification systems: the Library of Congress system or the Dewey decimal system. The *Library of Congress system* uses a combination of letters and numbers to arrange books by subject area and within the subject area. The *Dewey decimal system* uses numbers to designate major subject areas, and then a combination of letters and numbers to designate subdivisions under the major classifications. For example, *Violence in the Media,* by James D. Torr, is listed in the Dewey decimal system at 303.60973 (the 300s designate social sciences). The same book in the Library of Congress system is found under the call number P96.V5 V563 2001.

You do not have to memorize the codes for the system your library uses, and you need no specialized knowledge to use it yourself. However, if you have access to the stacks, familiarizing yourself with the call numbers for your particular field will enable you not only to locate the books you have found listed in the library catalog but also to browse in appropriate sections for other books that may prove valuable. If you are writing about violence in the media, browsing books in the 303.6 area may turn up some useful sources. As always, your librarian is the professional to turn to if you have any problems understanding the organization and location of materials in the library.

Availability

Unlike electronic media, books can only be used by one person at a time. You may find that the book you need is checked out. (You may even find that the catalog says the book is available, but it is not on the shelves. If that is the case, ask a librarian for help.) If the book has been checked out, ask about *placing a hold* or having the book *recalled* so that you can use it. Keep in mind that when a book is recalled, the person who has the book usually has about two weeks' notice before the book is due back at the library.

If you are searching for books in a large library system with more than one library, set the search template to search all locations. It is common for library systems to hold the same book in different locations. A book that Fred Hutchins found on Cotton Mather was listed as missing at his satellite library branch, but it was available in two libraries on the main campus.

You may also be able to borrow the source through an interlibrary loan. Until recently, a librarian had to arrange for such a loan, and it often took weeks for the materials to arrive at the requester's library. Many libraries now have an electronic form on their computer system that enables patrons to request such loans directly. A rush loan can now be arranged within a couple of days, but you will probably have to pay a fee for such a service.

Public libraries are not the only places books are held. You may be able to borrow sources from the home or professional library of someone with an interest in the field you are studying. For example, your communications professor may have a relevant book on media literacy that you can borrow. If you are willing to purchase the books, you may also be able to find useful sources in new and used bookstores, especially once you know the titles and authors you need.

Books on Reserve

Most college libraries have a *reserve reading room* or a *reserve shelf,* where you find books that instructors have asked a librarian to pull out of the stacks and set aside for use in particular classes. However, the books remain available for anyone to use, with certain restrictions. A book placed on reserve may be checked out only for use in the library or, at best, may be taken out overnight. When a book is put on reserve, the online catalog entry usually notes that fact. In some library catalogs, you can set the search template to search only for reserve books instead of the entire library collection. Should you discover that a book you need for your research has been put on reserve, plan to read it and take notes while in the library. Try to use reserve books as early in the term as possible because you can be sure that other students will soon be competing with you for the same books.

Using Electronic Books

Although the vast majority of books are print based, some books are available electronically. Some are free and available at Web sites such as the following:

Project Gutenberg	www.gutenberg.net
Alex Catalogue of Electronic Texts	www.infomotions.com/alex
Electronic Text Center	http://etext.lib.virginia.edu/ebooks

Most of the works available at these free sites are older classics in literature or social thought, such as the complete poetry of Emily Dickinson or Karl Marx's *The Communist Manifesto.* Therefore, they may be particularly useful for research papers in the humanities and social sciences. You can typically access electronic books as Web pages, which you can save to your computer or download as text files.

There are also many commercial Web sites that sell electronic texts, such as www.ebooks.com. The titles available at these sites are more diverse in subject and more current than the free electronic books. These books can be downloaded to handheld electronic book readers, as well as to personal computers.

You can search electronic book sites in much the same way that you would search a library catalog: by title, author, and sometimes by subject. In addition, many electronic book sites offer the advantage of allowing keyword searches within the full text of books.

Searching for Sources

Once you have accessed or downloaded an electronic book, you can easily perform your own keyword search within the full text. For example, if you are studying the insect imagery used in Emily Dickinson's poems, a search for *bee* would turn up a variety of poems in which the word appears. You can usually access your Web browser and word-processor search function by pressing Control-F (Windows) or Command-F (Macintosh).

Searching for Sources

6

Finding Periodicals

Articles from periodicals (journals, magazines, and newspapers) are essential for most research projects. In fields where knowledge changes rapidly, such as science and technology, articles have replaced books as the primary way in which professionals exchange information and ideas. Even in fields such as history and literature, you need to check periodicals to make sure your research is up to date. Subjects involving current affairs, such as *government energy policy* and *national health insurance*, must be heavily researched in newspapers, newsmagazines, and journals of political commentary.

Understanding Types of Periodicals

Periodicals fall into two broad categories — professional and popular — according to their purpose and audience. *Professional periodicals* such as scholarly journals and trade magazines, which publish recent research by experts in the field, have a specialized audience. Because some journal articles use terminology and methods aimed at an audience of specialists, you may find much of the material hard to understand at first, depending on the field and the journal. However, you should become acquainted with such materials and perhaps work through one or more journal articles with your instructor so that you can incorporate specialized material in your paper. Journal articles are especially important sources to use if your audience already has knowledge in the field or if your hypothesis is specialized.

specialized hypothesis   The Banks model for multicultural transformation offers an effective framework for secondary education reform.

nonspecialized hypothesis   Diversity education requirements in high schools can benefit the community.

The specialized hypothesis would probably need more support from scholarly sources to achieve its purpose and communicate effectively with its audience. Later in college, especially in your major, the information in scholarly journals will become increasingly accessible and valuable to you as you find yourself learning how to write for increasingly specialized audiences.

Popular periodicals include magazines and newspapers intended for a broad audience. These publications may be focused in topic (like *Popular Mechanics* or *National Geographic*), but they are not written for an audience of experts. Other popular periodicals, like many newspapers or general-interest magazines, contain articles on a variety of topics. Popular publications range widely in their reading level, audience, and purpose. Magazines like *People, Sports Illustrated,* and *Details* offer easily accessible entertainment for mass-market audiences; these kinds of periodicals are typically the least useful for research projects. Reputable and long-standing publications like *Atlantic Monthly, Harper's,* the *New York Times,* the *Los Angeles Times,* the *Wall Street Journal,* and many others offer excellent analysis and social commentary by respected writers.

Although popular periodicals are not considered authoritative publications, they can be good sources for real-world examples to supplement the research you find in journals, books, and other scholarly sources. David Perez, for example, found a newspaper article in the *Houston Chronicle* about a Brazilian village invaded by fire ants. He decided to use the story as an additional illustration of some points made by his other sources.

Using Periodical Databases

You may be lucky enough to find a useful article on your topic while browsing the newsstand shelves or reading the morning paper, but in most cases you will need an organized search plan to secure the best newspaper, magazine, and journal articles. A good first step is to use a *periodical database* (sometimes called an *electronic index*) — an electronic storage and retrieval system that will direct you to specific periodical articles. In addition to publication information, many databases also provide abstracts and the complete text of articles. Periodical databases are usually accessed through your library's home page (look for a link titled

"Databases" or "Electronic Resources"). You may even be able to access some databases through the Internet from off campus. Ask a librarian or read the library Web site's help screens for information on how to access periodical databases through the Internet.

Understanding Types of Periodical Databases

Your library's periodical databases probably include a large comprehensive service such as ProQuest, InfoTrac, LexisNexis, or EBSCOhost. These resources allow you to search a number of smaller databases all at once or to limit your search to one or more specific databases. For example, ProQuest includes separate databases for trade and industry publications, newspapers, and a variety of academic disciplines. Unless you select particular databases within the service, your search results may include scholarly journals, popular magazines, and newspapers from wide-ranging fields all mixed together. In the initial stages of your research, you may want to conduct a broad search of this type to determine what sources exist on your topic, what subjects it is referenced under, what disciplines and publications cover it best, and the names of major authors who write about it.

If a comprehensive database search produces too many results, you can focus your search by selecting a specialized database relevant to your topic (the specialized database may or may not be part of a larger database service). For example, you can select *Medline* medical information database when researching health-related topics, or *Sociology Abstracts* for topics in sociology.

Specialized databases mainly index scholarly and trade journal articles. Here are a few examples of specialized databases:

- Ethnic Newswatch
- CINAHL (Cumulative Index to Nursing & Allied Health Literature)
- ERIC (Educational Resources Information Center)
- ABI/Inform Trade and Industry
- Anthropological Index Online

Conducting a Basic Search for Periodical Articles

A large, general academic database such as EBSCOhost, which references thousands of popular and scholarly periodicals, is a good place to start a search. As you can see in Figure 6-1, many smaller databases are available within the EBSCO service. To determine which smaller database seems right for your search, read the brief descriptions and, if needed, link to the list of periodicals a database references. For example, let's say

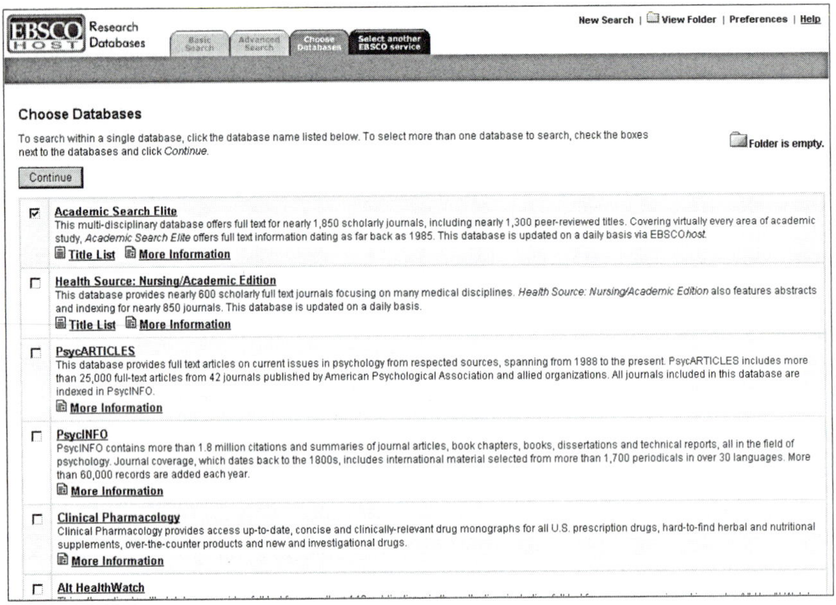

Figure 6-1 EBSCOhost's list of databases.

your hypothesis is "Media literacy classes should be offered in high school because of advertising's harmful effects on young people." You want to include some scholarly sources, but you are not sure which field the literature would be published in (communications, psychology, and sociology are three possibilities). In this case, Academic Search Elite is probably the best choice within EBSCOhost because it references a variety of journals from different disciplines.

After selecting Academic Search Elite, you might first try a basic key-word search for *media literacy* (see Figure 6-2). Note that this database's basic search template does not allow you to select specific search fields; by default, the database will look for your keywords in article *citations* (author, title, and publication information), subject headings, and abstracts. (To expand your search to the full text of articles, you can click the check-box near the bottom of the screen).

This particular search produces over two hundred results, more than you had expected. At this point, you decide to remain in the basic search mode but refine your search by entering *media literacy AND advertising*. Remembering that you are specifically looking for sources in professional journals, you also click the "Refine Search" tab and select the check-box next to "Scholarly (Peer Reviewed) Journals" to filter out results in popu-

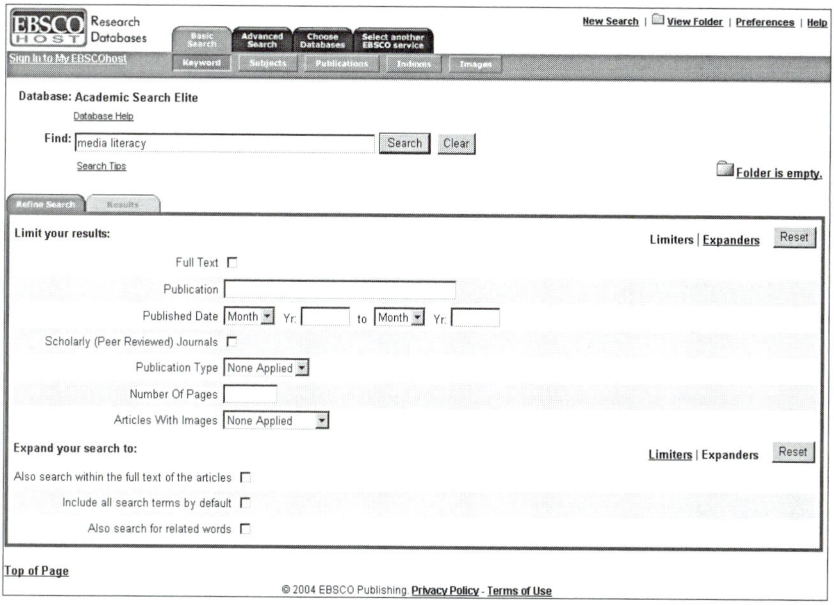

Figure 6-2 A basic keyword search on a periodical database.

lar periodicals. Clicking on "Search," you discover that you have effectively narrowed the original 224 articles to a manageable eight hits.

Using an Advanced Search Template for Periodical Articles

Because articles in periodical databases — especially large, general services — can be very wide ranging in topic, advanced Boolean searches are often useful for filtering out irrelevant results. Boolean searches are easy to construct on advanced search templates. For example, a student who wanted to find information on discrimination against Muslim immigrants began with the ProQuest search shown in Figure 6-3. Because she wanted to check for coverage of her topic in both popular and professional publications, she decided to leave the "databases" setting as the default, which searches all ProQuest databases. This search retrieved all records under the subject heading *immigration* that also contained *discrimination* in their abstracts. (Because *discrimination* was an important keyword, the student wanted to make sure that it appeared in the abstracts. She decided that searching for it as another subject field, though, would be too limiting.)

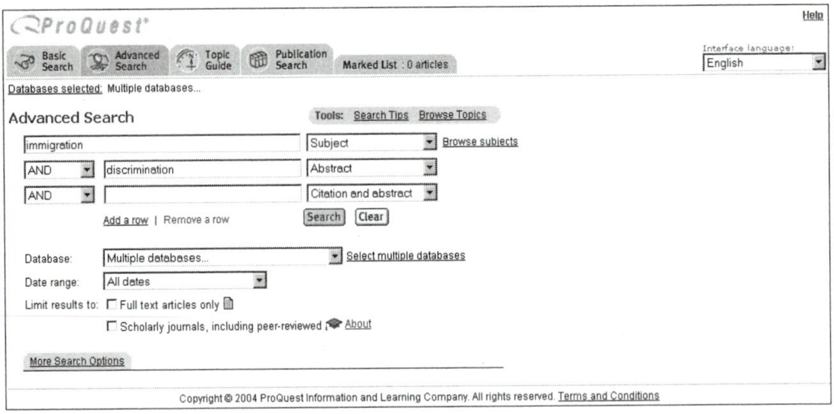

Figure 6-3   An advanced search on a periodical database.

When the search retrieved 377 results, the student knew that she would have to further narrow her search. Scanning the titles of the hits and reading several abstracts, she noticed that many articles focused on Hispanic immigrants. Other articles dealt with discrimination in European societies. To filter out these irrelevant hits, she added these lines to her original search, setting the fields more broadly this time to search citations as well as the full text of articles (ProQuest's version of an "all fields" search):

The student had to select "add a row" on the advanced search template to add the final line to this search. By using *wildcards* (see page 50), she ensured that the database retrieved articles containing the word *Arab*, *Arabs*, or *Arabic*, and excluded articles including *Europe*, *European*, or *Europeans*. This time, the search retrieved forty-three results from a variety of publications.

Now the student decided to check the coverage of the topic in specific types of sources. First, she clicked the "scholarly journals" sort tab, refining the list to six articles from professional journals. She clicked "all sources" to bring back the original list of forty-three, then clicked "newspapers" because she knew that newspaper articles might describe individual cases of discrimination. This reduced the list to fourteen sources from various newspapers.

In scanning the list of newspapers the student noticed a lot of coverage in the *New York Times*. Knowing this newspaper's excellent reputation, she decided to isolate the search results to that publication. She selected the "Databases" link, clicked "clear all databases" to remove the previous selections and then scrolled down and chose the *New York Times Index*. Clicking on "Continue" brought back the advanced search template that still displayed the original four-row search she had carefully constructed. She clicked "search" and this time got a list of six articles, all from the *New York Times*. Of course, the student could also have manually reentered the same search into a completely different database.

Advanced searches may also be combined with other limiters such as a particular date range, full-text only, inclusion of graphics, and other factors to help you find useful sources. Read the screen or the database's "help" feature to see what limiters can be applied, or ask a librarian for help.

Evaluating Results of a Database Search

The hits you retrieve from a database include information that will help you screen sources for usefulness. Figure 6-4 shows some questions you can ask yourself to determine which sources to further pursue. After scanning the search results shown in the figure, the student looking for articles on discrimination against Muslim immigrants decided that the first article on the list seemed especially promising. The article was current, the title relevant, and the publication reputable.

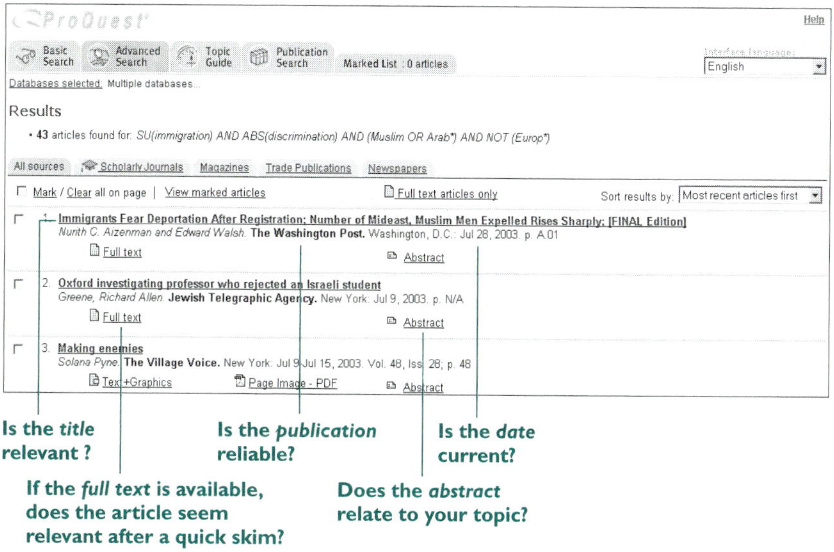

Figure 6-4   Evaluating the results of a database search.

It is also helpful to scan abstracts. Abstracts cover the key elements of an article, allowing you to quickly gauge whether an article will fit your information needs. If an article does not sound like it will directly relate to your paper's hypothesis and main points, remember that it could contain detailed supporting information that you may need.

Finally, you can scan the full text of an article (if available) by quickly reading the introduction, the first sentences of paragraphs through the body, any section headings, and the conclusion. On most databases, your search terms will be displayed in the document in bold print or a different color, so you can quickly read passages where these terms occur. You can also use your computer's "Find" function to search for particular words or phrases in the document. To access this function, try pressing Control-F (Windows) or Command-F (Macintosh).

When you find database citations or articles that are worth keeping, you can often download them to a disc or e-mail them to yourself. Open the article's data record and look for the appropriate links (often at the bottom of the document). Many databases also offer a personal folder in which you can store search results. However, the contents of the folder may be deleted at the end of your session.

Using Print Indexes

Articles are also referenced in reference books known as *print indexes*. Before the widespread use of electronic referencing, print indexes such as the *Humanities Index* and the *Social Sciences Index* were the primary resources for finding articles. They still play a prominent role in many libraries, particularly in certain specialized disciplines or for older articles.

These indexes appear as hardbound volumes in the reference section of your library. Each volume is labeled with the year it covers. The titles of recently published articles are cataloged in paperbound supplements typically covering a month or two. At the end of the year, the supplements are incorporated into hardbound annual volumes.

Although they reference many of the same periodicals as databases, print indexes are organized, and therefore searched, very differently. Within the volumes, articles for the year covered are listed alphabetically by subject and author, so it is very important to know of authors or subject headings related to your topic.

Because many periodical databases go back only a limited number of years, you will probably do better to use print indexes when researching sources for events that took place two decades ago or more, especially if you are interested in investigating sources written close to the time the events were happening.

Because many print indexes are specialized by discipline, they may also provide focus that is sometimes hard to achieve in electronic resources. For example, by using the *Women's Studies Index* you are certain to reference only articles deemed useful in that field. Paper-based indexes can also provide a change of medium for screen-weary researchers.

Each print index has its own format and subject directory, so take the time to familiarize yourself with it. Indexes use abbreviations that are explained at the beginning of each volume. Be sure to consult these explanations before using a print index.

Using Print Indexes to Find Scholarly and Professional Journals

Two very important print indexes that will help you find scholarly sources are the *Humanities Index* and the *Social Sciences Index*. These resources may well provide you with all the sources you need for research papers in the social sciences and the humanities. (The online versions are the *Humanities Abstracts* and *Social Sciences Abstracts*).

The *Humanities Index*, which covers well over three hundred periodicals, lists articles according to subject in the following academic disciplines:

archaeology	language and literature
area studies	literary and political criticism
classical studies	performing arts
folklore	philosophy
history (not included until 1974)	religion
	theology

The *Social Sciences Index* covers about four hundred periodicals and lists articles according to subject in the following academic disciplines:

anthropology	medical science
area studies	political sciences
economics	psychology (not included between 1945 and 1974)
education	
environmental science	public administration
law and criminology	sociology

Many of the journals cited, and perhaps even the indexes themselves, are not available in small libraries. Nevertheless, if they are available you may be able to quickly locate excellent sources for your project.

Other indexes cover narrower fields. These specialized indexes, which reference scholarly and professional periodicals, include the following:

- *Applied Science and Technology Index*
- *Art Index*
- *Business Periodicals Index*

- *Education Index*
- *General Science Index*
- *Hospital Literature Index*

For the titles of other specialized indexes, see the Appendix, which contains a selective list of indexes to scholarly and professional journals in many major fields. If you need to find additional sources, consult *Bibliographic Index: A Cumulative Bibliography of Bibliographies*. This work briefly describes all the periodical indexes you will probably ever need.

Using Print Indexes to Find Popular Periodicals

Print indexes are still an extremely useful source for finding popular periodicals. This section will cover three print indexes that have been in use for a long time and are an established part of many libraries: the *Readers' Guide to Periodical Literature*, the *New York Times Index*, and the *Book Review Digest*. These indexes are often available in online versions as well. For additional print indexes to popular periodicals, see the Appendix.

The *Readers' Guide to Periodical Literature*. Often referred to as simply the *Readers' Guide*, this index has long been one of the most important resources for finding articles in popular periodicals. Its references range on a wide variety of subjects published in periodicals aimed at a cross section of American readers. This index is also available online (as *Readers' Abstracts*). Here is a sampling of the magazines indexed by the *Readers' Guide* and the subjects they cover:

American City and County: local government policy, city planning, urban problems

Atlantic Monthly: current affairs, short fiction

Consumer Reports: evaluations of the performance of commercial products for the general consumer

Discover: reports of happenings and issues in science, written for a general readership

Foreign Affairs: political topics, for readers who are well versed in current events

The Nation: political issues, aimed at a politically liberal audience

National Review: political issues, aimed at a politically conservative audience

New Republic: political issues, aimed at a politically conservative to moderate audience

Psychology Today: reports on recent research in all branches of psychology, designed for the general reader

Scientific American: reports of recent scientific research, written for scientifically informed readers

Time: news items from the current week, written for the general public

United Nations Monthly Chronicle: issues pertaining to the work of the United Nations

Vital Speeches of the Day: transcripts for those who want to know exactly what was said by political, business, and academic leaders.

The print version of the *Readers' Guide* has been published since 1900 as a series, each volume covering one or more years. If you need material from the nineteenth century (to read about public reactions to an event at the time it happened, for example) go to *Poole's Index to Periodical Literature,* which covers 1802 to 1906.

The *Readers' Guide* lists both authors and subjects alphabetically. For example, if you were looking for articles on immigration published in the last twenty years, you would look at several volumes of the *Readers' Guide,* checking listings under "Immigration." In the August 2003 volume of the *Readers' Guide,* you would find the information shown in Figure 6-5.

To find an author's work in the *Readers' Guide,* look alphabetically for the author's last name. Under it you will find all articles by the author,

The topic of interest — Immigration and Customs Enforcement Bureau (U.S.) *See* United States. Dept. of Homeland Security. Bureau of Immigration and Customs Enforcement
Immigration and emigration
Related topics — *See also*
Alien labor
Assimilation (Sociology)
Asylum, Right of
Deportation
Illegal aliens
Refugees
Repatriation
United States. Immigration and Naturalization Service
Article title — America Slams the Door (On Its Foot): Washington's Destructive New Visa Policies. J. N. Paden and P. W. Singer. — **Authors**
Periodical title — *Foreign Affairs* v82 no3 p8-14 My/Je 2003
Body Count [War on terrorism] A. Gourevitch. *The Washington Monthly* v35 no6 p37-9 Je 2003 — **Periodical date (May–June 2003)**
Volume and issue number — Driving While Immigrant. D. Cole. *The Nation* v276 no18 p6, 30 My 12 2003
Immigrants From Mexico [Editorial] *America* v188 no8 p3 Mr 10 2003 — **Page numbers**
It's Child's Play to Fake It [L-1 visa fraud] B. Grow. *Business Week* no3823 p83 Mr 10 2003
A Loophole as Big as a Mainframe [L-1 visas] B. Grow. il *Business Week* no3823 p82-3 Mr 10 2003
Subtopics — **International aspects**
Ranking the Rich. graph tab *Foreign Policy* no136 p56-66 My/Je 2003
Laws and regulations
See Immigration and emigration

Figure 6-5   From the *Readers' Guide to Periodical Literature.*

arranged alphabetically according to title, disregarding *A, An,* and *The.* (The word *about* above an author's name indicates that the author is the subject of an article written by someone else.)

The *New York Times Index.* The *New York Times* is generally regarded as the most important newspaper in the United States, and its print index is still an important resource in many libraries. In annual volumes, the *New York Times Index* lists all major news accounts and feature articles that have appeared in the *Times* since 1913, arranged alphabetically according to subject. To locate articles on a specific topic or event, choose the volumes that cover the relevant time period and then look alphabetically in the volumes for the subject. To check the *Times Index* for very recent events, use the supplements published every two weeks. At year's end, these supplements are republished as the new annual volume. The *Times Index* is also available as an online database (both separately and as part of ProQuest).

Newspaper articles are particularly useful for topics that require you to know precisely what facts and impressions were reported at the time an event occurred or to sample public opinion over a particular period of time. Examples of such topics include the following:

> *attitudes toward Prohibition at the time the Eighteenth Amendment was being ratified (1917–19)*
>
> *reactions throughout the South to the Supreme Court decision of 1954 outlawing segregation in public schools*
>
> *the extent to which the American public was misinformed about the testing of atomic bombs in Nevada after World War II*

While researching public opinion preceding an event, such as an election or the ratification of a constitutional amendment, be sure to check the *Times Index* volume not only for the calendar year of the event but also for the previous year, especially if the event took place early in the year. Similarly, when investigating the reactions to an event, check the *Times Index* volumes for both the year of the event and the following year.

Every daily issue of the *New York Times* (beginning with the first issue in 1851) has been reproduced on microfilm, and many libraries have a complete set. Find the date, section, and page number of a particular news item in the *Times Index;* then request the filmstrip of the *Times* for that date and run it through a microfilm viewer.

Even if your library does not subscribe to the *Times* on microfilm, consult the *New York Times Index* for the year the event occurred; then you can find the exact days on which important events were reported. Use those dates to locate information in newspapers that your library does have because most newspapers usually publish important stories at the same time.

The *Times Index* offers another convenient feature: its brief summaries of many articles may help you decide whether to spend time searching for and reading a particular story.

Figure 6-6 shows a sample from the *New York Times Index*. The entry "Immigration and Refugees" in the bound volume of the *Times Index* for 2003 indicates several articles about the subject, with one editorial referring directly to immigration policy.

IMMIGRATION AND CUSTOMS ENFORCEMENT BUREAU.
See also
Cocoa, My 29
IMMIGRATION AND REFUGEES. See also
Africa, My 19
Architecture, My 18
Colombia, My 17
Computers and the Internet, My 30
Congo (Formerly Zaire), My 16
Cuba, My 16
Great Britain, My 23, 24, 29, 30, 31
Israel, My 20
Labor, My 18
Lewiston (Me), My 22
Libraries and Librarians, My 18
Medicine and Health, My 21, 26
North Korea, My 23, 30
South Korea, My 16
Terrorism, My 22, 28, 30, 31
   Criminal charges are filed against Tyrone Williams, owner of tractor trailer where 18 illegal Hispanic migrants were found dead in Victoria, Texas; investigators say Williams admits taking $2,500 for taking migrants from Mexican border; truck may have had 100 people packed inside; survivors fled when doors were opened at truck stop; at least dozen are hospitalized; photos; map (M), My 16,A,20:1
   Eighteen suspected illegal immigrants are found alive and near sweltering tractor-trailer at southern Texas highway rest area, few miles from where 17 immigrants were recently found dead after being trapped in similar trailer; truck's driver is arrested; Tyrone M. Williams, driver in first case, appears in court on charges of conspiracy to smuggle, transport and conceal illegal immigrants; death toll in case rises to 19; six survivors remain hospitalized; US Atty Michael T Shelby says investigators seek to identify conspirators involved in both gathering immigrants from Central America and Mexico and then smuggling them across border and employers who lure people with promise of job; says Atty Gen John Ashcroft has expressed keen interest in case; photo (M), My 17,A,13:1
   Memorial service is held in Houston for illegal immigrants who died after being transported from Mexico and abandoned in stifling truck trailer near Victoria, Tex, by driver Tyrone Williams; photo (S). My 19,A,17:3
   Editorial says gruesome deaths in Texas of 19 undocumented immigrants in airless trailer truck serve as reminder that Mexican Pres Vicente Fox and Pres Bush have failed to deliver on their ambitious pledge to craft landmark immigration agreement, My 19,A,20:1

An editorial about immigration policy appeared in section A, page 20, column 1 of the May 19, 2003, issue of the *Times*. The abbreviations (S), (M), and (L) in the other entries indicate short, medium-length, or long articles.

Figure 6-6   From the *New York Times Index*.

Searching for Sources

The *New York Times Index* is most useful for social science subjects such as modern history, economics, and political science. The *New York Times* also reports extensively on literature and the arts.

The *Book Review Digest*. The *Book Review Digest* publishes excerpts from book reviews that appeared within a year after a book was first published. The *Book Review Digest* does not cite every published review but only a sample of critical responses, both favorable and unfavorable.

Each annual volume of this digest (beginning in 1905) indexes reviews of several thousand books, according to both title and author. It covers popular and scholarly works, both fiction and nonfiction, and it draws its material from more than eighty English-language periodicals. To use the *Book Review Digest*, you need to know the year in which a book was first published. Then you should look up the title or the author in the volumes both for that year and for the next year because some books are not reviewed during the calendar year in which they are published. A book published in November 1991, for example, might not have been reviewed until January 1992.

The *Book Review Digest* presents the initial critical reactions to a book, helpful especially if you want to compare immediate responses with later judgments made by critics and scholars after the work had a chance to influence other writers or after public tastes changed. Examples of research assignments requiring you to use the *Book Review Digest* would be "Initial Critical Reactions to Ernest Hemingway's *The Sun Also Rises*" and "Changing Critical Evaluations of Willa Cather's *My Antonia*."

The value of the *Book Review Digest* is not limited to literary topics. For example, you might want to know how reviewers reacted to a book that presented a new view of a well-known person or event or one that unveiled a new social or scientific theory such as evolution, relativity, or psychoanalysis.

Finally, check a book you want to use as a source in the *Book Review Digest*; you can find out very easily whether reviewers found that book informative and reliable.

Acquiring Articles from Print-Based Periodicals

If you have found the title of an article that promises to be a good source and the full text is not available through an electronic database, you need to find out whether your library has a copy of the periodical in which the article appeared. Periodicals are generally listed in the online catalog — search for them by title. If you used a database, the citation for the article will often indicate whether your library holds the periodical in print form. You can also look for a periodical holdings notebook near the indexes or search terminals. If you do not find a periodical listed in the catalog, check with a librarian to see whether your library subscribes to it. If not, he or she might be able to suggest other strategies for retrieving the article.

Most libraries have a periodical section in which you can find current issues of each magazine and newspaper that your library regularly receives. Most of your research, however, will require that you consult back issues of certain periodicals, and these may be kept elsewhere or may have been transferred to microfilm. Again, the online catalog will tell you where periodicals are located, or you can ask your librarian how back issues are handled in your library.

Acquiring Articles from Web-Based Periodicals

Many periodicals now offer Web sites to accompany their print versions, and in most cases you can access these sites for free. (You may be asked to establish a free account, with a username and password.)

Finding Periodical Web Sites

If you know the name of a magazine or journal that you are interested in, use the title as a keyword in an Internet search engine.

If you want to learn the names of online periodicals in your subject area, look in a subject directory (see pages 88–90 for more on subject directories). Click on a subject related to your topic and then look for a link titled "journals" or "magazines." You can also conduct a keyword search, entering your subject area plus the word "journal" or "magazine." "Scholarly Journals Distributed via the World Wide Web" at <http://info.lib.uh.edu/wj/webjour.html>, a Web resource compiled by the University of Houston Libraries, gives a comprehensive and searchable list of journals that either are fully online or are supplements to more complete print-based publications.

You can also search for individual articles using Internet search engines (covered in Chapter 7). You can use a general search engine (such as Google or Lycos), or you might try the following specialized directories, which will help you find popular periodical articles online:

FindArticles	<www.findarticles.com>
MagPortal	<http://magportal.com>
NewsDirectory.com	<www.newsdirectory.com>

Using Periodical Web Sites

Most periodical Web sites offer full-text articles, but they usually cover only the last few years. Sometimes only a selected list of articles from the print edition is available online; in other cases, the Web site includes articles that did not appear in the print version. Archived articles can be searched for by keyword, by date, and sometimes by subject, using search templates within the site. Sometimes you may have to pay a small fee to access an archived article. If this is the case, the site might offer a brief abstract or portion of the article to help you decide whether you want to purchase the full text.

If you are working with periodicals that appear both in print and online, what you see on the screen may be somewhat different from what appeared in the printed version of the periodical. Often the online version will include more information, such as links to related articles or other Web sites, or multimedia displays such as video, a sound link, or a slide show. Sometimes, though, the online version is just a shorter form of the print article or only an abstract. The text on the screen should tell you what is included.

Searching for Sources

7

Finding Internet Sources

The Internet is an *inter*national *net*work connecting millions of computers and computer networks all around the world. Many of these computers, both large and small, are operated by organizations or individuals who have set up electronic sites that can be accessed by users of the Internet. These sites belong to a wide variety of owners — universities, libraries, government agencies, the military, nonprofit organizations, and a host of commercial enterprises.

The databases on the Internet usually index entries from only as recently as 1995 or so. In general, the Internet is therefore most helpful for recent topics or topics for which scholarship has recently changed. If you want to find sources about the Persian Gulf War (1991) that were written at the time, you might not find much on the Internet aside from historical analysis. If you were looking for information about the more recent war with Iraq (2003–2004), you would find more information than you could possibly use.

Using the four student papers in Chapter 22 as examples, we could say that for subjects like *Cotton Mather* and *Emily Dickinson* you would certainly need to use mostly print sources, although the papers on these subjects do each cite a few online sources. For subjects such as *fire ants* and *recent immigration,* the Internet is more useful. Even here, however, you should make it no more than a partner of your other sources, albeit possibly a major one. In general, Internet sources should serve as supplements to printed library sources. Just how necessary or valuable they are will depend on the nature of your project.

In Chapters 5 and 6, we covered the use of the Internet as a gateway to library catalogs and periodical databases, so this chapter will focus mainly on strategies for using search engines to locate Web sites.

Understanding Types of Web Sites

Web sites make available materials published by academic institutions, corporations, government agencies, nonprofit organizations, and individuals. These Web sites offer material ranging from information about the work these organizations do; to laws, speeches, and press releases; to texts of historical and literary documents. On the Internet, you will also find first-person accounts and opinions on various topics, as well as pages offering bibliographies with links to a multitude of other online documents and related Web sites. For example, if you were investigating issues surrounding U.S. immigration, the following organizations' Web sites might be helpful:

The Statue of Liberty–Ellis Island Foundation at <www.ellisisland. org> — to learn about immigrants' experiences in the early part of the century

Center for Immigration Studies at <www.cis.org> — for current immigration news, research, and policy analysis

Human Rights Watch at <www.hrw.org> — to investigate advocacy groups that are working on immigration issues

The Web is also a good source of information from government agencies. A search engine can lead you to the home pages for the U.S. House or Senate, the White House, federal agencies, your state government, and in many cases county and city governments. Sites such as FirstGov.gov at <www.firstgov.gov> and FedStats at <www.fedstats.gov> serve as gateways to government information and can quickly help you find numerous documents that would be difficult to procure in print. These sites offer search templates as well as extensive menus organized by agencies and types of information. For example, if you were using FirstGov.gov to research the U.S. defense budget, clicking on "Defense and International," then "Defense Reports and Publications" would lead you to a downloadable version of the 2004 Defense Budget.

The Web also offers a variety of reference information that can help you look up specific facts or background information on a topic. You can access encyclopedia entries, look up words in an online thesaurus or dictionary, find famous quotations on various topics, check almanacs, or consult maps. Almost any good Internet subject directory offers a "Reference" link. Try the Internet Public Library at <www.ipl.org> or Yahoo! Reference at <education.yahoo.com/reference>.

Some sites can give you access to texts and pictures that you would otherwise have to travel long distances to examine in person. For example, if your topic were African American slave narratives, you could read full texts of rare books and essays at a Web site called African American Women Writers of the 19th Century at <http://digital.nypl.org/ schomburg/writers_aa19>. If you were researching an art-history topic, you could view digital representations of more than 3,500 works of art at the Web site of the Metropolitan Museum of Art in New York at <www.metmuseum.org>.

As you can see, the Internet offers an impressive variety of material for researchers, which is the main problem with using the Internet for research. Just about any individual or group can set up a Web site and say whatever they want about any subject. If you find material on the Internet that seems of value to your project, you must determine whether the site offers credible information. Information on sites created by well-known periodicals like the *Atlantic Monthly* and organizations like the American Cancer Society, for example, is as reliable as the print material they create, but information on unfamiliar sites needs to be checked carefully for reliability. In Chapter 10, you will learn more about evaluating Web sites (and other types of sources).

Understanding Web Addresses

To research on the Internet, it helps to understand the structure of an Internet address, referred to as a URL (Uniform Resource Locator). Here's a typical URL, in this case, for the African American Women Writers of the 19th Century site at the New York Public Library:

protocol domain name   directory paths   filename
http://digital.nypl.org/schomburg/writers_aa19/toc.html

As the labels indicate, a URL has four basic elements: protocol, domain name, directory paths, and filename.

- The *protocol* is the kind of computer link that the URL represents. The protocol *http* stands for *hypertext transfer protocol*, which allows the exchange of hypertext documents.
- The *domain name,* or *server,* is made up of three basic parts. The prefix *digital* simply indicates the name of the computer where the New York Public Library stores information accessible on the World Wide Web. Many URLs have the prefix www, and others have no prefix before the domain name (for example, *amazon.com*). The second part identifies the owner of the site, the person or group that has put the information on the Web. The third part identifies the

Searching for Sources

general group to which the owner belongs. In this case, the suffix *.org* indicates that the owner (the New York Public Library) is a non-profit organization. Common suffixes include the following:

.com	commercial
.edu	educational institution
.gov	government
.mil	military
.net	network organization
.org	nonprofit organization

- The *directory path* (or *paths*) may be quite long. In this example, the directory path begins with a folder called *schomburg,* and within that is a folder called *writers_aa19*. Some URLs end in a folder name instead of a filename (accessing the folder automatically launches a file within it called *index.htm*, the site's home page).

- The *filename* is the name of the specific Web document being accessed. Filenames for Web pages end in either *htm* or *html*.

Sometimes directory paths and filenames get quite long. They may involve multiple folders, or they may be constructed of complicated-looking code. When you come across a long URL and must enter it into your browser's address bar, it is often best to type just the domain name, then search the site for the specific page you want to access.

Follow all spelling and punctuation precisely when you type URLs into a browser, as well as when you document them. With one typographical error, the URL won't work.

Using Search Engines

Sometimes you know the address of a particular Web site you want to consult. In most cases, though, you will be searching for Web sites that might offer information on your research topic. To find them, you need to go to a search engine, a resource that allows you to perform keyword searches on millions of Web documents. You may have already used search engines without considering how they work, but to efficiently find the best sources on the Web you will need to understand how search engines operate. Here are some leading search engines:

Google	<http://google.com>
AltaVista	<www.altavista.com>
Infoseek	<http://infoseek.go.com>
Lycos	<www.lycos.com>

Some Internet resources search other engines and return the most promising results from each. These *meta search sites* include the following:

WebCrawler   <www.webcrawler.com>
Dogpile   <www.dogpile.com>
ProFusion   <www.profusion.com>
Ixquick   <www.ixquick.com>

For the most part, search engines are commercial ventures, so you may find ads on them and prominent postings of search results from businesses. For example, David Perez's search for *fire ants* on Lycos returned a short list of commercially sponsored links at the top of the page offering products such as pest-control kits. He had to scroll past this list (which is clearly labeled "Sponsored Links") to retrieve useful research information.

Conducting a Basic Search for Web Sites

Figure 7-1 shows a common sight (and site) on the Internet: a basic search template. When you enter a word or phrase (sometimes referred to on the Web as a *search string*) in the box and click "Google Search," the

Figure 7-1   Google's basic search template.

search engine conducts keyword searches of the Web pages it references. Unlike periodical databases and book catalogs, search engines do not typically search data records that are organized in fields such as subject, title, author, and abstract. Instead, most search engines search entire Web documents for the search string you enter. Because this type of search makes it easy to retrieve many irrelevant results, selecting effective keywords is extremely important. Learning how to select the best keywords requires a good deal of thought and experience; in many cases, you may still need to browse long lists of results. One very important skill is the ability to think of synonyms for the words that first come to mind because quite often the search will be more effective when you substitute another term for the one you had used originally. Also, you can import subject and keyword terms from successful searches in other resources. For example, in your Web search you might be able to use the terms that worked well in an earlier search of the EBSCOhost periodical database.

Once you think of some good keywords, you will probably want to combine them using Boolean connectors. Most Internet search engines support Boolean logic, as well as the use of wildcards and truncation. (See Chapter 4 for more on these topics.) You can usually use these in a search engine's basic search template; however, they may not work in exactly the same way in all search engines. For example, it may not be necessary to capitalize *and, or,* and *not* connectors on all search engines. You may find that some resources only allow Boolean searches from their advanced search page. Check the "help" feature for each search engine you are using to determine how to use these terms. (You typically must select the Advanced Search page to find the help link.)

Let's say a student investigating the topic *government funding of AIDS vaccine research,* for example, typed the term *AIDS* into Google's basic search template. This retrieved over 30 million hits, so she followed with these limiters:

AIDS U.S. government research, resulting in 4,550,000 hits
AIDS vaccine U.S. government research, resulting in 130,000 hits

Like many search engines, Google automatically conducts an *AND* search for side-by-side words, so the student did not need to type the Boolean connector between keywords. She could have placed quotation marks around *AIDS vaccine* and *U.S. government,* but she did not want to restrict her search only to Web pages containing those exact phrases (some Web pages, she reasoned, might contain the phrase "vaccine for AIDS" instead of "AIDS vaccine"). Surprised to still see such a huge number of hits, though, at this point the student thought more specifically about the information she needed and entered *AIDS vaccine U.S. government re-*

search funding shortage, resulting in 7,880 hits. Finally, she tried adding *politics* to the search string and retrieved 1,890 links. Although this is still far too many sources to read, the decrease in results indicates much more focus in the articles. Because Google lists the most relevant articles first, the student was able to find several good sources toward the top of the list.

Using an Advanced Search Template for Web Sites

Like periodical databases and library catalogs, search engines offer advanced search templates that can help you limit and expand your searches. The advanced search features vary between search engines, so it is best to familiarize yourself with the specific resource you are using before plunging into a search.

If you examine the advanced search templates for the major search engines listed in this chapter, you will find many of the common filters explained in Table 7-1, as well as various other features. These limiters and expanders can be set in conjunction with each other in order to construct complex searches. For example, if you conduct a basic Web search for *media literacy for children,* you would likely turn up a lot of irrelevant sites. Noticing that many of these sites are about financial grants for media-literacy projects, you might construct an advanced search like the one shown in Figure 7-2.

Table 7-1 Common Filters on Advanced Search Templates

Limiter/Expander	Allows you to ...
Domain	Limit results to more reliable sites hosted by educational institutions (*.edu*) or government entities (*.gov*).
Location	Search only for Web pages from a specific geographic location.
Date	Restrict results to Web pages posted or updated within a certain date range.
Medium	Choose the medium you are searching for: mp3, video, text, images, etc.
Search-string location	Specify where the search engine will look for the search string: in the Web page title, text, URL, or any of these.
Search-string occurrence or format	Search for Web pages containing an exact phrase, all, at least one, or none of the words in a search string.
"Safety" rating	Restrict or permit adult-oriented content.
Language	Find Web pages published in a certain language.

Searching for Sources

Google™
Advanced Search Tips | All About Google
Advanced Search

Find results	with **all** of the words		10 results ▼
	with the **exact phrase**	media literacy	Google Search
	with **at least one** of the words	children	
	without the words	grant	

Language — Return pages written in — any language ▼
File Format — Only ▼ return results of the file format — any format ▼
Date — Return web pages updated in the — anytime ▼
Occurrences — Return results where my terms occur — anywhere in the page ▼
Domain — Only ▼ return results from the site or domain — .gov
e.g. google.com, .org *More info*
SafeSearch — ⊙ No filtering ○ Filter using SafeSearch

Figure 7-2   An advanced search on Google.

Rather than returning thousands of hits, this search retrieves 404 results. Because the results are ranked by relevance, several potentially useful articles can be found toward the top of the list. Let's say, though, that you wish to focus your search even more by adding one more filtering requirement:

Occurrences Return results where my terms occur [in the title of the page ▼]

This time a rare thing happens for Web searches — no results are found! You return the "Occurrences" filter back to its original setting ("anywhere in the page") and decide to change the domain being searched to *.edu* (for educational institutions). Now you see two promising hits near the top of the search results: one is an article titled "Media Literacy Is Important for Children," posted on the University of Kentucky Web site, and the other is a site called *Tune In: The Children's Media Literacy Project,* hosted by North Carolina State University.

Using Internet Subject Directories

Some Web search tools organize the sites they index into menus of categories and subcategories. Following are examples of these subject directories:

Librarian's Index to the Internet   <http://lii.org>
The Internet Public Library   <www.ipl.org>
Yahoo!   <http://yahoo.com>

To use these subject directories, you work much as you did when reducing a subject to a topic for your paper. Beginning with the general category *health* at the Internet Public Library, for example, you can select the
subcategory *nutrition and diet* and end up with a listing of several potential sources (see Figure 7-3).

Unlike search engines, subject directories are put together by human
editors who choose, evaluate, and index the sites that go into the resource's
database. The Internet Public Library is prepared by staff at the University
of Michigan School of Information, so the Web sites it references have been
checked by university staff for reliability and coverage. Like many directories, it also lists reference works such as almanacs and calendars, and it
offers links to electronic books, newspapers, and other resources.

The menus are chosen by the designers of the directory. You can
browse these categories and subcategories (as illustrated in Figure 7-3),

Figure 7-3   Results of browsing a subject directory.

then scan the results when you arrive at what seems the most specific menu the subject directory provides for your topic. Another strategy is to type in keywords to search the entire directory or to search only within a specific category. At commercial sites such as Yahoo!, you may have to scroll down through advertisements and commercial links to reach the subject directories useful for research.

New directories are continually being developed and many of them are very specific. For example, WWWomen.com at <http://wwwomen.com> is a directory related to women's issues. To find other specialized Web directories, see the Appendix.

Evaluating Results of a Web Search

When you are looking for a few good sources, Web search results numbering in the hundreds or thousands can be daunting. If you have reasonably narrowed your search but still see an overwhelming number of hits, don't worry — search engines try to present the most useful results at the top of the list. They use artificial-intelligence methods to rank search results according to the location of the search string (whether it is found in the title, the headers, the top of the page, the body of the document, the hyperlinks, and so on). If the search string occurs in a significant place in the document (such as in the title), the link occurs higher in the list of results. If you enter more than one word in the search template, most search engines give higher placement to sources that feature your search string as a phrase.

A search engine cannot read your mind, however, so you should not rely too heavily on relevance ranking. One student looking for sources about the role of sports in child development began with a basic search for *child development AND organized sports*. Figure 7-4 shows a few hits from his search, along with some questions that will help you evaluate Web search results. After scanning the results and answering these questions, the student decided that the third link seemed the most helpful: Its title and lead-in text (sample passages containing keywords from the source) were the most relevant, and the domain name indicated that the site was sponsored by an organization. The link, in fact, uncovered a useful policy statement from the American Academy of Pediatrics.

Once you have screened your search results and uncovered some promising sources, you will still need to evaluate each of these sources in more depth. See Chapter 10 for a discussion of this process.

Using Other Web Resources

Web pages are the most commonly used Internet resource, but there are other ways to use the Internet for research. Some of them are Web

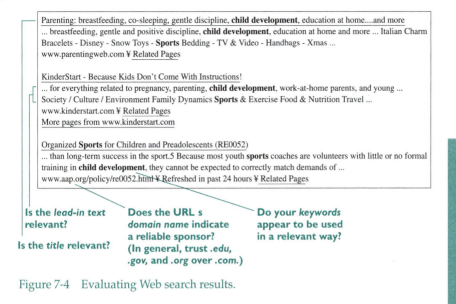

Parenting: breastfeeding, co-sleeping, gentle discipline, **child development**, education at home....and more
... breastfeeding, gentle and positive discipline, **child development**, education at home and more ... Italian Charm
Bracelets - Disney - Snow Toys - **Sports** Bedding - TV & Video - Handbags - Xmas ...
www.parentingweb.com ¥ Related Pages

KinderStart - Because Kids Don't Come With Instructions!
... for everything related to pregnancy, parenting, **child development**, work-at-home parents, and young ...
Society / Culture / Environment Family Dynamics **Sports** & Exercise Food & Nutrition Travel ...
www.kinderstart.com ¥ Related Pages
More pages from www.kinderstart.com

Organized **Sports** for Children and Preadolescents (RE0052)
... than long-term success in the sport.5 Because most youth **sports** coaches are volunteers with little or no formal
training in **child development**, they cannot be expected to correctly match demands of ...
www.aap.org/policy/re0052.html ¥ Refreshed in past 24 hours ¥ Related Pages

Is the *lead-in* text relevant?

Is the *title* relevant?

Does the URL s domain name indicate a reliable sponsor? (In general, trust *.edu*, *.gov*, and *.org* over *.com*.)

Do your *keywords* appear to be used in a relevant way?

Figure 7-4   Evaluating Web search results.

based, but they lead to message postings instead of Web sites. Others use protocols different from those of the Web.

Discussion Groups

Discussion groups are large-scale electronic seminars or forums devoted to a particular topic, ranging from *The X-Files* to *ecology* to *computer software* to *teaching English*. When you join such a group, you will be in contact with people throughout the world who share an interest in that subject. Discussion groups fall into two main categories: mailing lists and newsgroups.

Discussion groups are likely to prove most beneficial as research tools for those who are actively engaged in a particular academic discipline. Much of their value comes from listening in on the conversations of other people who are thinking out loud about questions in their chosen fields. Of course, when you have joined a newsgroup or mailing list, you will eventually want to add your own opinion to the dialogue. Also, when working on a research paper, you can ask questions, knowing that someone will give you an interesting and possibly valuable response.

In addition, discussion groups can be useful for getting leads about additional sources for your topic and for doing field research, such as sampling public opinion.

Mailing Lists. *Mailing lists,* also known as *listservs,* give you the chance to communicate via e-mail with a group of people who share your interests in a topic. Messages (comments, questions, and answers) go to a central computer called a list server, which then relays the messages to everyone who has subscribed to the list. You can, however, choose to respond either to the individual sender of a message or to everyone.

Once you know the name of a list you want to join, send an e-mail to the host to find out how to subscribe to it. The procedure may be as simple as stating "subscribe [list's name] [your name]." (There is no reason to mention your e-mail address because it automatically accompanies any e-mail you write.) If you first need to see what lists are available on your topic, you can write to a list server or visit one of these Web sites:

Google Groups	<http://groups.google.com>
Topica	<www.liszt.com>
Tile.Net	<http://tile.net/lists>

One of our students, Mary Kim, was researching the possible connection between breast cancer and diet. To find discussion groups relating to cancer, she sent this message:

To: listserv@listserv.net

Subject: send list

Message: list global/cancer

When she received by return e-mail the names of several cancer-related discussion groups, she chose the one dealing with breast cancer, of course. This was her next message:

To: listserv@listserv.net

Subject: (leave blank)

Message: subscribe breast-cancer Mary Kim

In a few minutes, she received an e-mail response stating, "Your subscription to BREAST-CANCER list [breast-cancer discussion list] has been accepted." She also received a description of the group's purpose and guidelines for participating in the discussion. Instructions for canceling the subscription were also included. Mary saved these to use when her research was done.

Many listservs make their messages available not only as e-mail but on Web pages that are frequently updated. They may also offer resources in a related Web site. Check with the list owner or see the listserv instructions for the listserv you want to use.

Newsgroups. A newsgroup is a type of discussion group whose postings can be accessed through a Web browser. For those just beginning to wrestle with research papers, newsgroups are more likely than mailing lists to yield results.

Newsgroups operate slightly differently from mailing lists. Here all the messages go to a virtual bulletin board, and you have to go to it every time you want to see what has been posted. With a mailing list, the messages go to your inbox and are kept on file there, just like all your other e-mail. This might seem quite convenient, but if a huge number of these messages starts to accumulate, you may wish you were using a newsgroup so that you could review the postings without having to erase them as you move along. In a newsgroup, however, the server removes old messages periodically, forcing you to keep an eye on changes. Be sure to copy anything that seems useful before it is erased.

For a schedule of newsgroup lists, you can visit Google Groups at <http://groups.google.com> or Tile.net at <http://tile.net/lists>. These Web sites allow you to search newsgroup listings by keywords or phrases. David Perez, for example, searched Tile.net using the keyword *ecology* and came up with a few relevant newsgroups. Posting a question about fire ants, he received several useful e-mail responses, one of which provided an ecologist's firsthand accounts of the destruction caused by fire ants in her region. Fred used this information in his paper, citing it as "Personal Communication" (following the American Psychological Association–style documentation guidelines he was using).

A Few Words of Caution. When participating in discussion groups, keep the following in mind:

- *Frame any questions you ask a discussion group fairly specifically.* David Perez would not have gotten very far if he had merely asked, "Can anyone tell me about fire ants?"

- *Do not ask an obvious question.* Such a question would be one that the group members assume everyone in the group already knows the answer to. To avoid being *flamed* with angry replies for asking such a question, look at the group's home page and read the Frequently Asked Questions (FAQ) link.

- *Be sensitive to the nature of the group's topic.* For example, don't show up at a discussion group for Vietnam veterans and request battle stories about how bad it was.

- *Remember that discussion groups are not always reliable sources of information.* Although some groups edit postings, mainly to exclude offensive or inappropriate material, generally anyone can write almost anything to these groups.

Resources for Advanced Internet Users

Before there was a World Wide Web, researchers on the Internet had to use several older protocols, such as gopher, FTP (file transfer protocol), and telnet. These protocols do not use hypertext, so, instead of beginning with *http://*, URLs for the materials they provide access to start with *gopher, ftp,* or *telnet.* Most of these materials have been incorporated into the Web, but those of you who enjoy expertise with the computer and have a fair amount of patience for relatively slow retrieval methods may want to venture into these areas.

Gopher stores vast amounts of information in layers so that you pursue your objective by moving from the very general to the more specific, one stage (menu) at a time. (Gopher got its name in part because it burrows deeper and deeper into layers of information.) If your college has a gopher system, follow the screen instructions to access the system. If an Internet search returns an address that starts with *gopher://*, once you click on that address, you will see instructions for navigating the menus.

FTP lets you download (transfer) files from another computer into yours. *Full-service FTP* lets you transfer files between any computers for which you have passwords or access privileges. *Anonymous (restricted-access) FTP* lets you retrieve only publicly available files from archives of text, music, or art.

Some Internet sites allow you to access their files through gopher or the Web, and then to use FTP to copy or print what you find. Depending on the type of information you are seeking and your mode of access, learning FTP could be very valuable as a means of collecting documents. Be sure to consult a librarian to learn how to use this resource because the method varies from place to place.

Telnet protocol provides access to other computer databases, where you will be working with directories and menus, from general to specific. In effect, telnet connects your computer to another and makes it possible to use that computer as if it were your own. The procedure of telnetting differs from one computer network to the next, so you need to follow the directions posted at your location or ask for help. Although it is no longer common, some library Web sites will switch you into telnet mode as you enter their catalogs. Others offer a telnet link to the catalog in case you are having trouble with the Web browser. Telnet connections typically ask you to identify the type of monitor you are using when you access them. If you don't know, take the first menu choice (usually "VT100").

8

Finding Other Kinds of Sources

Although you can produce a fine research paper based entirely on books, periodicals, and perhaps Web sources, other resources may give you still more information and ideas. These include other kinds of material available within your own library, the resources of other libraries and nonacademic organizations, and television and radio programs. In addition, for some topics in certain fields, you may find it useful or may even be required to do field research in the form of interviews and surveys.

Other Materials in Your Own Library

Special Collections

Some libraries maintain separate collections of materials such as books, periodicals, personal letters, and manuscripts. A special collection sometimes relates to rather specific areas of interest: a particular author's works, the history of a particular place, or a fairly narrow field (cave exploration, Broadway musicals, or aviation engineering). Other special collections are kept separate from the main collection because their holdings are fragile, rare, or otherwise unusual. Information about special collections can usually be found on your library's Web page. Typically each special collection has its own catalog. Some special collections, such as photographs or multimedia displays, are digitized and available on the Web.

Microforms

In addition to books and periodicals, your library probably has a collection of *microforms,* materials available on *microfilm* (rolls of film on which printed materials are reproduced in miniature) or *microfiche* (sheets of microfilm containing images of many pages of printed material, arranged in rows). To read microforms, you need a special machine. In some libraries, an aide will help set up the microform reader; in others, you must load the reader yourself, following instructions posted nearby. Using such readers is simple, and you should be able to operate one easily after a couple of attempts. Also, most microfilm readers can print out copies of material you want to examine further, often for a small fee.

Many source materials have been preserved on microforms to save space, avoid wear and tear on delicate holdings, and increase usefulness. The most common sources available on microforms are periodicals, particularly newspapers; others include old and rare books and even facsimiles of manuscripts. Some sources, such as graduate dissertations, may be published only as microforms.

The Vertical File

Some printed sources may not be classified as books or as periodicals and so will appear in neither the library catalog nor the periodical indexes. Such materials include pamphlets, brochures, and clippings from hard-to-get periodicals on specialized topics. You can find these resources by using the *vertical file,* a collection of various materials that is usually kept in file cabinets. A librarian can explain how to use a vertical file and tell you whether and how the file is indexed.

Audiovisual Materials

Many libraries contain media sections that house films, videotapes, pictures, slides, and sound recordings. If your topic concerns the performing or visual arts, architecture, or the social or natural sciences, you will often find materials useful to your research in the audiovisual collection. You most likely will be able to search for audiovisual materials in the online catalog. You may be able to set the search field labeled *format, material,* or *medium* to look only for audiovisual material. In addition to materials on the arts, you can find valuable documentaries and interviews, especially in those fields having to do with human and animal behavior and society.

Other Print Sources

Private businesses, nonprofit organizations, special-interest groups, and various levels of government agencies publish reports and pamphlets in great numbers. Usually these materials can be obtained free of charge by writing to the organizations or contacting them through their

Web site. In most cases, no catalog is available to which you can refer, so you may have to describe what you are looking for and hope the answer meets your needs. The *Monthly Catalog* of the U.S. Government Printing Office (GPO) lists all federal government publications that are available to the public, their prices, and the addresses from which they may be ordered. Your library should have a copy of the catalog, and you can ask your librarian where it is kept. Be warned, however, that you may wait a month or more for materials ordered. You can also access the GPO's Web site at <www.gpoaccess.gov>.

Television and Radio Programs

Many radio and television broadcasters, including National Public Radio and the Public Broadcasting Service (PBS), regularly present programs about the performing and graphic arts, the natural and social sciences, politics, and other topics. These programs are often repeated several times, so you may be able to watch broadcasts originally shown before you started your research project. Many libraries acquire tapes of programs aired on PBS and other stations, so check your library. If your topic has to do with a current issue, be alert for interviews and documentaries scheduled on any station. (The programming schedule may be available on the Web.) Transcripts usually require four to six weeks' delivery time, so, in most cases, you will have to make your own transcription. If possible, record the program and later transcribe word for word those portions of it you want to use, rather than trying to take notes during the program.

Audiovisual Material from the Web

The Web is a great source not only of text material, as discussed in Chapter 7, but also of audiovisual content. The Web offers a huge variety of images, sound recordings, and video that may provide useful information for your project. For example, National Public Radio archives recordings of many of its programs and makes them available online at <www.npr.org>. Web sites focusing on biology may use video animations to demonstrate the functions of internal organs. The Web also offers many types of photographs: historical, fine art, and current events, to name a few.

To access and use these media, you will need the appropriate software and some knowledge of the types of files involved. Table 8-1 gives an overview of the types of files you may find on the Internet and the kinds of programs you will need to access them.

Many files in these formats can be downloaded and saved, but some files are large and must be saved to a hard drive or disc that will hold large files. To save a multimedia file, right click on its link and choose

Table 8-1   File Formats for Audiovisual Material on the Web

Medium	File Format	How to Access
images	.jpeg .gif .tiff	Web browser or Image viewer
sound recordings	.midi .wav .mp3 .ra	Web browser, Media Player, or Real Audio
video	.ram (RealVideo) .mpeg .mov .avi	Web browser, Media Player, Quick Time, or Real Video

"Save Target As" (note that this does not work for all formats, however). For images, put the cursor on the image, right click, and select "Save Picture."

In some cases, you may even be able to present some of these media to your audience. See Chapter 15 to learn about incorporating audiovisual material into your paper. Whether you use an entire source or just a piece of information from it, be sure to carefully document audiovisual material that you find on the Web.

Interviews and Surveys

For some research projects, you may want to engage in some first-hand investigation to confirm what your sources have written or to learn more about what you have read. In some courses, especially in the social sciences, you may be required to obtain some information on your own, whether by interviewing knowledgeable people or by sampling public opinion through a poll or a questionnaire.

Both interviewing and surveying call for careful planning and consultation with your teacher to be successful. However, do not be discouraged by the unfamiliarity of these approaches. Knowing how to ask questions effectively can be an important asset in many situations.

Interviews

You may want to set up an interview with a person whose knowledge and opinions would be useful to your research project. Perhaps a faculty member is an authority on your topic, or a local public official administers a program relevant to your research. Depending on your topic, you may well find that interviews with people who possess special knowledge or have undergone unusual experiences will yield valuable information.

If you would like to interview someone who lives too far away from you to meet in person, consider doing an interview by phone or e-mail. In fact, e-mail may be an attractive option even for a local interview because it does not require that you and the interviewee be available at the same time. The following discussion assumes a face-to-face interview, but most of the same advice applies to interviews conducted by other means.

Setting Up Interviews. When you request a personal interview, prepare thoroughly and carefully for the meeting. Here are some guidelines for doing so:

- Write, telephone, or e-mail as early as possible, explaining to the person just why you want the meeting. Specify your field of inquiry as precisely as you can, and explain why you think this interview can help you get a better grasp of the topic you are researching. Let the person know that you will limit the interview to a few pertinent questions that will not take up too much time.

- Review your questions with your instructor. Forming brief questions that will bring out the kind of information you need is an art, and you may need help the first time. You might even offer to send the questions to the interviewee in advance of the actual interview.

- Ask ahead of time whether the interviewee minds if you bring a tape recorder to the interview. If you meet objections, don't persist. Bringing the machine and asking permission just before the session starts puts the other person under unwelcome pressure to let you proceed. After all, taking notes will serve your purposes almost as well.

Conducting Interviews. The attitude you assume will be important to the success of your interview. Keep in mind that the authority is a research source and that your main concern is to find out what the person knows or believes about some aspect of your topic. At the time of an interview, you are gathering sources to test the hypothesis you have chosen to guide your research. This means that you have not yet arrived at a particular conclusion regarding your topic. Thus your job is to listen carefully to the person's responses to your questions and summarize major points in your notes. If you enter into an interview with a biased point of view, your source may catch the tone of your remarks and give you little, if anything, in the way of useful information or opinions.

Also keep in mind that you are asking a favor of a busy person; never let yourself think that you are generously offering an opportunity to share ideas with an intelligent listener. Following are some guidelines for conducting successful interviews:

- Arrive on time. In fact, for your own comfort, try to be at least five minutes early. Most people value punctuality.

- Bring a large pad or notebook and several pens or pencils in case one of them stops functioning. Look as though this meeting is important to you.

- Come prepared with a written series of questions aimed at eventually leading to the specific information you are seeking. You may not need to stick doggedly to the list because the answers to some questions may come out quite naturally before you ask for them. Having a list prevents you from forgetting to ask all your questions, and it can help you control the flow of the interview. Furthermore, the interviewee will respect you for being so conscientious.

- If the interviewee has agreed to be taped, be sure the recorder is ready to work immediately, fresh batteries and tape already in place.

- Write a note thanking the person for the interview.

You may find it helpful to read the following examples, describing how two students went about planning and conducting their interviews.

Example 1: Planning an Interview. Jeremy, a sociology student, decided to base his research project on a unit of the course concerning society's reaction to antisocial behavior by young people. He narrowed his preliminary topic to *the effectiveness of curfews in reducing antisocial behavior by teenagers.*

Jeremy had become interested in curfews after seeing a TV news segment in which a group of teens were being questioned in a nearby town by police officers who wanted to know what the teens were doing out on the street during the nighttime curfew period. Jeremy's initial feelings about curfews, based on the TV segment, were that they were very difficult to enforce and, if enforced strongly, might actually make teenage antisocial behavior even worse in the long run.

After meeting with his instructor, Jeremy agreed that research derived from interviewing might provide the best information for his topic because curfews were relatively new approaches to crime prevention, especially in the area in which he lived. With further thought, he decided he would try to interview the mayor of each of three towns that had instituted curfews within the past two years. In this way, he would gather information on how the curfews were working, at least from the official and administrative point of view. After talking to his instructor again, Jeremy came up with the following questions for the mayors or other knowledge-able officials.

- Has your curfew succeeded in reducing crime by young people to the extent you expected it would? Are there any before-and-after statistics?

- Have police reported any major problems in enforcing the curfew? What are the penalties for those who break the law? Are parents penalized for their children's noncompliance?

- I understand that several legal challenges to your curfew are in the courts. What groups or individuals have initiated these challenges? On what grounds? Do you have any doubts that your law will withstand such challenges?

- Have any businesses or social organizations objected to the curfew? Are exemptions allowed for special events?

- Have you seen any change in the relationship between the police and young people since the advent of the curfew law?

- Would you say, overall, that the curfew law has improved the quality of life for most citizens of your town?

Example 2: Conducting an Interview. Ben, a political science student, chose the North American Free Trade Agreement (NAFTA) from a list of subjects assigned by his instructor. In his reading of magazine articles and essays from journals such as *Foreign Affairs*, Ben felt that several of his questions were not answered as clearly as he wanted. At his roommate's suggestion, he set up an interview with an economics professor, who he believed would supply him with a few answers that would confirm his hypothesis that NAFTA would turn out to be harmful to the U.S. econ-omy. Ben felt confident that his research up to that point had given him sufficient knowledge of his topic to enter the interview without a specific questioning strategy. This attitude proved embarrassing.

After exchanging pleasantries with the professor, Ben plunged right into the questioning with "Can you tell me why anyone would want to sell us on a treaty that will cost U.S. workers so many jobs?"

After a moment's thought, the professor told Ben that he should have done more background reading before coming to see her. Saying that she did not have time to fill him in on all the details of the proposed treaty, she asked to end the interview. Ben protested that he had read numerous commentaries before reaching his opposition to NAFTA, but his defense did not satisfy the professor. Later, perplexed at his embar-rassing loss of a source, Ben complained to a friend that the professor had been unreasonable.

He received a little sympathy and a good piece of advice. His friend had written several papers that involved interviews, and she pointed out that he had forgotten the fundamental purpose of the interview — to gain more information about the topic. Ben's opening question had led the economics professor to believe that Ben would not listen to her ideas because he had already formed a strong opinion. Also, because she probably supported NAFTA, judging from her accusing Ben of ignorance on the subject, she did not want to spend time arguing with him.

Ben's friend recalled some of her instructor's advice on approaching an interview: Remember that your objective is to learn something, not to show how much you know or what you think. Give any experts you consult a chance to let you know how they view the topic and what they believe are the major points to be considered. The best way to open an interview is, therefore, with a rather general approach, free of any indication that you have reached a conclusion.

In short, tempting as it may seem, do not give in to the urge to impress the expert with your own knowledge and good judgment. Throughout the session, keep opening up possibilities for the other person to impress you. After all, the other person is the expert, or else you would not have asked for an interview.

Deciding to test his friend's advice, Ben called on another economics professor, who agreed to a half-hour interview. Ben began his questioning in this way: "I've been doing a fair amount of research on NAFTA, and I hoped you could help me understand some of the complex issues it raises."

The professor spoke initially about the provisions of the treaty, almost all of which Ben already knew. Ben waited patiently before asking: "How might this treaty affect American workers in industries that could employ Mexican workers, who earn much less than Americans performing the same work?"

The professor's response seemed, at first, to support Ben's opinion that U.S. workers would suffer, but the professor went on to show ways in which American labor might benefit. He finally shared with Ben his judgment as to the overall effect of the treaty, carefully detailing his argument with specific examples of both positive and negative outcomes. Ben was able to close the interview by asking for clarification of several puzzling points that had originally led him to undertake the interview.

Ben had asked both professors if they minded his taping the interviews, and both agreed. His roommate had interviewed a doctor in a Veterans Administration hospital about the quality of care received by Vietnam veterans, and that person refused to be recorded. Maybe the doctor felt uneasy because he could not be sure who might end up hearing his comments, which were in fact fairly candid. Some people, however, just plain feel nervous with a recorder running, and you should cheerfully respect their wishes, particularly if you want the interview to go smoothly.

Surveys

We will assume for this discussion that the main sources for your research paper will come from a library. If, at some point, you want to make a poll or questionnaire the central feature in a research paper, you must consult your instructor to obtain far more complete guidelines than we have space for in this book. Our suggestions are intended to help you decide whether to venture into this mode of research. We surely do not want to discourage anyone, because creating one of the sources in your own paper adds an exciting personal touch to the project.

Someone might ask whether opinions gathered from the general public by a student researcher can be regarded as authoritative sources, but that is not the relevant question. A more useful way to think about polling would be to ask how sampling people's opinions can enhance the research project. Until you write a paper based primarily on field research, the opinions you gather can serve only as interesting complements to the judgments found in your other sources.

When to Do a Survey. When newspapers, magazines, radio and television stations, or Web sites tell us what ordinary people are thinking about an issue, you may want to test these reports to get a firsthand sense of public opinion. You can legitimately consider doing a survey when your topic deals with an issue that directly affects the lives of some people on campus or in the surrounding community. Consider the following issues:

- AIDS education
- sex education in public schools
- school vouchers
- drug use
- teenage pregnancy
- taxes
- violent crime
- police handling of sensitive situations
- women's opportunities in the workplace
- sexual harassment
- the war with Iraq
- the quality of public education
- college admission standards
- affirmative action
- gay and lesbian rights

Searching for Sources

A check on the accuracy of media polling may seem necessary in certain situations. You may think that the media asked questions in such a way that the answers did not truly reflect public opinion. For example, maybe they forced respondents to choose between only two alternatives and you think that many people actually prefer a compromise between the two or some other option entirely. You may believe that their sampling method was flawed. They may have selected people from one or two social or geographical groups who could be most easily approached within their reporters' deadlines.

In 1936, when polling was first becoming part of American election campaigns, a poll conduced by *Literary Digest* magazine predicted that the Democratic presidential candidate, Franklin Roosevelt, would be defeated for reelection. On Election Day, however, he won a landslide victory. The error lay in conducting the poll by telephone. In those days, a great many American households could not afford phones, and those that could were disproportionately Republican.

Planning a Survey. If you plan to conduct a survey, you need to make several important and interrelated decisions. Ask yourself the following questions:

- *How many questions do I need to ask?*   Ask enough questions to get a clear sense of public opinion on the issue and to make sure that you are not oversimplifying it. Try to keep the number to a minimum so that the people you survey won't feel imposed on and so that you won't have too much material to analyze and work into your paper. The way you conduct the survey may also affect the number of questions you choose to ask, or vice versa.

- *How many people do I need to poll?*   The answer to this question is closely related to your polling method. If you need only a small sample, you may simply decide to interview all the people individually. However, if you need many respondents, it may be easier and faster to do an e-mail poll. In addition, keep in mind that more responses mean more material to analyze. Ask your instructor what size sample seems appropriate for your particular objectives.

- *How should I choose the people to poll?*   Do you want to survey everyone in your dorm or your online discussion group? The first twenty people who agree to take one of your questionnaires? An equal number of men and women? Students or nonstudents? Think about whether you want to focus on — or to exclude — members of a group whose opinions relate directly to your hypothesis. For example, the student writing on immigration restricted her sample population to people born in the United States whose parents were also born here so that she could avoid opinions that were influenced by a natural sympathy for immigrants. If you do not screen the respondents ahead of time, you may need to include some questions about personal background in the questionnaire to help determine whether to include the responses of particular respondents who are not a part of the group you want to survey.

- *How will I find the people I want and actually do the survey?* If you are going to hand out questionnaires at a bus stop or subway entrance, use only a few questions, and keep them brief and simple. Be ready for a good many refusals and hasty responses. If you feel you need to ask quite a few questions or complex questions, plan on catching people in the cafeteria or letting them take the question sheets with them and return them to you. (*Warning:* If people take the questionnaires with them, you will need to give out two or three times as many as you hope to receive because many people will forget to return them or change their minds about participating in the survey.)

Unlike questionnaires, surveys by e-mail or phone enable you to ask follow-up questions that may help to clarify the answers to your original questions. However, it also makes the survey feel more personal and less anonymous — and therefore may discourage people from participating or make their responses less candid. In planning the survey, you must weigh all these considerations — the number and nature of the questions, the size and composition of the sample, and the method of sampling — to decide how to proceed.

Stages of Work. Whatever you decide about how to develop and administer the survey, be sure to give yourself plenty of time to complete the job. In addition to the actual sampling, the work falls into the following stages:

- *Select and formulate the questions.* Start by going to the periodicals that have reported public opinion on your topic and using their questions as a basis for your own survey. You may want to rephrase some of the questions, especially if you suspect that the phrasing encouraged answers that did not reflect the true opinions of those polled. Because the wording of survey questions requires a good deal of sophistication about language as well as polling techniques, check the phrasing with your instructor.
- *Prepare the questionnaires.* If you are distributing the questionnaires by hand, type the questions for easy readability, and leave plenty of space for comments. Reproduce more question sheets than you think

Searching for Sources

you will need. If you are doing an e-mail survey, be sure it is clear where the respondents should type their answers. For any survey method in which you do not get immediate responses, give people a deadline for responding and, for questionnaires on paper, clear instructions for where and how to return them.

- *Review the responses and form conclusions.* In analyzing the responses and reporting them in your paper, you should throw out questions that seem to have confused or misled the respondents. In writing the paper, do not simply list all the questions and the numbers of people who responded. Rather, tie all the pieces of information together into a coherent package that can be discussed in relation to the views of experts on the topic or to the results of polling by the media. Before going into detail about your findings, take time to tell readers why you conducted the survey and how you chose your sample group.

Reviewing Part Two

The following questions and exercises will help you reinforce and practice the skills covered in Part Two. For additional practice, visit <bedfordstmartins.com/writingresearch>.

Questions

1. Suppose you are looking for a particular biography of Queen Elizabeth I of England, *Elizabeth the First* by Paul Johnson. How can you find this book in the library catalog? How can the catalog help you locate other books about Queen Elizabeth?

2. How is each of these pieces of information, found in entries in the library catalog, useful to researchers?

   author   date of publication

   title   number of pages

   subject   notation about a bibliography

   call number

3. What are the differences between print-based periodical indexes and electronic periodical databases? What are the advantages and disadvantages of each?

4. For each of the following topics, what types of sources would be useful? How would you search for those sources?

   - the latest government recommendations about energy conservation
   - a seventeenth-century book (all known copies are owned by British libraries)
   - the inaugural address of President John F. Kennedy
   - the kinds of jobs accepted by recent graduates of your school
   - the history of the town in which your college is located
   - your city's or town's model program for pest control
   - the major works of a particular artist
   - the position on a controversial issue taken recently by the governor

5. What are the similarities in searching for books, periodicals, and Internet sources? What are the differences?

6. Define each of the following terms and explain their significance in searching for sources: data record, data field, basic search template, advanced search template, Boolean logic, truncation, filtering.

7. Why is it highly unlikely that you could effectively search electronic resources such as library catalogs, periodical databases, and the Internet without talking with librarians? In consulting these people, what questions would you be likely to ask?

8. What might surveys and interviews add to a research paper? For which kinds of projects might the results of surveys and interviews be most useful? What are some problems associated with using surveys and interviews, and what steps can be taken to address these problems?

Exercises

1. Use the library catalog to look up a fairly recent work of fiction by a well-known author. Consult the library's classification guide to find the shelf where the book should be located. Use the *Book Review Digest* to find out if the book was reviewed during the year it was published or the following year. Report your findings.

2. Using microfilms of the *New York Times*, find the most important story reported on the day and year you were born. (The lead story is usually in the upper right corner of the front page.) Then, in the *New York Times Index*, find a listing for this article and the next *Times* article on the same subject. Copy both listings, converting all abbreviations to the full forms of the words that they represent.

3. Use a periodical database to locate an article published during the past year, offering an opinion or commentary about your favorite hobby, pastime, or field of interest. Acquire the article, determine the author's topic and thesis, and explain briefly why you agree or disagree with this thesis.

4. Choose one of the topics listed under Question 2 in Reviewing Part One questions. Do a subject search in the library catalog to find the titles of three books related to the topic. Write out these titles and their call numbers, and describe briefly where in the library each is located.

5. Think of a fairly specific topic in psychology or medical science that interests you. Use a periodical database to discover how many articles have been written on that topic during the past three years. Use an advanced search template to reduce your findings to a manageable list of fewer than twenty. Record appropriate article and journal titles and explain the process you used to reduce the list.

6. Using a subject directory on the Internet (such as Yahoo! or the Librarian's Guide to the Internet), try to find one of the following

topics without doing a keyword search; that is, try to predict which subject headings would contain the information and then attempt to find your way to the topic. Write a one-page summary explaining which paths you took, what you found out about the subject directory's organization, and what kind of information you found for the topic.

- the Holocaust
- *The Matrix Reloaded*
- the National Football League, the Ladies Professional Golf Association, the Women's National Basketball Association, or Major League Baseball
- tennis
- golf
- the Atkins diet
- addictions
- Italian cooking, Chinese cooking, or another type of cooking
- gay and lesbian issues
- Native American issues
- AIDS prevention
- Swedish immigration
- care of tropical fish
- sportfishing
- Israel
- terrorism
- men's or women's fashion
- UFOs
- silicone implants
- senior citizens' issues
- Ronald Reagan
- John F. Kennedy
- Vietnam
- bees
- Koala bears
- group therapies

7. Using a search engine, construct a basic keyword search to find five sources on one or more of the following topics:
   - the effect of corporate downsizing on blue-collar workers
   - groups that deny the reality of the Nazi Holocaust

Searching for Sources

- the effects of the USA Patriot Act
- the effect of the antiterrorism bill of 1996 on legal immigrants and naturalized citizens
- the effect of the government's farm subsidy bills on small farmers during the last fifty years

8. Using a search engine's advanced search template, narrow the results for one of the searches you conducted in Exercise 7. Use at least two of the possible filters ("Find results without the words . . ." and "Only return results from the site or domain . . . ," for example). Write a brief paragraph explaining why you chose these filters and how they helped you narrow your search.

9. Join an interesting mailing list or newsgroup and report (in a couple of pages) on what issues seem to concern the group's members most.

10. Think ahead to possible uses of the Internet in your research project. Write a step-by-step plan for using the Internet as a resource for your research paper.

Part Three

Working with Sources

Working with Sources

9

Developing a Working Bibliography

Now that you have a good idea of the research aids available in your library, you can begin the process of searching for sources by developing a *working bibliography* — a list of possible sources for your paper. These titles may have come from the library catalog, from electronic databases or print indexes, from the Internet, or from bibliographies you saw in your background reading. Ultimately, you will use some of the information you find in these sources to support the thesis of your paper. Those sources that provide specific ideas and information for the paper will be listed in your *final bibliography*, which will be called Works Cited, References, or Bibliography, depending on which documentation style you are using. (See Chapters 18 through 20 for more on the various documentation styles.)

Setting Up the Working Bibliography

To begin putting together a working bibliography, decide on a format for recording information about possible sources. You could use three- by five-inch note cards for *bibliography cards,* or you could keep bibliographic information in a notebook. You could also set up a computer file or note-taking software. Then, whenever you come across the title of a book or an article that seems like it might be worth taking notes from, make a bibliography entry for it.

If you use cards, create a separate card for each item, and keep the cards in alphabetical order. Cards are handier for this purpose than a simple list because they can more easily be kept in order as you add and drop items from your working bibliography. If you are working with a word processor, you can keep these bibliographical notes in a special file, which you will constantly be updating. Some commercial note-taking software programs allow you to create separate entries for each source you consult, which you can search and sort by various keywords. The file you generate will, after you have pruned its contents, produce the works cited section of the final paper.

If your library catalog allows you to print entries as you search, you can save time in gathering your working bibliography. Similarly, you might be able to print results from electronic database searches. You can print out and organize lists of sources produced by a particular keyword, or separate each entry and sort, drop, and add entries alphabetically as you would cards. Be careful, though, not to find yourself collecting just any source you come across because of the convenience of printing.

Some libraries allow you to send an e-mail to yourself or to download to a diskette results from catalog and database searches. You can then easily add the results to your computer file or print out the entries and file them like cards. Before you rely on downloading or e-mailing search results, be sure the computer entries contain all the information you will need to locate the book or article. You ought to test the system before you do an extensive search to be sure you can successfully retrieve downloaded and e-mailed entries.

For a working bibliography entry to be useful, it must contain all the information you will need when you prepare the footnotes or endnotes and the works cited or references list for your paper. In addition, the entry should give you whatever information is needed to find the book or article in the library. If you are using cards, place in the upper right corner of every bibliography card the library call number or other locator information from the library catalog. If you are keeping your working bibliography in a notebook, place the locator information in the margins beside the bibliography entry, or use a separate page for each entry and place the locator in the upper right corner of the page. If you are using computer files, place the locator information at the top of the entry. Whatever method you use, take extra care to copy all bibliographical information correctly. Misspellings, incorrect punctuation, careless omissions, and other mistakes in copying can waste time in return trips to the library.

Books

To make an entry for a book, record the following information (see Figure 9-1):

- name of the author or the editor (last name first)
- title and subtitle of the book (underlined)
- place of publication
- publisher's name
- date of publication
- library call number (in upper right corner)

PS — call
1541   number
25

author —— Johnson, Thomas H. <u>Emily Dickinson: An Interpretive</u>
title —— <u>Biography.</u> Cambridge, MA: Harvard University —— publication
(underlined)   Press, 1955.   information

Figure 9-1   Bibliography card for a book.

Periodical Articles

For a periodical article, include the following information (see Figure
9-2):

- name of the author (if available)
- title of the article (in quotation marks)
- title of the periodical (underlined)
- volume number and date of publication
- numbers of the pages on which the article appears
- location in a library

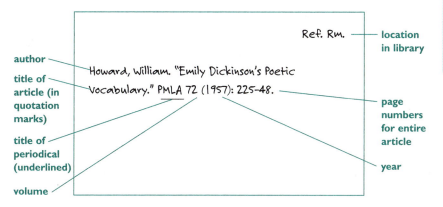

Ref. Rm. —— location
in library

author —
title of —— Howard, William. "Emily Dickinson's Poetic
article (in   Vocabulary." PMLA 72 (1957): 225-48. ——
quotation   page
marks)   numbers
for entire
title of —   article
periodical
(underlined)   year
volume —

Figure 9-2   Bibliography card for a periodical article.

For periodical articles that come from electronic databases, record the information listed above and then add the following:

- name of the database
- name of the database service (if different from the specific database)
- the name of the library you used to access the database
- date of access

Web Sites

For a document taken from a Web site, include the following information (see Figure 9-3):

- name of the author (if available)
- title of the document (in quotation marks), unless you are citing an entire Web site
- print publication information (if available), for documents also published in print format
- name of the site (underlined)
- date of electronic publication or last update (if available)
- URL
- date you accessed the page

The guidelines listed for books, periodical articles, and Web sites show you the basic information you should record for the most common types of sources. However, you also may find yourself using other sources

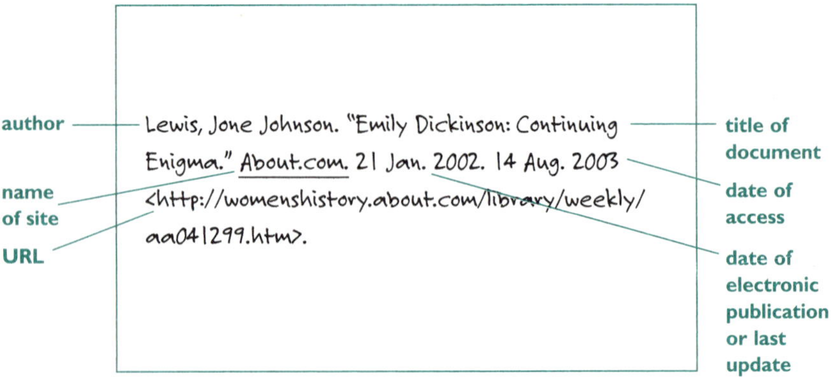

Working with Sources

author ——— Lewis, Jone Johnson. "Emily Dickinson: Continuing ——— **title of document**
Enigma." About.com. 21 Jan. 2002. 14 Aug. 2003
name of site <http://womenshistory.about.com/library/weekly/ **date of access**
URL aa041299.htm>. **date of electronic publication or last update**

Figure 9-3   Bibliography card for a Web site.

such as audiovisual media, lectures, or pamphlets. If so, consult Part Five for further details on the bibliographic information needed for those types of sources.

Gathering Potential Sources

You will almost always collect more titles for your working bibliography than will appear in your final list of works cited or references because many potential sources will, on closer reading, prove to be no help in the investigation of your hypothesis. The problem is that when you are looking through the library catalog or a periodical index, you may not have the full information needed to judge the usefulness of the source. Although you cannot add every interesting source you locate to your working bibliography, you should add every source that is likely to be useful for your project.

Many of these potential sources will turn out to be worthless for your purposes, so your working bibliography will shrink accordingly when you later critically evaluate your sources for usefulness (see Chapter 10). However, while you are dropping disappointing items from your list, you may be adding titles that are mentioned in the useful sources. You should, therefore, expect to be adding and dropping potential sources from your working bibliography throughout your research.

Four Students Gather Their Sources

Fred Hutchins began assembling a working bibliography while reading background sources about Cotton Mather. First, he came across several potentially useful titles at the end of the encyclopedia article on Cotton Mather. He then went to the library catalog to learn whether those titles were available in his library. Three books were available, two of which yielded information that helped support his eventual thesis. Furthermore, all three books contained bibliographies that led to other useful sources. From these sources, Fred was able to acquire a sizable working bibliography before he began a methodical search through the library catalog and periodical indexes.

Once he had followed up these early leads, Fred went back to the catalog. He did keyword searches using the subject headings that were related to his topic, such as *Mather, Cotton,* and *Puritans and Massachusetts.* Then, following up on clues from the background reading he had done, Fred did a keyword search for sources on *witchcra*ft and then *witchcraft and New England.*

Fred rejected a number of items, such as Christina Larner's *Enemies of God: The Witch-hunt in Scotland,* because their titles indicated nothing that applied to the Salem witch trials. However, he made out bibliography entries for any title that seemed likely to prove useful. Later, when he examined each of these books closely, he eliminated most of them from his working bibliography because he found that they were general overviews or surveys, much like those in textbooks, which repeated the same basic facts about Mather and his relationship to the Salem witch trials.

Finally, Fred searched through several periodical indexes, using *Cotton Mather* as a keyword in a search of abstracts, subjects, and titles. Some of the titles and abstracts he found clearly indicated little or no relationship to the witch trials, so Fred left them off his working bibliography. Others sounded vaguely useful, but these, too, Fred later rejected — either because they did not relate directly to his topic or because the information they provided had already been recorded in his notes. In the end, Fred used two periodical articles as sources. One was extremely valuable for its brief discussions and analyses of several theories attempting to explain the Salem witchcraft outbreak; the other provided information about an important subtopic in Fred's final paper.

Do not be misled by Fred's using just two periodical articles in his paper. His case is fairly unusual. Many papers, especially those dealing with topics in the sciences and the social sciences, list more articles than books as sources. (For example, see David Perez's paper on fire ants in Chapter 22.)

The student who researched the economic and social impact of new immigrants on the United States used the same basic strategies for gathering sources but with somewhat different results. Shirley Macalbe's works cited list contains three essays from two books of collected essays, five books that discuss immigration from particular viewpoints, one periodical article, two Web sources, and one personal interview. Along the way, Shirley interviewed more than twenty other people and sampled a number of books and Web sites that told of the experiences of individual immigrants, past and present, in their struggles to find security and success in America. She found most of these interesting and some of them quite moving. In the end, however, she decided that they were too personal and too subjective for the kind of general paper she had planned to write.

The student who researched Emily Dickinson used the same basic strategies for gathering sources but again with somewhat different results. Susanna Andrews's final list of works cited contains several books about Dickinson's life and works, two periodical articles (one of which she found online), an essay from a collection of literary criticism, two collections of the poet's works, and a collection of the poet's letters. Along the way, she skimmed numerous other books and articles, but most of these contained analyses of Dickinson's poems, with no useful references to the poet's life.

David Perez's research experience was far less extensive than those of the other students because the scope of his assignment was restricted to a report rather than an open-ended research paper.

The search for sources is a journey into the unknown that tests your imagination, perseverance, and ability to plan. Sometimes this search can be frustrating because many clues lead nowhere and seem to waste your time. Do not try to save time by hastily rejecting items whose titles do not indicate a clear and immediate relation to your topic. Remember that sources can help inform your paper in a variety of ways: by giving background, by exploring a situation similar to your topic, or by providing specific detail for one small part of your paper. Always follow up on ambiguous clues. The hastily discarded source may be the one that could have helped you the most.

Reassessing Your Topic

While searching for sources, you may reach a point where you doubt the topic is workable, either because you are finding far too many potential sources or because you have found too few. If, after several hours of intensive searching through various indexes as well as the library catalog and the Internet, you have discovered only two or three *possible* sources, your topic needs to be broadened. However, if you quickly find dozens of potential sources, you need to reduce the scope of the topic or sharpen the focus of your hypothesis. If when searching the library catalog you discover that many potential sources have been checked out or are in periodicals to which your library does not subscribe, you might want to consider refocusing your topic.

We hesitate to talk in terms of specific numbers because the number of sources does not directly indicate how much information you have collected. You might take a couple of pieces of information from just one or two paragraphs in one source, and then take more than a dozen lengthy notes from an entire chapter in another source. The crucial question is whether you have enough sources. Your research cannot be considered complete unless you read enough source material to have a comprehensive view of the topic.

Narrowing a Topic That Is Too Broad

We saw how one student limited his subject — *Cotton Mather* — to a reasonable topic — *what the witches meant to Cotton Mather* — after a conference with his instructor and a background-reading session in the library. Fred had some familiarity with his subject, which made it easy for him to take full advantage of the advice he received. However, another student, who knew relatively little about her subject — *abnormal psychology* — ran into trouble with her topic at a somewhat later step in the research.

Curious about the many strange paths human behavior often takes, this student decided to concentrate on just one disorder, schizophrenia. It

seemed reasonable to plan to discuss its cause and some of the therapies presently practiced in the effort to conquer this puzzling, distressing problem. During her preliminary research, the student formed this
hypothesis:

original hypothesis   Because the exact cause of schizophrenia is not yet known,
                           treatment is often difficult.

Her psychology textbook contained fewer than three pages on the
topic, and an encyclopedia covered it in just one column. So the topic did
not seem too broad. Only after the student had gotten fairly well into her
search for sources did she realize that there were far more books and articles on schizophrenia than she could hope to read. The college library
held more than a dozen books and hundreds of articles dealing directly
with the causes and treatment of schizophrenia. What she believed to be a
topic was actually a subject area, and a broad one at that. What should
she do? Go back to the background sources, which had not clearly indicated the trouble she ran into? She checked with her instructor, who
recommended that she look through her working bibliography to see if
the titles might suggest some direction in which she could reasonably
move. After all, why waste the time that had gone into the search for
those sources?

The student noticed that several of the titles mentioned the *nature* of
schizophrenia, others its *causes,* others its *effect on those living with schizophrenics,* and still others its *treatment.* She remembered from her background reading that doctors use several different methods of treatment
because of the uncertainty regarding the causes of the disorder. Although
she was interested in the treatment of schizophrenia, she realized from
looking at her working bibliography that this, too, was likely to prove too
broad for her paper. So she reviewed her background reading notes and
class lecture notes once more and decided to narrow her topic still further,
to one kind of treatment. Her new topic became *treatment of schizophrenia
in a community setting.* She also needed to form a new hypothesis and
decided on the following:

hypothesis revised   Treating severe schizophrenia in a community setting has
for focus   in some cases proven more successful than treating it in
                           traditional institutions.

The sharper focus provided by the revised hypothesis, as opposed to
the much broader original statement, saved the student from reading and
taking notes on matters that were not directly related to her paper's topic.
Also, the revised hypothesis has several key terms that helped the student search for sources and read them more efficiently. The word *severe*
warned her to skip over passages about milder forms of the disorder

that do not force sufferers to be committed to psychiatric hospitals. The term *successful* made her think about finding a valid basis for judging success — a difficult problem in this situation because schizophrenia is rarely, if ever, cured; the sufferer's symptoms only become less distressing. The student had to look closely to find the criteria used by her various sources to determine how much improvement could reasonably be considered "success." *Traditional institutions* reminded her that if she wanted to show that this method was successful, she had to compare it with well-established treatments rather than with other experimental approaches.

Thinking about her purpose, however, the student realized that this kind of hypothesis would simply generate a report on established facts. Because she had been assigned to write an analysis of an area of abnormal psychology, she tried adding a dimension of *analysis* by attaching a "because" clause:

hypothesis revised Treating severe schizophrenia in a community setting has
for purpose in some cases proven more successful than treating it in traditional institutions because of the greater opportunity for flexible, individualized approaches.

This revised hypothesis directed the student to sources that would help her achieve the purpose of her paper. The term *individualized approaches* indicated that she needed to find specific descriptions of patient-based approaches used for schizophrenia in a community setting. Finally, linking the two parts of the sentence with *because* told the student that she needed to show a cause-and-effect connection, either by using evidence from professional studies or by gathering enough detailed information about the approaches and the effects on the patients to demonstrate the link herself.

Revising a Topic That Is Too Narrow

You may never find yourself with a topic that is too limited to research; most newcomers to research tend to come up with topics that are too broad. Keep in mind the warning about topics that can be completely researched by reading just one source — *how bees communicate*, for example. Topics like this often lead to a brief report rather than an analysis or an argument paper. Avoiding "report" topics will also help you avoid erring in the direction of "too narrow."

A student who had read an article on lions in *Natural History* found himself with no sources beyond that article except for two brief summaries of that article, one in *Newsweek* magazine and another in the *New York Times*. His topic was *the effect of the severe drought of 1973 on the rearing of lion cubs in the Serengeti Plains of East Africa*. The *Natural History* article provided all the necessary information; *Newsweek* and the *Times* merely reported the story by summarizing the original article, so they could *not* be considered "different" sources because they did not present any new information or a different point of view.

Stuck after a long but futile search, the student went back to the step he had previously cut short — background reading. He had initially done nothing more than read about lions in an encyclopedia article on African wildlife. This time, he read several Web sites on lions and consulted a detailed article about lions in a specialized encyclopedia on wildlife.

As the student read additional background studies, he thought about ways to expand his topic. These ideas passed through his mind: "The lions had trouble due to a drought; are there other more common problems they face as parents? Is there a *mild* drought every year? [The article had dealt with a particularly severe one.] Do they normally have trouble feeding themselves as well as their cubs? Who gets fed first, the parents or the cubs?" His additional reading revealed that lions face famine every year in the Serengeti Plains because they do not follow the herds of antelope that migrate each winter to greener pastures.

The student now realized that he should broaden the problem from *the drought of 1973* to the *regular shortages of food* caused by droughts and the disappearance of the antelopes. He also broadened his focus to include the adult lions as well as the cubs. Thus he arrived at the topic *the ways in which lions manage to survive periodic food shortages.* At this point, the writer still could not see how to frame a hypothesis, so he deferred that step until he had gathered more sources. He was hoping to find some difference of opinion or at least different sets of data in the sources, or else he would once more be left with a topic that could be handled entirely through one source.

After collecting more than a dozen titles of potential sources, this time looking in a few scholarly periodical databases as well as popular indexes, he skimmed through them to see what they had to offer. (Chapter 10 explains how to go about this important step.) Sure enough, other observers of lions clearly had not seen the same thing or had drawn different conclusions about what they saw, especially about the roles played in the hunt by males and females. A quick glance at the sources enabled the student to form a reasonable hypothesis: "In her effort to survive under sometimes difficult circumstances, the female lion plays a more aggressive and critical role than the so-called king of beasts."

10

Evaluating Potential Sources

Once you have compiled what seems to be an adequate working bibliography, you are almost ready to begin reading the sources and taking notes. Before you undertake this challenging work, however, check to see if the sources provide enough ideas and information to allow you to do a thorough job of research. This is best done by skimming each source to gain a rough idea of what it says about your topic.

Skimming Your Sources

The purpose of skimming is to find out quickly whether a source is useful and, if it is, how much relevant information it contains. Skimming not only allows you to avoid a close reading of unhelpful sources but also gives you a chance to evaluate your hypothesis. A skimming of his sources told Fred Hutchins that his initial hypothesis needed expansion to include an account of Mather's complicated personality.

Quite often, you will find that a possible source's title was misleading and that the source contains nothing pertinent to your specific topic. For example, if your topic dealt with *the role parents play in adolescent alcoholism*, you would probably have included an article entitled "Teen Drinking Habits — Tragic Facts of Life" on your list of potential sources. Let's say you skim the article and find no reference to parental influence. Indeed, the article is a sermon, presenting several case histories involving teenagers who were injured as a result of drinking and concluding with a warning to adolescents not to drink. There are no documented facts or figures here — just a frightening picture of the perils of alcohol. You can safely drop this item from your list of sources.

If skimming leads you to reduce your list of potential sources too much, go back and look for more sources. If you cannot find any, check with your instructor to see whether you should try to broaden your topic or continue with what you have. Your instructor's advice will depend largely on how much information the remaining sources offer and how adequately they cover the variety of views that experts have expressed on your topic.

If skimming leaves you with a great many substantial sources, you may want to limit the topic or sharpen the focus of the hypothesis. Of course, several sources may offer much the same information and arrive at the same general judgment; in that case, you need read and take notes on only one of them, thereby reducing the overload of sources. It is not easy, especially when first undertaking research, to judge whether two or more sources duplicate one another. The main points to keep in mind are that you cannot afford to miss any valuable information, and that you must not leave out any of the various viewpoints on your topic.

Skimming Books

Skimming a book to determine its general content and organization can save you time when selecting sources for your working bibliography. Here are some skimming techniques you might find useful in evaluating books as possible sources:

- Read the table of contents to get a general outline of the whole book.
- Look for a chapter title that might be relevant to your research project.
- Turn to that chapter and read the headings that mark the subdivisions of the chapter. If the headings indicate that the chapter is devoted to a continuous discussion of ideas and details relevant to your topic, you have probably found a useful source.
- Read the first and last paragraphs of the chapter if you need further evidence of the chapter's content and its importance to your topic. Together, these paragraphs might provide a quick summary of the author's major points.
- Read the first sentence of each paragraph. By so doing, you are likely to take in a number of the author's main ideas, providing yourself with more information on which to base your decision about the relevance of the book to your research needs.
- Take note of any pictures, maps, or illustrated data appearing in the section you are skimming. Read the captions associated with the illustrations to get some sense of how the visuals relate to the con-

tent. Graphs and tables can be especially useful in helping you grasp the thrust of social science content.

Many books, especially scholarly works, provide indexes so that readers can find particular ideas and details referred to in different sections of the text. Indexes can facilitate your skimming because they provide page numbers for all topics mentioned in the book at hand, allowing you to find out quickly if the work has much to say about a particular aspect of your research topic.

When you are using an index, take the time to check all the headings that might be relevant to your topic, not just the obvious ones. For example, if your topic were *reading problems of grade-school boys as opposed to those of grade-school girls,* you would naturally look in a book's index under *reading, grade-school,* and *boys.* Some references would probably be listed under *reading,* but the other two terms might not appear in the index. In that case, you could look under synonyms such as *elementary school* and *male.* Do not stop at synonyms, however. Think of different ways to approach the topic that might lead you to other, possibly more fruitful headings, such as *learning disabilities,* or *disabilities, learning,* or *gender as a factor in learning.*

If you have reason to believe a particular book holds value for your research but offers few aids for skimming, such as nicely titled chapters and helpful illustrations, do not give up. The book is likely to have an introduction or a preface in which the author explains his or her approach to the subject. In this explanation, keywords and emphasized ideas will certainly catch your eye. Using these words and ideas in conjunction with the index, you should be able to locate passages to which you can apply skimming techniques.

Skimming Periodical Articles

Articles rarely come with outlines that might serve as tables of contents, but some of them, particularly those found in scholarly journals or electronic databases, include *abstracts* that summarize their theses and major supporting points. The abstract may indicate whether the article is worth a close reading. If the abstract does not mention material that is likely to help you, do not discard the source. Try some of these techniques to decide whether it is worth keeping:

- Quickly read the introduction and conclusion of the article. Most scholarly articles are structured so that the introduction and conclusion contain a summary of the article's approach to the topic and its findings.

- Skim the article by reading the first line of every paragraph to pick up the main ideas, much as you would a book's chapter.
- If the article is in electronic form, use your Web browser's "Find" command to search the document for relevant keywords. You can usually access this feature under the "Edit" menu, or you can press Control-F (in Windows) or Command-F (on a Macintosh).
- Skim any visual material included such as illustrations or tables, as you would for a book.

Skimming Web Sources

Many of the methods for skimming books and periodical articles can also be used for Web sources. To quickly assess the content of a specific document within a Web site, examine any visual material, and read the first and last paragraph, the section headings, and the first sentence of each paragraph. You can also use your browser's "Find" command to search for particular words or phrases.

When skimming Web sources, you should also take into account their unique structure. If the source is a page within a larger Web site, you may need to click links such as "Home," "Next," or "Table of Contents" to learn more about whether the source is worth further investigation. If a search engine has led you to the home page of an organization or institution's Web site, skim the major category links to see whether the site might contain information relevant to your hypothesis. Some large Web sites will allow you to conduct a keyword search of the entire site. You should also look for any information about the sponsor of the site to assess the credibility of the source. (For more on determining a source's reliability, see pages 130–31.)

Taking Notes While Skimming

When skimming a potential source, take brief notes that tell you how the source might prove useful, or why it is not useful. Write these notes on the backs of the bibliography cards or, if you are working on a computer, following the source entry.

To determine how useful a source may be, keep the following questions in mind:

- Is this information relevant to my topic?
- How much useful information does it seem to offer?
- Does this source support or contradict my hypothesis?

You do not have to take detailed notes at this time. Simply indicate the possible value of the source. (You may want to record the page numbers for the material related to your topic so that it will be easier to find later.)

Keep all bibliography entries that seem the least bit promising. If later you need to change your topic slightly, sources that originally seemed less useful may become quite valuable.

Judging the Usefulness of Sources

After you have skimmed your sources and determined their potential usefulness, you will need to conduct a more thorough evaluation of the sources that seemed promising. This section discusses some important points to keep in mind.

Relevance

With so much information available today, it is challenging to stay focused on sources that will be of use to your paper. Keep your hypothesis, your audience, and your paper's purpose in mind as you skim potential sources. For example, if your hypothesis is *college athletes should be allowed more financial benefits for playing sports,* a keyword search might also turn up articles on the Atlantic Coast Conference's desire to expand and the underrepresentation of minorities in top college sports jobs. No matter how interesting these issues may be, you must stick to the topics useful for your paper.

At the same time, don't expect all potentially useful sources to be exactly about your topic. Some of your sources, and probably the most important ones, *will* be listed under your topic's subject heading or contain your topic's keywords in its title or abstract. However, some very useful sources might relate to your topic in different ways: they might provide background information, analogous or parallel information, or detail.

- *Background.* If you are writing about problems caused by technology in modern medicine, for example, your paper might benefit from sources that describe the general evolution of technology in society.
- *Analogous or parallel information.* If your topic is government censorship in the United States, it might be useful to include information about censorship in other countries, or about other forms of government control. If you are writing about the overly complicated system of billing for medical insurance, descriptions of overcomplicated systems outside of medicine may help you make your points.

- *Detail.*   Your paper will involve specific, paragraph-level discussions to support its thesis, so you will need a wide range of details. For example, in a paper on *monopoly laws,* you may decide to include a section on Microsoft, which itself may include specifics on copyright laws for software. These details would be found in sources but not necessarily under the subject of *monopoly laws.*

Your paper's purpose will help determine what types of sources are relevant. If you are writing a paper for a science course, you will probably have to use several journal articles. If your topic focuses on a current social problem, you may not have to use an academic journal. For example, one can understand the controversy over the use of nuclear energy without expert knowledge of how a nuclear plant is constructed or how a nuclear reaction takes place. If you have any questions, ask your instructor what kinds of sources you will be expected to use given your particular topic.

Depth

In general, any source that treats your topic in depth will be more valuable than one that treats it superficially. You are looking for sources that give you a clearer, fuller understanding of some aspect of your topic and thereby provide grounds for accepting, rejecting, or in some way modifying your hypothesis.

When Fred Hutchins started skimming books on New England history, he found that all of them mentioned Cotton Mather and most summarized his involvement in the Salem witch trials. The information and conclusions presented in these books had probably been summarized from other historical works that had investigated the situation in far greater detail. (Ideally, it was these original sources that Fred thought he should read firsthand.) One of the general history books summarized Mather by saying he "was not a cruel, bloodthirsty persecutor of suspected witches; rather, his attitude toward the Salem witchcraft outbreak must be studied in the context of the times in which he lived, the traditions of his religion, and the erratic nature of his personality." Such a sweeping generalization is not necessarily wrong. In writing a research paper, however, you are expected to go beyond mere generalization to find specific evidence, in this case, primary accounts and well-founded interpretations of what the Salem "witches" meant to Cotton Mather. Otherwise, neither you nor your readers will have a sound basis for deciding whether your judgment is well supported.

Currency

Another important factor to keep in mind when evaluating sources is that some may be out of date. Especially in the natural and social sciences,

Working with Sources

knowledge is expanding so rapidly that theories, and even facts, are often revised or discarded within a year or two. Even history may be rewritten when new evidence comes to light or when a historian examines an old event from a new angle.

Therefore, if you investigate topics that involve current issues or recent developments in a scientific field, you *must* find the latest possible sources. A book on modern astronomy, for instance, is partly out of date even before it is published. This does not mean that most of what it says is inaccurate; rather, some of the facts and theories concern phenomena about which new, more powerful telescopes are yielding fresh information daily. Current social problems such as *child abuse* and issues such as *toxic-waste disposal* also demand that you work with the most recently published sources. Because the information in books can never be totally up to date, you need to rely heavily on periodical articles when researching these kinds of topics.

Bias

Writing and other sources of information are produced by people, and each person has a unique point of view. In addition, publications are typically supported by organizations, schools, governments, and businesses, and these entities have particular philosophies or interests that can affect the content of the information. This means that no piece of information can be entirely neutral or objective. News reports and even scientific reports have a *bias,* or *viewpoint,* just as do memoirs and letters to the editor. Information from Fox News has a different bias than information from the Public Broadcasting System; *U.S. News and World Report* has a more conservative political orientation than *Time* magazine. Given that each of your sources holds a particular point of view, your task is not to discard all the sources because they are not objective but to be aware of the nature of their biases and how these biases may affect *what kind* of information is presented and *how* it is presented.

Sometimes a source's viewpoint is apparent at first glance. For example, a book titled *Collegiate Sports: Opportunities to Excel* is likely to have a very different perspective on its topic from an article called "How 'Special Treatment' for College Athletes Has Undermined Educational Standards." At other times you will be able to determine a source's biases only by examining closely *which aspects* of a topic are being emphasized and *how* they are being discussed.

The bias of a periodical can often be determined by examining the nature and content of articles contained within it. For example, an article in the October 2003 issue of *Harper's,* "We're in the Army Now: The G.O.P.'s Plan to Militarize Our Culture," indicates a political position that is critical of the Republican administration. Although not every article in *Harper's* will share this exact orientation, the fact that it is published in the magazine (and featured on its cover) gives an indication of the periodi-cal's general bias.

Reliability

If a source is reliable, the information it presents is assumed to be rea-sonably accurate. A reliable source will have a bias, evident in its interpre-tations of the facts (and perhaps in what is included and omitted in the discussion), but at least you will know that most of its basic facts can be trusted. The author's authority, the publisher or sponsor's reputation, the level of review, and the purpose all contribute to a source's reliability:

- *The author's authority or qualifications.*   Find out what you can about the author's academic or professional background, area of expert-ise, and political or philosophical leanings. For the most reliable information, look for an author with a professional degree in the field or significant experience with the topic. You can also search your library catalog, periodical databases, print indexes, or the Web for additional works by the author and see if he or she has written anything else on the same subject. More publication on the topic usually indicates greater authority in the field.

- *The publisher's or sponsor's reputation.*   Sometimes it is easy to judge a source's reputation. The *Newark Star-Ledger* is far more reputable than a scandal-ridden tabloid you see at the checkout counter in a supermarket. You can assume that the American Cancer Society Web site contains reliable information because it is sponsored by a well-respected national organization. Other sources are harder to evaluate based on reputation. As you delve into your research, though, you may begin to recognize names of reputable publishers and organizations that are cited often in the literature on your topic.

- *The level of review of the information.*   Scholarly books and journals employ editors to ensure the accuracy of information. The content of popular magazines and newspapers also undergoes a review pro-cess, but magazines and newspapers are published under tighter deadlines than are books, and therefore their content may not be checked as thoroughly. You have probably noticed that newspapers sometimes print "corrections" to stories that have already been published. Web sites may be thoroughly reviewed, or they may not be reviewed at all. (See pages 131–33 for more on evaluating Web sites.)

- *The purpose of the source.*   A book or journal article written to share findings with others in the field is naturally more reliable than something written to entertain its audience or to sell a product or service. Accuracy may be less important in materials produced for entertainment or to advance a political agenda. These sources may heavily emphasize some facts over others for dramatic effect; in some cases, they simply misrepresent the facts. They may also use techniques such as *satire* or *hyperbole* (exaggeration to make a point) that can cause confusion about accuracy.

Coverage

While putting together your working bibliography, remember to look for works that express a variety of viewpoints on your topic. A paper that depends mainly on the opinions and interpretations of one writer is not only one-sided, but also potentially incomplete in its coverage. For example, look at the following list of books dealing with the strategies of the two major military commanders who faced each other during the American Civil War. The topic of the paper is *Lee and Grant: the old vs. the new style of warfare.*

Sources: 1. *Glory Road,* Bruce Catton
2. *Grant Moves South,* Bruce Catton
3. *Grant Takes Command,* Bruce Catton
4. *Mr. Lincoln's Army,* Bruce Catton
5. *The Civil War,* Bruce Catton
6. *Robert E. Lee,* Douglas Freeman
7. *Lincoln Finds a General,* K. P. Williams

This list of sources is so heavily weighted with Catton's works that his views are almost certain to dominate the paper. An experienced researcher would notice this imbalance and take steps to remedy the situation. Maybe some of Catton's books could be dropped if they largely repeated one another in regard to this topic. In any event, other historians' ideas must be added to the works cited list so that readers will be presented with a variety of historical judgments regarding these two military geniuses.

One further question about balance comes to mind when looking over this list of titles. Isn't something wrong when four of the titles focus on Grant while just one deals with Lee? After all, the topic suggests equal treatment of the two men. Good coverage of your topic within a variety of sources also allows you to cross-check information (see page 134) to get a better sense of its reliability and bias.

Evaluating Online Sources

The evaluation of online sources raises special challenges. Any member of a discussion group and any person or group who has established a Web site can make statements that reflect uninformed opinions and organizational agendas rather than expert judgment and established knowledge. Web pages sometimes mix information, entertainment, and advertising to a greater extent than other media, making them more difficult to evaluate for accuracy and bias. Also, the use of Web pages can be challenging because of the way they are searched for and retrieved. When linking to a Web page through search-engine results, you may arrive at an isolated document that does not clearly list an author or a sponsor.

Of course, the general guidelines discussed for judging the usefulness of sources apply to all sources of information, including the Internet. In addition, following are some specific guidelines to consider when deciding if a Web source is useful:

- If a Web site domain includes .edu or .gov, you can feel somewhat safe. Be wary of .edu addresses that contain the tilde (~) in the middle, however, because that symbol signifies a personal account within the institution.

- The top and bottom of a Web page and the menus along the side of the frame often contain useful information. Look for an "About this site" or "Frequently Asked Questions (FAQ)" link. These may tell you about the site's publisher, political or commercial affiliations, or date of last revision.

- If you retrieve search results that seem to have plunged you deep into a Web site that does not provide enough information to help you evaluate the page, you can find out more about the source's publisher or sponsor by truncating the URL. For example, a keyword search for *equal rights legislation* led one student to the following URL: <www.mith2.umd.edu/WomensStudies/GenderIssues/SexDiscrimination/GuaranteeingEqualRights/chapter2>. The link took her to a document titled "How Will States Be Affected by Ratification of the Equal Rights Amendment?" At first glance, the document seemed to contain useful information, but the student did not see the name of its author or sponsoring organization. To find out more, the student deleted the final term after the backslash in her Web browser's URL address box: <www.mith2.umd.edu/WomensStudies/GenderIssues/SexDiscrimination/Guaranteeing EqualRights>. Clicking on her browser's "Go" button, she arrived at a page revealing that the document was a chapter of a larger publication. Seeing that the publication was authored by the U.S. Commission on Civil Rights, a government agency, the student determined that the source was reliable. By further truncating the URL to <www.mith2.umd.edu/WomensStudies/GenderIssues>, she discovered that the document was part of the *Women's Studies Database*, a site sponsored by the University of Maryland, which contained several other sources that proved useful in her research.

- Hyperlinked menu items on a Web page may lead you to an entirely different site that needs to be evaluated on its own merits. These linked sites may be far different in quality than the page from which they are linked.

Using Primary versus Secondary Sources

If you picked a topic involving the constitutional amendment that granted women the right to vote, you would probably want to find out what the general public as well as the leading social commentators thought about the issue in the years immediately before its passage in 1920. A recently written historical account would get you started, but you might wonder whether the account missed something or even slightly distorted the picture of that historic crusade. Fortunately, you could check for yourself by reading some newspaper and periodical articles of that era that have been preserved in libraries, usually on microfilm. In doing so, you would be using primary sources.

Primary sources are materials closest to the events or people being researched, including the following:

- news articles based on direct observation
- reports based on direct observation
- surveys or interviews
- letters, memoirs, diary entries, or autobiographies
- speeches
- works of literature such as short stories, novels, and poetry
- works of art or other artifacts that can be directly observed

Secondary sources are materials based on primary sources. They contain description, analysis, and interpretation of the primary-source information or of other secondary sources. Secondary sources include the following:

- newspaper or magazine feature articles (articles not based on immediate events)
- works of argument or analysis based on primary sources
- materials that summarize and synthesize from a variety of primary and secondary sources
- critiques or reviews of events or works of art
- textbooks and most reference works

Working with Sources

For example, in historical research, newspapers and magazines published at the time of the event (as well as diaries and correspondence by people who observed the event) are the primary sources used by later historians, whose writings then become secondary sources for your research.

Searching the Internet is a good way to locate primary sources, especially government and organizational reports, firsthand accounts of incidents, and correspondence. If you want to find out what a Central Intelligence Agency report said about Iraq's Weapons of Mass Destruction Program in October 2002, to read stories written by immigrants to the United States, or to see photographs of events such as the Hindenburg airship disaster, you could find all of this material on the Internet.

Cross-Checking Sources

If you have achieved good coverage of your topic with a variety of sources from multiple perspectives, including solid anchors of information such as scholarly books, journals, and primary sources when possible, you will be able to cross-check information to gain a better sense of the truth about your topic.

Cross-checking, the process of verifying the validity of information by comparing how it is expressed by different sources, is an important critical-thinking tool in research. When a traffic accident occurs, police try to collect reports from all drivers as well as any passengers and witnesses to the incident. They inspect the vehicles and the place where the accident occurred. They may also consult the driving records of all the drivers involved and examine any existing information about previous accidents at the location. By collecting information from various perspectives around the event and considering the biases and limitations of each source, they establish their best representation of the truth about what happened. Although you will not be writing police reports on traffic accidents in your research, of course, the same kind of cross-checking approach will help ensure your own reliability as a writer.

By cross-checking information to review the validity of your sources, you can accumulate some useful expectations about the possible value of the work you are considering as a source for your paper. A librarian or your teacher can help with any remaining questions you may have about the usefulness of sources after you have analyzed them in these ways.

Creating an Annotated Bibliography

Once you have determined that a source will be useful, you may want to create an annotated bibliography entry for it. An *annotated bibliography* is a list of sources that includes standard documentation informa-

Working with Sources

tion for each source followed by a brief summary of the source's content and, if needed, an evaluation of its usefulness.

In some cases, you may be required to create an annotated bibliography for your research paper. Even if it is not required, you may wish to create one anyway for your own purposes. Doing so will save you time later if you are looking for a specific piece of information but are unsure of which source to consult. More importantly, annotations make it easier to understand the way that your sources relate to each other. A source, for example, may agree or disagree with, overlap, or support another source. When the time comes to write your draft, understanding these connections will help you integrate your source material more smoothly.

Here is an example of an MLA-style annotated bibliography entry that Shirley Macalbe created while researching immigration issues.

"Workers' Stories of Abuse, Exploitation Point to Need for Immigration Reform." AFL-CIO. 14 Nov. 2002. 27 Nov. 2003. <http://www.aflcio. org>. This article describes an AFL-CIO event in September 2002 as part of the union's campaign to improve the rights of undocumented immigrant workers. Labor leaders and immigrant workers spoke at a gathering on the Capitol steps in Washington, D.C., describing the many labor abuses these unprotected workers encounter and the important contributions they make to the labor force. This article showed surprising support for the immigrant workforce from an organization that represents American workers.

Reviewing Your Hypothesis

After skimming and evaluating the sources, review your notes to check the direction your hypothesis is taking. If you see that the sources do not fully support the hypothesis, modify your hypothesis to make it conform to the sources. Do not plow straight ahead. Stop and consider what you have just learned through skimming. Revising the hypothesis will bring it into sharper focus, and this will make the next step — reading the sources in depth — much easier.

11

Taking Effective Notes

Taking good notes is not simply a matter of copying as much information as you can, as fast as you can. You must be selective. Although you will surely end up with more information in your notes than will ultimately appear in your paper, you don't want to go too far in that direction. Yet you also want to be sure to record everything you will need to support your thesis. For notes to be effective, then, it is essential to keep your hypothesis firmly in mind at all times.

Using a Preliminary Outline as a Guide

Eventually, after you complete your research and settle down to writing the paper, you will need to construct an outline in which you organize all the information you have collected. Looking at the outline, you will be able to fit each group of notes into its appropriate place in the overall framework.

Now, wouldn't it be nice to have that outline in place *before* you begin taking notes? Then you would have a good idea of where each note fits into the paper. Furthermore, such an outline would make it easier to judge whether a particular piece of information is truly relevant and therefore worth recording in a note.

Using your background reading and hypothesis, you should be able to construct a preliminary outline consisting of key questions (subtopics) that you hope to resolve through the research. Once you have the outline, you can assign each note to one of the subtopics by writing the subtopic at the top of the note card. This preliminary outline is called an *ongoing outline* because, as you get well into the note taking, you are likely to see reasons to add to or modify the subtopics that make up this outline. When it is time to construct the final, rather detailed outline before writing the paper, this ongoing outline will prove quite helpful.

Following are two sample preliminary outlines, one for Fred Hutchins's research on Cotton Mather, the other for Susanna Andrews's research on Emily Dickinson. Each is based, at this early stage, on the student's projection of how he or she would support the research hypothesis and purpose.

Cotton Mather

1. CM's position in the Salem community
2. CM's role in the trials
3. CM's character and personality
4. CM's writing about witchcraft
5. CM's religious beliefs
6. The witchcraft trials: data, evidence, punishment
7. Definition of "witch"

Emily Dickinson

1. ED's character and personality
2. ED's ideas about poetry
3. ED's published poems; others' reactions to them
4. ED's family tree

Using a Statement of Purpose as a Guide

Instead of an outline, or along with an outline, you may find it helpful to write a statement of purpose once you have a plan for carrying out your research project. Some instructors may even require you to present a statement of purpose for their approval before you get very far into the project.

Writing a statement of purpose is a good way to bring together your ideas and make some decisions about the kinds of sources you will need to find. In addition, having this statement at hand while taking notes will help you avoid wasting time pursuing ideas that, although interesting in themselves, are not directly relevant to your research project.

Here is the statement of purpose written by the student who did his research paper on fire ants. After examining this statement, read his paper in Chapter 22 to see whether he carried out the assignment in line with the ideas presented here.

Working with Sources

Statement of Purpose

By using *Solenopsis invicta*, a South American fire ant, as an example, I will support the concept that an ecosystem can suffer great damage from invasion by an aggressive alien species. What I have already read about *S. invicta* shows why ecologists consider this ant a threat to biodiversity. To demonstrate the extent of the threat, I will try to find scientific sources that deal specifically with *S. invicta*'s destructive capacity. These sources must be as up to date as possible because scientists are undoubtedly learning more about this troublesome ant every day. I also want to instill in my readers a greater appreciation of the work being done by ecologists to preserve native species and their habitats. Finally, I will explain what scientists are doing, or hope to do, to control this particularly destructive creature.

Practical Aspects of Note Taking

When taking notes, you cannot know just how each piece of information will finally be used in the paper. One thing is certain, however: you will present your information in a different order from that in which you recorded it. Therefore, you will want a flexible method of note taking that makes it easy to find the best possible arrangement of your information. You can use note cards, a notebook, or a word processor; each method has its advantages.

Using Note Cards

Use four- by six-inch cards, and record just one idea, or a small group of closely related facts, on each card. Write notes on only one side of each card. (If you need to photocopy your notes, you will be glad the backs are blank.)

The main advantage of note cards is that you can spread the cards out on a table and arrange them into groups representing the subtopics of the paper. These groups (subtopics) will become the major sections of your paper. Because you may decide to shift a note from one subtopic to another, having your notes on cards gives you flexibility while you are rethinking the organization of the paper. Another advantage of using cards rather than a loose-leaf notebook or a word processor is that this space restriction will help you avoid the time-wasting tendency to use too many words and record more information than necessary.

Using a Notebook

If you feel more comfortable using a notebook, perhaps because you are worried that cards are easy to lose, write on just one side of each page and leave a fair amount of space between notes. This will allow you to cut each page into separate notes that can be grouped under subtopics when you are ready to organize the paper.

Whichever you use, cards or a notebook, be generous. Do not try to squeeze as many notes as possible into the space available. The satisfaction gained from being thrifty cannot compensate for the frustration of trying to untangle a tightly bunched, loosely connected set of facts and ideas. Each card should focus on just one idea.

Using a Word Processor

If you are preparing your paper on a word processor, you can create a separate file for your notes, using subtopic headings to organize them. Your notes can include your own ideas as well as material from your reading. If your subtopics change, you can move notes around accordingly. Periodically you can print out the notes to get an overview of the information you have collected so far. When you start drafting your paper, you can move notes from the notes file into the file that contains your rough draft.

If you paste sections of your computer notes into your paper, do not lose track of source material amid your own words and ideas. Cite all borrowed material and be sure to place quotation marks around direct quotations.

Make a backup copy of any computer files at least twice per hour. Then, even if you accidentally delete or otherwise lose a file or part of a file, the bulk of your painstakingly gathered research materials will be safe.

Entering Information onto Cards

It is important to develop a single format for putting information onto cards and then to follow it consistently. Later you may want to thumb through the stack of cards to look for a particular piece of information or simply to find any piece of information that might strengthen a particular section of the paper. In either case, you want to know at a glance if a card has what you want. Using a consistent format makes this easy.

Follow these guidelines when preparing your cards:

- *Include identifying source information.* In the upper right corner of each card, identify the author of the source. (Do not include the title unless you are using more than one work by the same author.) For paginated sources, also be sure to add the numbers of the page or pages from which you are taking the information. We need to stress this seemingly minor point: *Your working bibliography should include complete publication information for each of your sources.* If you forget to write identifying data on your notecards, you could lose hours retracing your steps when the time comes to insert notes into your research paper to show exactly where you found your information.

• *Use only the front of the card when recording information.* Don't be tempted to save money by finishing up on the back. You may miss that piece of information when reviewing your notes. If you run out of space on the front, continue the note on a new card and staple the two cards together.

• *Highlight keywords and ideas.* Leave lots of white space to make it easier to review your notes. Main points should easily catch your eye. Underline or highlight major ideas. Minor points should be clearly subordinate to the major ideas they support, so use numbers or letters to indicate subordination or sequence. (See Figure 11-1.)

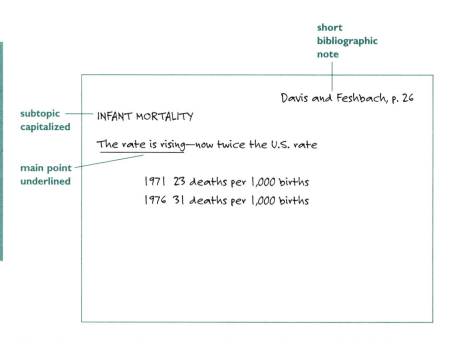

Figure 11-1   A series of notes on an article about infant mortality in the former Soviet Union in the 1970s. (The second and third cards, on page 141, show how a long note is continued from one card to another.)

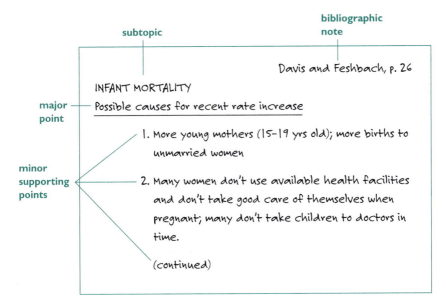

subtopic

bibliographic
note

Davis and Feshbach, p. 26

INFANT MORTALITY

major
point — Possible causes for recent rate increase

minor
supporting
points

1. More young mothers (15–19 yrs old); more births to unmarried women

2. Many women don't use available health facilities and don't take good care of themselves when pregnant; many don't take children to doctors in time.

(continued)

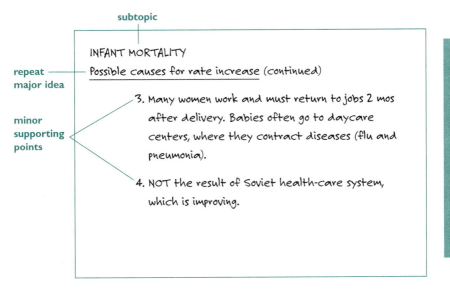

subtopic

INFANT MORTALITY

repeat
major idea — Possible causes for rate increase (continued)

minor
supporting
points

3. Many women work and must return to jobs 2 mos after delivery. Babies often go to daycare centers, where they contract diseases (flu and pneumonia).

4. NOT the result of Soviet health-care system, which is improving.

Figure 11-1 *(Continued)*

Working with Sources

- *Indicate the subtopic under which the information falls.* Write the appropriate subtopic, taken from your ongoing outline, at the top of each card, using more than one subtopic if a note seems to refer to more than one. Quite often, you will discover new subtopics while reading the sources. When Susanna kept reading references to a man who had published a few of Emily Dickinson's early poems, that man became worthy of a subtopic all to himself. As soon as you see a new subtopic emerging, add it to the ongoing outline. When taking a break from reading, go over the previous note cards and add the new subtopic where it fits. Reviewing earlier notes from time to time helps keep the scope of your project clearly in mind.

- *Be accurate.* When taking a note on a passage that contains numerical data and statistics, be extremely careful to copy the information accurately. If you are taking handwritten notes, write all figures with care; for example, a hastily written 9 can later look like a 7. Do not misread zeros in large numbers, writing "2 million" for "200,000."

- *Clearly distinguish paraphrases and direct quotations in your notes.* Keep track of the difference between paraphrased and quoted material. Forgetting to identify material as a direct quote on a notecard can lead to unintentional plagiarism (see Chapter 13). For more on entering quotations onto note cards, see pages 152–57.

- *Clearly distinguish your own commentary from source information.* At times you may need to express your own observations about the topic on your note cards. These comments may take up an entire card, or they may follow source notes on a card. In either case, distinguish your own thoughts from the source material. For example, you can place square brackets ([ ]) around your thoughts or write the term "personal commentary" on the card. Without clear and consistent labeling, you may plagiarize when drafting by mistaking source material for your own commentary.

In this discussion of creating a format for note entries, we focused on working with note cards. The same principles apply when using a notebook or a word processor, even though the mechanics will be a bit different. Your notes will be easy to read and easy to incorporate into your paper if you follow the suggested guidelines.

12

Paraphrasing, Summarizing, and Quoting

As we have said, effective note taking consists of more than copying relevant passages out of your sources. In fact, the more direct copying you do, the less useful your notes are likely to be. This section explains why.

Note taking for a research paper has three fundamental objectives:

- to record the general ideas that will form the skeleton of your research paper
- to record specific pieces of information that expand on these general ideas
- to preserve the exact wording of some statements so that you can quote them directly in the paper

Many students waste time copying long passages, word for word, because they have been misinformed, that research papers should contain a large number of quotations. This is just not so. In fact, the opposite is true. *For most research assignments, you should restrict the use of direct quotation to, at most, 20 percent of the paper.* (This limit does not apply to literature topics for which you must quote from the literary works you are discussing — primary sources — as well as from secondary sources.) For some topics, especially in the physical sciences, excellent papers can be produced without using any direct quotations.

One important reason for limiting the amount of quotation is that by restating in your own words most of the ideas that appear in the sources, you show that you understand what you are writing about. Furthermore, you will be reading a wide variety of sources, each written in a distinctive style and with a particular bias. So, if you were to string together a good many quotations from these sources, the paper would end up with a very uneven style and a confusing assortment of perspectives.

Finally, producing a convincing paper from a collection of quotations is almost impossible. Even though it might seem easier to quote than to paraphrase and summarize, the resulting paper would amount to a confusing, loosely related set of statements. Actually it is easier to express most of the ideas and information in your own words than it is to try to piece together dozens of quotations into a smoothly flowing, coherent essay.

Before we continue, we should establish an important principle: *in most cases, you must document all paraphrases, summaries, and quotes.* Any use of source material that is not common knowledge, whether it be material changed into your own words, isolated facts and statistics, or direct quotes, will need to be documented appropriately. These principles are discussed more fully in Chapters 17 through 20, but it is important for you to understand the basic documentation requirement now because it underscores the importance of careful note taking. Whether you are writing a paraphrase, summary, or direct-quotation note, be sure to include identifying source information (usually the author and page number) on the note card. Later, when you are incorporating notes into your paper and must create in-text citations, you will be glad that you took careful notes indicating where you found each piece of source material. Each note card should also have a corresponding working-bibliography entry containing the source's complete publication information.

Paraphrasing

To *paraphrase* is to express another person's idea in your own words. The value of paraphrasing goes far beyond meeting the requirement to express what you have read in your own words. For one thing, a good paraphrase usually takes fewer words than the original to convey the essential meaning. Even more important is the increased understanding that comes from trying to paraphrase what you are reading. Psychological experiments have shown that putting a difficult idea into your own words makes a stronger impression on your memory than merely copying the idea word for word. In fact, if you have trouble restating the idea, you probably do not thoroughly understand it.

In general, therefore, paraphrase any ideas that go into your notes unless there is a good reason for quoting the exact words in the source. (Several common situations that call for quotation are discussed later in this chapter.)

The following examples reveal two benefits to be gained from paraphrasing: brevity and clarity.

original	Will reputable scientists ever accept the claim that extrasensory perception and other paranormal powers really exist? It appears that many of them have.
paraphrase	Many scientists today believe in the reality of ESP and other paranormal powers.

The idea of "reputable" is not needed in your note; you know that you are looking only for real scientists — not those who simply call themselves scientists, as do some people who work with ESP.

The sample paraphrase is a good example of what it means to use your own words: the paraphrase restates the passage's idea using language and sentence structure clearly different from that in the original. When you paraphrase a passage, it is not acceptable to borrow most of the wording and sentence structure from a source, changing only a few words here and there.

original	Contrary to popular belief, exercise has never been shown conclusively to prolong life.
partial paraphrase; so close to the original as to be plagiarism	Contrary to popular thinking, exercise has never been conclusively demonstrated to lengthen life.
good paraphrase	No one has ever proved that exercise lengthens life.

In the partial paraphrase, the writer borrows significant aspects of the original. As you can see in the good paraphrase, which uses different language, sentence structure, and word order, it is not necessary to record "contrary to popular belief" if that is not the point you are interested in. Being careful to exclude unnecessary information from your paraphrase will help avoid the partial paraphrase that can slip into plagiarism, a serious problem discussed at length in Chapter 13.

original	Olfactory receptors for communication between different creatures are crucial for establishment of symbiotic relationships.
two reasonable paraphrases	The sense of smell is essential to cooperation among different animal species.
	Cooperation between different animal species is made possible by their sense of smell.

Working with Sources

The original, which comes from a biology journal, shows how difficult highly technical periodicals can be. Obviously the note taker had already learned some of the specialized vocabulary of the field or had looked up the meanings of the technical terms. Notice that either paraphrase would be much easier to understand than the original when reviewing notes and organizing information into a paper.

Summarizing

A summary greatly reduces the length of what you have read, which might be anything from a long paragraph to an entire periodical article. Writing effective summaries requires good judgment because you must decide what can safely be left out of the notes without losing or distorting the basic idea.

The essential consideration when writing a summary is to ask What is my purpose in using this material? Sometimes the entire passage contains valuable information. At other times, only part of the passage seems useful. So some summaries will be quite a bit shorter than others. Do not make a summary so short that it leaves out something that seems relevant to the hypothesis.

When working on a single paragraph, you may find that it contains a clearly stated topic sentence aptly supported by several details. In that case, you can simply paraphrase the main idea and then decide whether you need to note briefly any of the details, either for use in your paper or to reinforce your understanding of the main idea. In the following example, as in much professional writing, the main idea is stated early in the paragraph.

original

The payoff of a fast economy is clear. Capitalism loves speed because, as Benjamin Franklin well observed more than two centuries ago, time is money. This system of relentless turnover converts speed — of innovation, movement, and communication — into practical advantage. A culture of speed is produced by driven people. A successful capitalist is not a capitalist who does things the way his father did, or at his father's speed. Goods that do not move take up shelf space. People who do not move or change are *over the hill, same old same old*. Within a capitalist society there will be those who take pleasure in a slow tempo, but they are not, as a rule, winners in the contest for wealth or power.

works cited entry

Gitlin, Todd. *Media Unlimited: How the Torrent of Images and Sounds Overwhelms Our Lives.* New York: Metropolitan, 2001. Print.

Working with Sources

Gitlin, p. 76

MEDIA CHANGES

Effects of market-driven economy on communication

In a capitalistic society, speed is rewarded and new
ways of doing things are expected. This affects many
aspects of society, including communication.

Figure 12-1   Summary note card.

Whether you should include certain details on your note card depends on your hypothesis. If your use for this source goes no further than
noting the connection between capitalism and the speed of change, you
probably do not need any of the paragraph's subpoints. However, if you
intend to develop the idea that communication is also affected by the
"culture of speed," you may want to include some of the passage's subpoints. The note in Figure 12-1, which the student made by typing into a
word processor, would be used to associate changes in communication
with capitalism's rapid change.

Often your summary of a paragraph will consist of a general idea
derived from just a few details that directly relate to your hypothesis.
Assume when reading the next example that you are working with the
hypothesis "Most scientists believe that some form of life probably exists
on planets circling other stars in the universe."

original   Our solar system consists of nine, maybe ten, planets,
              which are circled by more than sixty moons, plus around
              5,000 fairly large rocks, called asteroids. In addition, the
              Sun's neighborhood is home to an untold number of
              comets, fifty of which appear in our skies periodically,
              and many megatons of cosmic dust. Ever since Galileo's
              discovery of Jupiter's four largest moons in 1610, Earth-
              lings have wondered about the possibility of extraterres-
              trial life. Only in the last five years, however, have
              astronomers been able to do much more than speculate

Working with Sources

about the existence of other solar systems, for Earth-bound observers were hindered by our atmosphere, which blurs even the best images gathered by their strongest telescopes. In 1990 a breakthrough occurred when the Hubble telescope was placed in orbit high above that atmosphere. Recently our Eye in the Sky has been transmitting pictures of actual Jupiter-sized planets hurtling around distant stars. Those seen so far are thought to be too close to their stars to sustain life as we know it. But new discoveries are emanating from Hubble at an amazing clip!

summary   The Hubble orbiting telescope has recently revealed the existence of planets circling stars, but none so far seems at the right distance from its star to support life like that on Earth.

The background information about the numbers of objects in the solar system, and about Galileo's discoveries, has been left out of the summary because you do not need it to understand the main idea — that although we now know that some other stars have planets, none as yet could sustain our kind of life. This illustrates the value of trying to keep notes brief. If some of the background information had been new to you, you might have been tempted to add it to your notes just because it was unfamiliar. Doing so, however, would not have helped you when it was time to write the paper. Always rely on your hypothesis to guide you in deciding whether information is truly relevant to your purposes.

Quoting

Once you accept the principle that you should paraphrase or summarize most of the ideas that go into your notes, you will be better able to judge when quotation can be both appropriate and effective. The four common reasons for quoting from your sources are conciseness, accuracy, memorable language, and authority.

Sometimes your best efforts at paraphrasing will produce a version that is either longer and clumsier than the original or somewhat inaccurate. In either case, you should quote all or part of the original statement. On other occasions, a source may express an idea so brilliantly that you want to preserve its beauty and power. Finally, you may want to support an idea or one of your conclusions by quoting a key statement or two from an established authority on the subject. None of these reasons for

Working with Sources

quoting is, however, an excuse for avoiding the effort necessary to create a successful paraphrase. You must learn to recognize those special times when these reasons are likely to be valid.

Examples of four situations in which direct quotation is desirable are presented here, along with some further advice on when to quote rather than paraphrase or summarize.

Conciseness

You find that you cannot paraphrase an idea without using many more words than the source.

This situation occurs when you decide to introduce a specialized term into your paper. You think it should be defined, but your attempts to paraphrase a definition are long and awkward. In that case, you should quote at least part of the definition from the source.

excerpt from paper	Noam Chomsky can be considered a reductionist — someone who believes that "all complex phenomena are ultimately explained and understood by analyzing them into increasingly simple and supposedly more elementary components" (Pronko 497).
works cited entry	Pronko, N. H. *Panorama of Psychology.* Belmont, CA: Wadsworth, 1969. Print.

(The note refers to the source of the definition, a textbook that the student used solely for the definition and not for any information related to Noam Chomsky. That textbook must, however, be included in the list of works cited for the research paper, and the student therefore made out a bibliography card for the source as well as a note card for the quotation.)

Note that this source is not out of date even though it was published in 1969 because the definition of a term such as *reductionist* does not change with time.

Accuracy

You find that you cannot effectively paraphrase an idea without distorting the author's meaning.

If, for example, a writer said that "virtually all women have experienced fantasies in which they were born as men," any paraphrase is likely to be more or less inaccurate.

questionable paraphrases

Most women wish they were men.

The majority of women have dreamed that they were men.

Almost every woman has a dream or daydream in which she has been born a male.

The first paraphrase grossly distorts the meaning; the second comes closer to the actual meaning, but it is not entirely accurate; the third is accurate but longer than the original. In such cases, it is better to quote the source and let your readers draw their own conclusions. Then they can compare their interpretations with those you put forth in your paper.

Memorable Language

You believe that the words or ideas expressed by your source are so vivid or powerful that the meaning cannot be captured in a paraphrase.

Restrain yourself in this matter; beware of quoting someone merely because you feel you cannot say the same thing as well in your own words. However, an example of brilliant language that cries out for quotation comes from a speech by British Prime Minister Winston Churchill, in which he referred to the behavior of Russia as "a riddle wrapped in a mystery inside an enigma."

Similarly, you should quote famous remarks whether or not the word choice is brilliant or difficult to paraphrase. President Harry Truman once advised timid politicians, "If you can't stand the heat, get out of the kitchen."

Finally, you may come across a remark that is so startling that your readers deserve to see the original. The brilliant biologist J. H. S. Haldane described Albert Einstein as "the greatest Jew since Jesus." Such a striking comment would surely lose a great deal if paraphrased.

Authority

You want to support a conclusion you have reached in your research by quoting the words of an expert on the subject.

The authors of many of your sources are probably experts on their subjects, at least in the sense that their ideas have been thought authoritative enough to be published. Still, you need to be selective in this regard. Choose writers whose credentials are known. Reporters for *Newsweek* or the *Washington Post* are experts only on journalism, although they may be fairly well informed on the topic at hand. An author referred to in an earlier source (or in a biographical sketch accompanying her article in *Scientific American*) as "a leading gerontologist" can be treated as an expert in the study of aging.

Keep in mind that you cannot rely entirely on expert opinion, whether quoted or paraphrased. You must also work to support your conclusions with hard facts and clear reasoning.

Quoting Out of Context

Because you are always quoting just a small part of any source, you must take great care to see that your quote accurately reflects the general meaning and attitude of the author or source. This principle applies to paraphrasing as well. The next example shows how someone read a passage hastily and then produced a serious misrepresentation of the original material, grossly distorting the author's meaning.

<table>
<tr>
<td>student's source</td>
<td>It is currently very fashionable among popular social critics to blame television for the recent widespread increase in juvenile crime statistics. The argument usually pursues this line of reasoning: Many parents today neglect their children by allowing them complete freedom in watching TV. The shows these children choose to watch often present violence in an attractive form, and some have even gone so far as to depict clever ways of committing crimes. Many of these children later reenact the violent acts they have witnessed on TV in order to recapture the thrills.

I contend, however, that this widely accepted explanation of a serious social problem is too simplistic.</td>
</tr>
<tr>
<td>quotation out of context</td>
<td>Sociologist Jane Doe joins those people who denounce violence on television as the primary cause of the sharp increase in the number of crimes committed by young people: "Many children later reenact the violent acts they have witnessed on TV in order to recapture the thrills" (41).</td>
</tr>
</table>

Apparently the student missed the two signals that tell the reader that Jane Doe disagrees with the points listed. First, the words "It is currently very fashionable among popular social critics . . ." carry a mocking tone. Second, the words that open the next paragraph, "I contend, however, that this . . . is too simplistic," clearly assert the author's position.

Working with Sources

Blending Quotation with Paraphrase

One very effective way to use source material without quoting too often is to combine quotation with paraphrase. In the following example, you can read the context surrounding Winston Churchill's famous remark about Russia, and you will see the advantage of quoting just the most pertinent part of a source. In 1939, Churchill was attempting to alleviate British fears that Russia might not enter the war against Nazi Germany. Part of that speech is presented here, along with a note card showing how quotation can be blended with paraphrase or summary. (The student's hypothesis was "Before and during World War II, Churchill demonstrated a clear understanding of other nations and the ways their leaders thought.")

original speech by Churchill	I cannot forecast to you the action of Russia. It is a riddle wrapped in a mystery inside an enigma; but perhaps there is a key. That key is Russian national interest. It cannot be in accordance with the interest or safety of Russia that Germany should plant itself upon the shores of the Black Sea, or that it should overrun the Balkan states and subjugate the Slavonic peoples of Southeastern Europe. That would be contrary to the historic life interests of Russia.
works cited entry	Churchill, Winston. "The Russian Enigma." BBC Broadcast. London. The Churchill Society, London. 1 Oct. 1939. Web. 27 November 2003.

The note in Figure 12-2 supplies a connection between Churchill's words and the student's hypothesis — that when others were confused (in this case, about Russia), Churchill's intuition or plain old political savvy led him to the truth. The note shows this point better than a lengthy quotation from the speech.

Entering Quotations onto Note Cards

When writing a note, you must be precise in placing the quotation marks and accurate in recording the author's words. This need for accuracy when quoting can be better understood if we examine some problems that can occur when you are reviewing notes in preparation for writing the paper.

Problem 1.   Because quotation marks are small, they can be overlooked when you are transferring information from your notes to your paper. To avoid missing a quotation mark or two, use very heavy strokes or even the marks « and » (guillemets). This will ensure that you do not confuse quotations with paraphrases. (See Figure 12-3.)

Working with Sources

Churchill, "The Russian Enigma" — title is included because more than one source by Churchill is being used; no page number is listed because the source is an unpaginated Web document

C. on Russian foreign policy
(late 1939)

The English were wondering whether R. would go to war against Nazi Germany. C. described R's policy as "a riddle wrapped in a mystery inside an enigma." He added that the key to the riddle was "Russian national interest" and this led him to predict that R. would enter the war.

subtopic

Figure 12-2   An example of blending quotations with paraphrase.

Arthur, pp. 30-32 — page numbers of section being summarized

SEXISM
Correcting sexism in language

In getting rid of sexism, teachers must avoid awkward and ugly constructions such as he/she. «Like badly tattered fig leaves, they call attention to what they are trying to conceal.» (30)

Three suggestions: (1) Do away with most feminine suffixes, such as -ess and -ette; (2) provide substitutes for man and woman suffixes, ex: mail deliverer instead of mailman; (3) avoid he/she and him/her constructions by using it when sex is not specified.

summary with direct quotation clearly marked

page number of quotation

Ref.
Room

Arthur, Herman. "To Err Is Huperson, to Forgive, Divine." American Educator 4.4 (1980): 30-32.

corresponding working bibliography card

Working with Sources

Figure 12-3   An example of a carefully recorded quotation.

Problem 2.   If a note summarizing several pages of a source includes a quotation, you must record the page number where the quotation appeared, as well as the page numbers of the full passage being summarized. Be sure to record the page number of each direct quotation. (See Figure 12-3.)

Problem 3.   Sometimes you will want to leave words out of the middle of a quotation because they are not relevant to your purpose. A reader is entitled to know about such an omission, so you must use *ellipsis points,* which are three dots in place of the omitted words. The following example shows how a quotation can be shortened by the use of ellipsis points. (The passage also demonstrates a smooth blend of quotation and paraphrase.)

student's source   Muldrow is by temperament a primitive whose profoundest ambition is to shuck what traces of civilization persist in him.

To criticize Muldrow for being unlikable would be accurate but off the point, given Dickey's unstinting pains to have him so. I suspect that in each successive draft of **omitted words** the novel (which was long in gestation: it arrives six years after Dickey's second novel, *Alnilam,* and twenty-three after his best-selling first, *Deliverance*) he strove to make his hero hardier, terser, chillier; Muldrow is, like the knife with which he dispatches so many victims, a thing of patiently honed steel.

works cited entry   Leithauser, Brad. "Haunted by the Good War." Rev. of *To the White Sea,* by James Dickey. *New Yorker* 27 Sept. 1993: 101-04. Print.

excerpt from student's paper   As for the relentless brutality of Dickey's heroes, critic Brad Leithauser observed about Sgt. Muldrow in *To the White Sea:*

Muldrow is by temperament a primitive whose profoundest ambition is to shuck what traces of civilization persist in him.

To criticize Muldrow for being unlikable would be accurate but off the point, given Dickey's unstinting pains to have him so. I suspect that in each successive draft of the novel . . . he strove to make his hero hardier,

Working with Sources

> terser, chillier; Muldrow is, like the knife with
> which he dispatches so many victims, a thing of
> patiently honed steel.

The ellipsis points let readers know that something was omitted. They must then trust that the omitted words were not essential to the point being made in the paper. In this case, the dates of the earlier novels interrupt the student's comment and would distract the reader's attention.

You might ask why one should not also drop the long phrase about the knife in the last sentence — "like the knife with which he dispatches so many victims." The knife is not extraneous; it symbolizes the man's character, thereby supporting the notion of his brutality.

Notice that the paragraphing in the source is shown in the set-off quotation, as recommended by the Modern Language Association (MLA).

Ellipsis points are three dots, separated from each other and the surrounding text by spaces.

You chose to omit some words.	"However, the mating of a horse and a donkey . . . yields a mule, which is always sterile."
Source chose to omit some words.	The major sign would be a "period of deepening corruption . . . when the devil would make more violent assaults than usual" on humankind (Levy 33-34).

If you omit words from the end of a quoted sentence, add a fourth dot immediately after the third dot, indicating the period that ends the sentence. If a parenthetical reference appears at the end of the quotation, place it ahead of the fourth dot (the period).

> For Mather, "denial of the Devil's power in this world implied the denial of other spirits, including angels . . ." (Levin 200).

If you are omitting a whole sentence or more, consult the *MLA Handbook for Writers of Research Papers,* Seventh Edition, for guidelines.

Caution: If you replace part of a sentence with ellipsis points, make sure you have not inadvertently changed the meaning of the sentence.

Problem 4.   One last problem occurs when you want to quote a remark that was quoted by your source. The possible danger here is that

Working with Sources

when you review your notes you may become confused. You must clearly indicate whether the quotation marks enclose your source's words or those of the person your source was quoting. Devise a format that will leave no doubt in your mind when you review the notes. We believe the easiest solution is to add a parenthetical note on your card to clarify the source. Figure 12-4 shows the note card a student created for the following source:

student's source   Of all the Concord circle, Emerson was perhaps the most widely read in science. He was familiar with Sir Charles Lyell's work in geology and was well aware that Christian chronology had become a mere "kitchen clock" compared with the vast time depths the earth sciences were beginning to reveal. "What terrible questions we are learning to ask," brooded the man sometimes accused of walking with his head in the clouds. He saw us as already divesting ourselves of the theism of our fathers.

Working with Sources

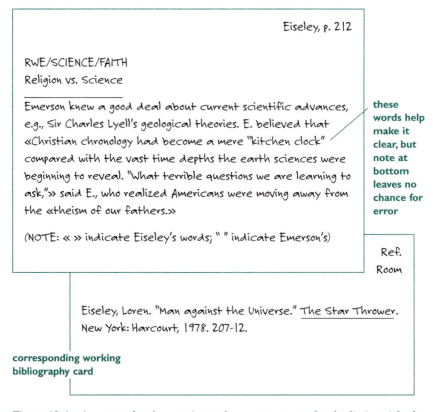

Eiseley, p. 212

RWE/SCIENCE/FAITH
Religion vs. Science

Emerson knew a good deal about current scientific advances, e.g., Sir Charles Lyell's geological theories. E. believed that «Christian chronology had become a mere "kitchen clock" compared with the vast time depths the earth sciences were beginning to reveal. "What terrible questions we are learning to ask,"» said E., who realized Americans were moving away from the «theism of our fathers.»

(NOTE: « » indicate Eiseley's words; " " indicate Emerson's)

these words help make it clear, but note at bottom leaves no chance for error

Ref.
Room

Eiseley, Loren. "Man against the Universe." The Star Thrower. New York: Harcourt, 1978. 207–12.

**corresponding working
bibliography card**

Figure 12-4   An example of quotations whose sources are clearly distinguished.

Other Alterations of Quotations

If the final punctuation of a quotation is a period, it may be altered to improve the flow of your sentence or to insert parenthetical documentation in MLA style. Capitalization at the beginning of quoted sentences may also be changed. Generally, if you introduce a quotation with the word *that*, the first word of the quotation should be lowercase. If you introduce it with a comma, the first word should be capitalized. Here are some examples created from a quotation that Shirley Macalbe used in her paper:

<table>
<tr>
<td>final period changed to a comma</td>
<td>"On balance, the economic benefits of immigration . . . tend to exceed private and in some areas public costs," says Muller (133).</td>
</tr>
<tr>
<td>final period moved to follow parenthetical citation; initial capital letter changed to lowercase</td>
<td>Muller asserts that "on balance, the economic benefits of immigration . . . tend to exceed private and in some areas public costs" (133).</td>
</tr>
</table>

If the final punctuation is an exclamation point or a question mark, however, it cannot be altered in this way.

Aside from these situations, MLA style does not allow other alterations within a quotation. For example, you may not alter wording, spelling, or capitalization within a quote. If an error, such as misspelling, occurs in the original quote, do not fix it. Instead, place the term *sic* (Latin for *thus* or *so*) in square brackets immediately following the error to indicate that it occurred in the original: "The band Led Zeplon [sic] created innovations in the use of the electric guitar that still influence today's rock music."

Note Taking for Nontextual Sources

Sources such as visual material, lectures, and television and radio transmissions pose special challenges for note taking. For these types of sources, use note-taking methods similar to the ones you would use for a print source, but keep the following guidelines in mind.

- Make a working bibliography card for these types of sources, just as you would for a written document. (Consult the chapter in Part Five for the documentation style that you are using to see what information is required for the entry.)
- Pay particular attention to the source's major and minor points because accuracy is just as important for nontextual sources as for other sources. Avoid paraphrasing or quoting material out of context.

Working with Sources

- Use a recording device when quoting from transmissions or live events so that you can replay and check the exact wording. Otherwise, paraphrase or summarize these types of sources.

- When you do not have a text version that you can consult at your leisure for television or radio programs, lectures, and other live events, take preliminary notes during the event or transmission and then, in a second stage, selectively expand the notes that will be most useful for your research paper.

- Check the programming schedule either in the local newspaper or online; some broadcast networks such as National Public Radio, PBS, or the Discovery channel may transmit the same program more than once in a one- or two-week period.

- Use Web sites that supplement programming with additional information, which some networks offer. These supplements may help clarify the program's content or add new dimensions to it. Radio stations often offer links to audio recordings of transmissions, and educationally oriented television stations may sell videotapes of some programs.

- Insert such visual material as photographs, charts, and tables into the text of your paper. Be sure to properly document any images that you use (see pages 265–66). If you don't want to include a copy of the visual in your paper, you can paraphrase or summarize what you learned from the source. Figure 12-5 is an example of a summary note card for a visual source.

An Extended Example of Effective Note Taking

As Paul Oster was researching the topic *dangerous effects of ozone layer depletion,* he was shown a source by a fellow student who was working on the same subject. The article's title, "Study of Cloud Patterns Points to Many Areas Exposed to Big Rises in Ultraviolet Radiation," is interesting in itself because it does not mention ozone. Paul might not have found this source under *ozone layer* in a periodical index unless the indexer had actually read the article and therefore knew it dealt with the ozone layer. Some indexers will go entirely by the title when it seems as specific as this one. However, Paul would have been able to find this item only if he had in mind various subjects related to his topic (in this case, *ultraviolet radiation*).

As he read the article, Paul realized that his understanding of the role of the ozone in the dangers of ultraviolet radiation had been incomplete. Paul's working hypothesis was "Although measurements of the ozone layer are not very precise at this time, it seems likely that the ozone layer

Yellowstone Caldera Map

YELLOWSTONE CALDERA LOCATION

The site of the Yellowstone Caldera takes up most of the center of Yellowstone Park, and much of present-day Yellowstone Lake lies within the depression created by the ancient explosion.

Figure 12-5   An example of a visual source and corresponding summary note card.

is being depleted, and that humans are the cause." Previously, he had imagined that wherever the ozone layer became too thin, the ultraviolet radiation would immediately affect all those living directly under the "hole" in the layer. From the article, he learned that some parts of the Earth are protected from ultraviolet injury by their cloudy climates. Tropical jungles and rainy London, as well as Seattle and the American Northwest, will experience the effects of ozone depletion quite a bit later than sunny southern California and the Saharan lands in North Africa. This news created a new subtopic for Paul's research — *the role of climate* (or *clouds*).

Now let us watch Paul closely as he takes notes on this article.

Working with Sources

Study of Cloud Patterns Points to Many Areas Exposed to Big Rises in Ultraviolet Radiation

By WILLIAM K. STEVENS

This paragraph states the article's thesis; no note is needed.

Depletion of the earth's protective ozone layer is exposing some areas of the world, including parts of the United States, to biologically harmful doses of ultraviolet radiation, but some other areas will not become vulnerable for another 20 to 50 years, according to a new study.

The paragraph provides new information on the role of clouds. (card 1)

The reason for the variance, the authors of the study say, is that patterns of cloud cover vary from one area to another. Clouds as well as ozone block ultraviolet radiation, and the actual pattern and amount of radiation reaching the ground cannot be calculated globally unless this is taken into account.

The list of affected places may be useful. (card 2)

By making the calculation in that manner, experts in California have concluded on the basis of satellite data that large parts of North America, most of central Europe, the Mediterranean, New Zealand, South Africa and the southern half of Australia, Argentina and Chile are now being subjected to significant increases in harmful radiation. In the United States, the affected areas are the Midwest, the Southwest including southern California, and part of the Northeast. Hawaii is also being affected, according to the study.

This shows the researchers' expertise; Paul may want to consult the source of the information, given at the end of the paragraph. (card 3)

The research was done by Dr. Dan Lubin, a research physicist at the California Space Institute at the Scripps Institution of Oceanography in San Diego, and Elsa H. Jensen, an aerospace engineer with the Sea-Space Corporation, a satellite

Working with Sources

note
card 1

Stevens, p. C4

EFFECT OF CLIMATE

Clouds also block UV rad—this effect must be considered in measuring danger.

note
card 2

Stevens, p. C4

DANGER—LOCATIONS

Satellite info shows areas subject to "significant increases" in UV rad—

Cent. Eur.; Medit. area; N.Z.; S. Africa; southern Australia; Argentina & Chile

in U.S.: Midwest; Southwest (inc. S. Calif.); parts of Northeast; Hawaii

note
card 3

Stevens, p. C4

A BIBLIOGRAPHICAL NOTE

Dr. Dan Lubin, res. physicist, Calif. Space Inst.
Elsa Jensen, aerospace engineer, Sea-Space Corp. (satellite instrument co.)

See report in Brit. j. Nature Oct. 26, 1995

note
card 4

Stevens, p. C4

EFFECT OF UV-B

UV-B causes skin cancer & cataracts; injures immune sys.; also upsets natural ecosystems.

(Note cards continued on page 163)

Working with Sources

A clear, brief statement of the dangers of radiation. There is no need to note the role of the ozone layer, which Paul already knows. (card 4)

The date is important; the rest is familiar to Paul. (card 5)

This needs to be paraphrased for possible use. (card 6)

A paraphrase is needed; absolute accuracy is important. Keywords: *calculated, estimated, average, 2.5% per decade, five years.* **(card 7)**

The paragraph gives more specific information about the future threat. (card 8)

Paul needs to paraphrase the description of the relationship between cloud cover variance and UV exposure, including a quotation, to ensure accuracy. (card 9)

instrument and software company in San Diego. Their report appeared in the Oct. 26 issue of the British journal *Nature.*

Ultraviolet-B from the sun, a form of radiation that can cause skin cancer and cataracts, damage the immune system and disrupt natural ecosystems, is normally blocked by a layer of ozone in the stratosphere. Industrial chemicals, principally chlorofluorocarbons used as refrigerants, destroy stratospheric ozone.

Under an international agreement, the production of chlorofluorocarbons is to cease at the end of this year. But because the chemicals persist so long in the atmosphere, ozone depletion is expected to continue for decades.

"Whether or not you can assert that ozone depletion is an environmental problem" at any given time "depends very much on where you are," Dr. Lubin said.

He and Ms. Jensen calculated that at the estimated average global rate of ozone depletion, about 2.5 percent per decade, large parts of continental Europe, North and South America, Australia and Southern Africa would be bathed in increased UV-B radiation in five years.

But the British Isles and Ireland, for instance, are not expected to experience a significant increase for another 30 years, and it is not expected for 20 to 50 years in parts of central Russia, most of China, Japan, North and South Korea and the Indian subcontinent. Mexico, northern Australia, New Guinea and areas of South America north of São Paulo, Brazil, are also not expected to experience increases for decades.

In the United States, the South and Pacific Northwest should not experience increases for another 20 years, according to the calculations.

A major factor in determining whether biologically significant amounts reach the earth, Dr. Lubin said, is the natural variability of cloudiness in a given area. When cloud cover varies widely from one year to the next, the ultraviolet radiation that people and other organisms are exposed to also varies. Increases in the radiation because of the depleted ozone layer probably do not

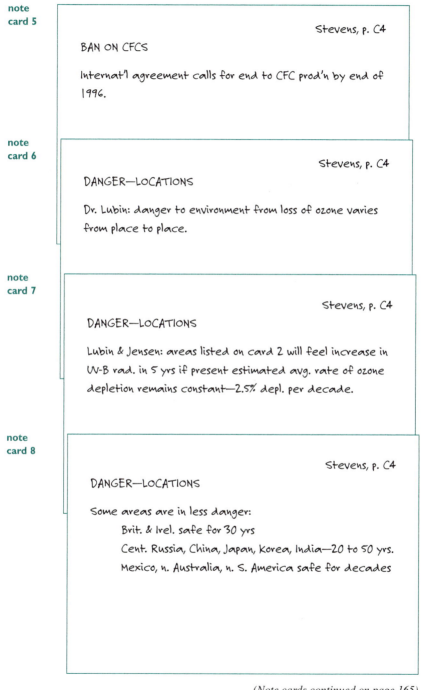

note
card 5

Stevens, p. C4

BAN ON CFCS

Internat'l agreement calls for end to CFC prod'n by end of
1996.

note
card 6

Stevens, p. C4

DANGER—LOCATIONS

Dr. Lubin: danger to environment from loss of ozone varies
from place to place.

note
card 7

Stevens, p. C4

DANGER—LOCATIONS

Lubin & Jensen: areas listed on card 2 will feel increase in
UV-B rad. in 5 yrs if present estimated avg. rate of ozone
depletion remains constant—2.5% depl. per decade.

note
card 8

Stevens, p. C4

DANGER—LOCATIONS

Some areas are in less danger:
Brit. & Irel. safe for 30 yrs
Cent. Russia, China, Japan, Korea, India—20 to 50 yrs.
Mexico, n. Australia, n. S. America safe for decades

Working with Sources

(Note cards continued on page 165)

have a biological effect until they exceed this natural variability, Dr. Lubin said.

This material is important for telling how the theory was derived. (card 10)

To calculate natural variability, Dr. Lubin and Ms. Jensen combined satellite data on global ozone trends from 1978 to 1993 with satellite data on solar radiation reflected from clouds from 1985 to 1990. This produced a base line of natural variability, against which the researchers compared trends in UV expected from ozone depletion. The comparison enabled them to determine how long it takes for the expected UV trend to become significant.

Here is important information on the measurement of UV radiation from place to place. (card 11)

In determining the present amount of UV-B striking the earth, an indirect analysis of this sort would not be necessary if there were abundant UV detection instruments around the world. But the instruments are sparse, and most have not been in position long enough, over a broad enough area, to detect any trends, especially in the temperate zones where most people live.

Instruments have shown for certain that UV-B has risen significantly in Antarctica, where ozone depletion has been the most severe. A few measurements in temperate zones also indicate an increase.

Working with Sources

note card 9

Stevens, p. C4

EFFECT OF CLIMATE

Dr. Lubin: How much UV rad. reaches earth is greatly affected by amount of clouds covering area throughout the year. If this changes much from yr to yr, danger also varies. Increases due to ozone depl. "probably do not have a biological effect until they exceed this natural variability."

note card 10

Stevens, p. C4

EFFECT OF CLIMATE

Lubin & Jensen came to their theory this way: They took (1) satellite info on global ozone 1978–93 and (2) sat. info on solar rad. reflected by clouds 1985–90. Putting these together, they saw how cloud cover affected UV rad. Then they could predict variation in rates of rad. increase from place to place.

note card 11

Stevens, p. C4

MEASUREMENT

At present we have very few rad. measuring devices around the earth; the few in operation have not been working long enough to yield reliable data, esp. in temperate zones, where pop. is concentrated.

Only Antarctica has given definite results; ozone depl. is most severe there.

Working with Sources

Distinguishing Very Useful Information from Not-So-Useful Information

Paul Oster now went to another source, an article titled "Russian Spy Plane Is Turning Its Sights from U.S. to Ozone." Judging by its title, the article seemed unlikely to offer as much information as the previous one had. However, Paul did not want to chance missing something valuable.

Russian Spy Plane Is Turning Its Sights from U.S. to Ozone

By MALCOLM W. BROWNE

No note is needed; there is no specific information here, and the use of the plane will be shown.

No note is needed; the plane's features are irrelevant to the hypothesis.

The note needs to mention that the plane reaches 67,000 feet and carries more than U.S. planes. (The information lets readers know that we can expect better measurements in the near future.)

No note is needed; Paul already knows the 1975 date, and the hole's existence is Paul's research topic.

For the first time since the end of the cold war, a Russian high-altitude spy plane has been put at the disposal of Western European scientists, who will use it to study depletion of the protective ozone layer over Arctic regions.

The European Science Foundation announced this month that Russia would provide a specially modified Myasishchev M-55 airplane for high-altitude Arctic studies during the winter and spring months of 1996 to 1998. The M-55 Geophysika is roughly equivalent in purpose and performance to America's U-2 reconnaissance plane, which has been renamed the ER-2 and flies research missions for NASA.

However, it can carry much heavier loads than the American plane, enabling it to fly large analytical instruments to altitudes up to 67,000 feet.

Depletion of the earth's stratospheric ozone, which protects human beings and animals from dangerous solar ultraviolet radiation, was detected in 1975 by a high-flying U-2. Since then, depletion of the ozone layer has progressed to the point at which a gigantic hole in the ozone layer opens over Antarctica every southern spring.

No note is needed unless noncompliance seems important, for Paul knows about these pollutants from his background reading; he also knows the date of the U.S. ban on Freon.

No note is needed; Paul already knows that the effect of CFCs is long-lasting, and the very general description of chemical reactions is familiar from his background reading.

The note needs to mention ice clouds' role in the chemical action. (This is news to Paul.)

The note should mention how the plane's data will be used.

Less severe but marked depletion of the ozone layer has also begun to occur over the Arctic during the northern spring, and there has been pronounced thinning of the ozone shield even over temperate regions in recent years.

Most atmospheric scientists attribute the ozone depletion to increasing quantities of chlorofluorocarbons and similar Freon compounds released into the atmosphere by human activity. Freons have been used for many years as refrigerant gases in refrigerators and air-conditioners, as foaming agents in plastic, as insulators, as solvents for cleaning computer components and in many other applications. Although the United States banned Freon propellants in aerosol sprays in 1978, some nations continue to manufacture Freon-propelled sprays.

Although production of these chemicals is now prohibited in most industrial nations, their effects on the ozone layer are expected to increase and linger for many years. At high altitudes, Freons are broken down by ultraviolet radiation from the sun, producing chlorine compounds that react with ozone. This initiates a chain reaction, in which the destructive chlorine compounds are regenerated, becoming available to destroy still more ozone.

According to the European Science Foundation, which is based in Strasbourg, France, the M-55 provided by the Myasishchev Design Bureau, the Russian Central Aereological Center and Aviecocenter will be able to study the chemical reactions believed to occur on the surfaces of fine ice particles that make up polar stratospheric clouds. These clouds, which appear in early spring, seem to play a pivotal role in catalyzing the chemical reactions that lead to the destruction of ozone.

The leader of the scientific team, Dr. Leopoldo Stafanutti of the Italian National Research Council, hopes to combine measurements made by the M-55 with mathematical models of possible physical and chemical changes occurring in the stratospheric clouds. This, he hopes, will lead to methods by which forecasts can be made regarding changes in the ozone layer.

Working with Sources

A note is needed; the precise information on areas being investigated is useful. Paul already knows the sources of aerosols (natural/human).

Participants in the Airborne Polar Experiment include some 20 research institutions in Russia, Italy, Germany, Britain, Finland, Norway, Sweden and Switzerland. The group plans particularly to study lee wave clouds, clouds of ice particles that form downwind of mountain peaks, in Scandinavia and the Urals. The plane will also analyze the chemistry and physics of polar stratospheric clouds in the Siberian Arctic, where no comparable measurements have ever been made, the foundation said.

No note is needed; Paul already knows the sources of aerosols (natural/human).

A secondary object of the flights, each of which may last up to six hours, will be to catalogue all types of aerosol particles present in the European and Arctic atmosphere up to the plane's operational ceiling. Aerosols come from both natural sources (like volcanoes) and human activity (such as the burning of soft coal).

No note is needed; this is not relevant to Paul's research.

The M-55 has been scrutinized by Western observers only a few times since NATO intelligence experts spotted it at a Soviet airfield in 1982. Six of the planes were built, five of which remain in military service. The civilian version, the Geophysika, is a single-seat airplane with two jet engines, twin tail booms and wings 133 feet long, and it has a huge instrument bay that can carry more than 3,000 pounds.

As you can see, much of the material in the article was not very helpful, but the several notes Paul recorded would become pieces in the final analysis of his topic. Of course, someone who read this article as a first source would not have been familiar with some of the information that Paul had already read about and, therefore, would have taken more notes than Paul needed to take.

Working with Sources

13

Avoiding Plagiarism

Plagiarism — the use of someone else's writing or ideas without proper documentation — can be a very perplexing subject. You encounter undocumented information every day in periodicals, advertisements, radio, and television, so the emphasis on documenting sources for academic papers may seem confusing. The existence of various documentation styles (Part Five covers four of these styles) can also add to the confusion. If you are from another culture or are new to the conventions of academic research, you may not be familiar with the emphasis on giving credit for intellectual ownership of ideas and language, especially when mass media like the Internet and newspapers do not seem to emphasize individual authorship. Finally, distinguishing between your own ideas and the ideas you learn from sources can be challenging after many hours spent researching a topic.

For these reasons, students often have trouble seeing plagiarism from the instructor's point of view. Many tend to feel that instructors exaggerate the seriousness of the offense. Conversely, many instructors think students treat the problem lightly because avoiding plagiarism sometimes takes a lot of effort. The basic fact remains, however, that plagiarism is a serious offense in academic writing. Plagiarism policies exist at virtually every college or university in the country, and the consequences for plagiarism expressed in these policies can be very serious, ranging from failing the assignment or course to being expelled from the institution.

When your instructor emphasizes the seriousness of plagiarism, he or she is doing so because proper documentation of sources is important in academic writing. Avoiding plagiarism is not just a matter of avoiding consequences; it is a matter of practicing ethical responsibility and establishing your own credibility as a writer. The purposes of carefully documenting all borrowed material in your paper include the following:

- *Giving credit where credit is due.* You must acknowledge the work of researchers who have gone before you. (If another writer were to use an interesting idea from something you had written, you would surely want your work acknowledged as its source.)

- *Telling your readers where to find more information about your topic.* You may have raised some questions that would send a curious reader back to your sources for answers. Or a reader might want to verify your interpretation of what you read; for instance, someone might want to be certain you had not quoted out of context.

- *Giving knowledgeable readers some idea of how authoritative a particular statement is.* Let the reader know whether the author of the source is an expert in the field or simply a reporter summarizing recent developments for the general public.

- *Providing the date of initial publication.* The date that your source was originally published is important because information changes through time. Magazine articles and books may be reprinted, so you must record the original publication date (as opposed to the date an article was posted electronically, or the year the book was printed). For instance, Sigmund Freud spent more than forty years developing the psychoanalytic theory of personality, and over that period he revised some of his earlier ideas considerably. Therefore, a well-informed reader might want to know just when Freud made a statement that you quoted in your paper. For this reason, you must be careful to find out the year the source was first published.

- *Giving an overall sense of how thoroughly you carried out your research.* The list of works cited reveals at a glance the range of your investigation of the topic; the notes indicate how thoroughly you have read the sources.

Most instructors recognize that plagiarism can be unintentional or intentional. Unintentional plagiarism can occur because of negligence (such as poor note taking) or from a misunderstanding of documentation rules. Intentional plagiarism can occur when a student purposefully tries to pass off another person's work as his or her own, either by copying material from one or more sources without providing documentation or by simply turning in a document written by someone else. These cases of intentional plagiarism are instances of theft. Plagiarism as a result of misunderstanding or inattention might not carry such moral connotations, but it is still considered plagiarism and may be treated just as severely as intentional academic theft.

The problem is essentially one of trust and attribution. Readers of your research paper assume that all ideas and judgments that are not accompanied by a note are yours. As a matter of personal integrity, you must acknowledge any idea, fact, or language that comes from a source. To avoid unintentional plagiarism, you must work hard to understand the documentation conventions and ask any questions that arise as you learn.

Understanding Documentation

You must document any ideas, facts, or quotations that you take from sources. The only exception is information that is considered general knowledge by your paper's audience. (See pages 234–37 for a more extensive discussion of material that must be documented.) Chapters 18 through 20 provide detailed coverage of how to format your in-text citations and list of sources, but here are some examples from the student papers in Chapter 22 to introduce the principles of documentation.

The following example is from Shirley Macalbe's paper, "The New Immigrants: Asset or Burden?" Shirley wrote her paper using MLA-style documentation.

documented idea   Nathan Glazer, a professor of sociology, explains that the American public is undecided about whether these new immigrants will make the United States a stronger nation or a weaker one (3).

works cited entry   Glazer, Nathan, ed. *Clamor at the Gates: The New American Immigration*. San Francisco: Inst. for Contemporary Studies, 1985. Print.

Susanna Andrews included the following quote in her paper, "Emily Dickinson's Reluctance to Publish," also using MLA-style documentation.

documented quote   Further disagreement with the image of the poet as a shy, unworldly creature comes from Clark Griffith, who sees her as a person whose sensibility was "responsive to the brutalities which life imposes on the individual, and acutely aware of the nothingness with which existence seems surrounded" (5-6).

works cited entry
> Griffith, Clark. *The Long Shadow: Emily Dickinson's Tragic Poetry*. Princeton: Princeton UP, 1964. Print.

Here is a documented fact from David Perez's paper, "*Solenopsis invicta*: Destroyer of Ecosystems." His assignment required APA-style documentation.

documented fact
> Mann (1994) tells us that the anti-fire-ant program included bombing large areas infested by *S. invicta*.

references list entry
> Mann, C. C. (1994, March 18). Fire ants parlay their queens into a threat to biodiversity. *Science, 263* (5153), 1560-1561. Retrieved from DPER database.

Plagiarizing Ideas

Sources can provide interpretation, opinions, analysis, definitions, comparisons, analogies, and other useful ideas on your topic. Sometimes students make the error of thinking that documenting these borrowed ideas is less important than documenting borrowed language. This is not the case at all. In academic writing, when you use an idea — for instance, a critical judgment that appeared in one of your sources — you must use documentation that tells who proposed the idea and just where you found it. Even if you arrived at the same judgment on your own, you need to acknowledge that the writer had the same idea. The following example shows a case in which a student created a good paraphrase but failed to credit it in her paper with an in-text citation.

original passage
> What we need to consider about the computer has nothing to do with its efficiency as a teaching tool. We need to know in what ways it is altering our conception of learning, and how, in conjunction with television, it undermines the old idea of school.

works cited entry
> Postman, Neal. *Technopoly: The Surrender of Culture to Technology*. New York: Vintage, 1993. Print.

plagiarism in student paper
> The big question about computers in education is not how well they teach us, but how they are changing our orientation to learning and challenging traditional notions of school.

At times it may seem challenging to separate your newly formed ideas from those of the sources you are reading, especially when you are writing a rough draft. However, with good understanding of documentation requirements and organized note-taking skills, you can distinguish source-based ideas from your own and document appropriately. If you are in doubt, use a citation. If you feel you may have omitted documentation at any point in your draft, such an oversight is easy to correct. Simply reread your paper, with your notes at hand, and check each significant idea or fact to see whether you have given proper credit. Add any source citations you omitted.

Plagiarizing Language

When you borrow ideas, the in-text citations alone indicate that they are not your own original ideas. When you borrow language, however, you must take an additional step. In addition to using citations, you must use quotation marks. Without quotation marks, the use of another writer's language is considered plagiarism even if the passage is otherwise documented. Here is an example:

original passage	Don't we remember how it was as a child, to enter a story innocently, only to emerge at the other end utterly wrung out, red-eyed, and in some intangible way transformed?
works cited entry	Kenison, Katrina. Foreword. *The Best American Short Stories*, 2003. Ed. Walter Mosely. New York: Houghton, 2003. ix-xii. Print.
plagiarism in student paper	Stories often have the effect of making us feel utterly wrung out, and transformed in some intangible way (Kenison x).

Even though the student documents the source with an MLA-style parenthetical citation, the lack of quotation marks around *utterly wrung out* and *transformed in some intangible way* constitutes plagiarism.

Many of your notes will consist of paraphrases and summaries; therefore, you might accidentally treat a direct quotation as though it, too, had been written in your own words. If in taking notes you followed our suggestion and marked off the quotations with large quotation marks, or « and », you can easily check the paper against the notes to be sure all quotations have been identified as such. If the markings on your note cards are not clear, however, you must go back to the original sources to determine which words in your notes are quotations and which are your own.

Plagiarizing Paraphrases

A student plagiarizes when the wording of his or her paraphrase is so close to that of the wording in source materials that it is practically a quotation — that is, when only a few words have been changed and the sentence patterns are virtually identical to those in the sources. As you learned in Chapter 12 (see pages 144–46), this is called *partial paraphrase*, a form of plagiarism. Following is an example involving a description of George Washington's plan for saving his forces from the British army, which had trapped him into defending a fortress on the shore of Long Island. The only means of escape required moving the men in small boats.

original passage   The other necessity, and this seemed the impossible one, was for Washington to find some way to get his army away without tremendous loss. The problem was that, when part of the force was on water, the rest, unable adequately to defend the fortifications, would become easy prey for the enemy. Unless he could somehow slip secretly away, Washington would have to sacrifice half his army.

works cited entry   Flexner, James T. *The Young Hamilton*. Boston: Little, 1978. Print.

plagiarized paraphrase   The other need, which seemed to be impossible, was for Washington to discover some means of getting the army away without enormous losses. His problem was that, when some of the soldiers were on the water, the others would be unable to defend their land position adequately and could be easily defeated by the British. Unless Washington could manage to slip away in secret, he would lose half his forces (Flexner 110).

Perhaps the only crime here is laziness, or perhaps the student knowingly borrowed the author's sentence structure and word order. From an instructor's perspective, the student's intent is not the issue. This student relied heavily on the original sentence structure and only "translated" the passage by finding synonyms for a few words. The flow of thought is a direct echo of the original. Although the note tells the reader where the information came from, it gives no indication that the wording is not entirely the student's own.

The solution is to rewrite the entire paragraph, changing the sentence structure and making different word choices:

acceptable paraphrase   Washington's brilliance as a field commander is shown by his plan for the army to escape by water before the British knew what was happening. Obviously, the soldiers could not simply board boats and sail away, because if the British attacked in the middle of the operation, most of the troops would be in no position to defend themselves (Flexner 110).

This paraphrase is distinctly different from the source, as it should be. The language no longer mimics the original, and the passage will probably integrate into the paper more smoothly because it is written in the student's own style. The passage would still need to be documented, of course, to credit the author as the source of the information.

Paraphrasing without Plagiarizing

It is not always easy to know how different from the original your paraphrase must be if you are to avoid plagiarism. A possible rule would be to enclose any words taken from a source in quotation marks, but this could lead to absurdities in many common situations. For instance, how would you paraphrase the following sentence without using the italicized words?

original   The typical *Inuit igloo* offers superior insulation against *temperatures* that fall as low as *–50° F.*

No synonyms exist for most proper nouns, such as *Inuit,* just as no synonyms exist for most numbers (exceptions: *dozen* for *twelve; score* for *twenty; decade* for *ten years*). As for *igloo,* the substitution of *ice house* or *house made from blocks of hard-packed snow* would be either inaccurate or very clumsy, and *temperature* can be replaced only by a slightly different idea, such as *coldness* or *freezing weather.* If you put quotation marks around these words in your paraphrase, the result would look rather silly:

absurd use of   A well-made "Inuit igloo" protects its occupants even
quotation marks   when "temperatures" outside reach "–50° F."

Obviously, any rule must be flexible enough to prevent this ugliness. In general, then, you can safely repeat specific numbers (*–50° F., 21 percent,*

Working with Sources

5,280 feet, 7 million people, $524.52), special terms for which there are no sim-
ple synonyms *(igloo, gross national product, income tax, influenza, touchdown,
amphetamine),* and even very simple words that would require bizarre sub-
stitutions *(horse, ocean, atmosphere, lung, father, high school, temperature).*

Remember, however, that sometimes even a single word taken from a
source requires quotation marks if it is especially colorful or represents
the writer's judgment. The following summary of an article quoted just
two isolated words, *ridiculous* and *absurd.*

student summary of article

In 1912, H. H. Goddard, director of research at
Vineland Institute for Feeble-Minded Girls and Boys
in New Jersey, was commissioned by the U.S. Public
Health Service to survey mental deficiency among
immigrant populations at Ellis Island. According to
paleontologist Stephen Jay Gould, Goddard's study
employed "ridiculous" criteria which led to "absurd"
conclusions regarding the native intelligence of
Jews and other unpopular European minorities.
Goddard's work played a significant role in the
passage of the Restriction Act of 1924, which,
according to Allan Chase, author of *The Legacy
of Malthus,* barred millions of Jews from entering
the United States and thereby escaping the Nazi
holocaust (Gould 14-15).

works cited entry

Gould, Stephen Jay. "Science and Jewish
        Immigration." *Natural History* Dec. 1980: 14-19.
        Print.

Plagiarizing Facts

Facts is a broad term that refers to statistics, observations, descriptions, eyewitness accounts, and a variety of other basic pieces of information. If facts come from a source and they are not general knowledge
among your audience, they must be documented. (See pages 234–37 for
more on common knowledge.)

original source

The Great Lakes shoreline is equal to almost 44 percent
of the circumference of the earth, and Michigan's Great

Lakes coast totals 3,288 mi/5,294 km, more coastline than any state but Alaska.

works cited entry

"Great Lakes Facts and Figures." *Great Lakes Information Network.* 15 July 2003. Web. 1 Dec. 2003.

plagiarism in student paper

The Great Lakes are so huge that their combined shoreline would stretch almost halfway around the earth.

Although the student included the source in his works cited list, he failed to include an in-text citation when presenting the fact in the paper. Because this information about the Great Lakes is not widely known, the lack of a citation asks the reader to believe that the fact came from the student, which is clearly not the case. Facts are typically detailed content involving numbers, descriptive terms, proper nouns, and names, so it is easy to skim an initial draft for undocumented facts and insert appropriate documentation.

Avoid the tendency to insert facts from remembered (as opposed to researched) sources such as a long-ago lecture, a television program you saw last month, or a magazine article you once read. Often your memory of such facts is not accurate. With the research skills you have learned, you should be able to find and verify them in sources that can be documented.

As you can see, the problem of plagiarism concerns not only the use of individual words but also the flow of thought, the presentation of ideas, and the use of facts, all of which combine to give a piece of writing its style and originality. The research paper assignment measures, among other things, your ability to express ideas effectively. Although this challenge can be frustrating at times, you will be expected to maintain a personal integrity that will prevent your surrendering to the temptation to borrow even "just a little bit here and there" from sources.

Working with Sources

Reviewing Part Three

The following questions and exercises will help you reinforce and practice the skills covered in Part Three. For additional practice, visit <bedfordstmartins.com/writingresearch>.

Questions

1. What is a working bibliography? How does it differ from the final list of works cited or references?
2. Briefly outline the different but related processes of skimming a book and skimming a periodical article.
3. Explain how you can tell whether a potential source is likely to be useful to you. Mention several specific criteria.
4. What signs might warn you that a topic is probably too narrow? Too broad? What steps can you take to resolve both problems?
5. Describe the different ways in which a source might be relevant to your paper.
6. How does a hypothesis help you read sources and take good notes?
7. What kind of information *must* you record in every note entry to avoid problems at later stages in the process?
8. Why do successful note takers keep each note as brief as possible?
9. What is the difference between a summary and a paraphrase? How are they similar?
10. What are the advantages of paraphrasing and summarizing rather than copying passages from sources?
11. When paraphrasing, do you have to change every word that appeared in the original? Explain your answer.
12. For what reasons might you quote rather than paraphrase a statement found in a source?
13. How might plagiarism become a problem even for honest writers of research papers?

Exercises

1. Write out the information for the following sources as you would on a bibliography card:
   • a 1952 book published in New York by Harcourt, Brace & World called A History of Western Philosophy and written by W. T. Jones.

- an article about the Japanese economy called How Japan Does It, written by Christopher Byron, published in Time magazine on March 30, 1981, and running from page 54 through page 60.
- an article in The Sixteenth Century Journal by N. M. Sutherland called Catherine de Medici: The Legend of the Wicked Italian Queen, running from page 45 through page 56 and published in volume 9 in 1978.

2. If you are currently working on a research paper and have developed a topic and hypothesis, follow the suggestions in this chapter to put together a working bibliography and evaluate the potential sources by skimming them. Turn in your notes.

3. In a popular magazine of your choice, read an article about a topic of current interest, such as *new energy sources, genetic engineering, political problems in Central America,* or *space probes of distant planets.* Then, using an appropriate periodical index, find an article on the same topic in a professional journal and read it. Write a paragraph or two contrasting the approaches used by the authors of the two articles.

4. Choose a nationally controversial topic, such as *the war on drugs, Medicaid payments for abortion, sexual harassment in the workplace,* or *affirmative action programs,* or any important issue facing your area of the country. Find articles in two different periodicals (newspapers included) that take opposite sides on the issue. Write a summary that points out the major differences in their views and the general tone of each article.

5. Take a full set of notes on the following excerpt from a lecture. Be sure to follow the direction indicated by the hypothesis when deciding what information belongs in your notes. Do not put too much information on individual cards. If you quote something, mark it clearly, and, in parentheses, give a reason for quoting — accuracy, memorable words, conciseness, authority.

topic: *the causes of violence in America today*

hypothesis: "Although some observers blame violence on television and the economy, the cause may lie in our past, going back to the lawless West and to Prohibition."

It is commonly assumed that violence is part of our frontier heritage. But the historical record shows that frontier violence was very different from violence today. Robbery and burglary, two of our most common crimes, were of no great significance in the frontier towns of the Old West, and rape was seemingly nonexistent.

Bodie, one of the principal towns on the trans-Sierra frontier, illustrates the point. Nestled high in the mountains of eastern California, Bodie, which boomed in the late

From Roger D. McGrath, "The Myth of Frontier Violence," *Harper's* Feb. 1985: 26–28, an excerpt from a lecture given November 1984 at California State University, Long Beach.

1870s and early 1880s, ranked among the most notorious frontier towns of the Old West. It was, as one prospector put it, the last of the old-time mining camps.

Like the trans-Sierra frontier in general, Bodie was indisputably violent and lawless, yet most people were not affected. Fistfights and gunfights among willing combatants — gamblers, miners, and the like — were regular events, and stagecoach holdups were not unusual. But the old, the young, the weak, and the female — so often the victims of crime today — were generally not harmed.

Robbery was more often aimed at stagecoaches than at individuals. Highwaymen usually took only the express box and left the passengers alone. There were eleven stagecoach robberies in Bodie between 1878 and 1882, and in only two instances were passengers robbed. (In one instance, the highwaymen later apologized for their conduct.)

There were only ten robberies and three attempted robberies of individuals in Bodie during its boom years, and in nearly every case the circumstances were the same: the victim had spent the evening in a gambling den, saloon, or brothel; he had revealed that he had on his person a significant sum of money; and he was staggering home drunk when the attack occurred.

Bodie's total of twenty-one robberies — eleven of stages and ten of individuals — over a five-year period converts to a rate of eighty-four robberies per 100,000 inhabitants per year. On this scale — the same scale used by the FBI to index crime — New York City's robbery rate in 1980 was 1,140, Miami's was 995, and Los Angeles's was 628. The rate for the United States as a whole was 243. Thus Bodie's robbery rate was significantly below the national average in 1980.

Perhaps the greatest deterrent to crime in Bodie was the fact that so many people were armed. Armed guards prevented bank robberies and holdups of stagecoaches carrying shipments of bullion, and armed homeowners and merchants discouraged burglary. Between 1878 and 1882, there were only thirty-two burglaries — seventeen of homes and fifteen of businesses — in Bodie. At least a half-dozen burglaries

were thwarted by the presence of armed citizens. The newspapers regularly advocated shooting burglars on sight, and several burglars were, in fact, shot at.

Using the FBI scale, Bodie's burglary rate for those five years was 128. Miami's rate in 1980 was 3,282, New York City's was 2,661, and Los Angeles's was 2,602. The rate of the United States as a whole was 1,668, thirteen times that of Bodie.

Bodie's law enforcement institutions were certainly not responsible for these low rates. Rarely were robbers or burglars arrested, and even less often were they convicted. Moreover, many law enforcement officers operated on both sides of the law.

It was the armed citizens themselves who were the most potent — though not the only — deterrent to larcenous crime. Another was the threat of vigilantism. Highwaymen, for example, understood that while they could take the express box from a stagecoach without arousing the citizens, they risked inciting the entire populace to action if they robbed the passengers.

There is considerable evidence that women in Bodie were rarely the victims of crime. Between 1878 and 1882 only one woman, a prostitute, was robbed, and there were no reported cases of rape. (There is no evidence that rapes occurred but were not reported.)

Finally, juvenile crime, which accounts for a significant portion of the violent crime in the United States today, was limited in Bodie to pranks and malicious mischief.

If robbery, burglary, crimes against women, and juvenile crime were relatively rare on the trans-Sierra frontier, homicide was not: thirty-one Bodieites were shot, stabbed, or beaten to death during the boom years, for a homicide rate of 116. No U.S. city today comes close to this rate. In 1980, Miami led the nation with a homicide rate of 32.7; Las Vegas was a distant second at 23.4. A half-dozen cities had rates of zero. The rate for the United States as a whole in that year was a mere 10.2.

Several factors contributed to Bodie's high homicide rate. A majority of the town's residents were young, adventurous, single males who adhered to a code of conduct that frequently required them to fight even if, or perhaps especially if, it could mean death. Courage was admired above all else. Alcohol also played a major role in fostering the settlement of disputes by violence.

If the men's code of conduct and their consumption of alcohol made fighting inevitable, their sidearms often made it fatal. While the carrying of guns probably reduced the incidence of robbery and burglary, it undoubtedly increased the number of homicides.

For the most part, the citizens of Bodie were not troubled by the great number of killings; nor were they troubled that only one man was ever convicted of murder. They accepted the killings and the lack of convictions because most of those killed had been willing combatants.

Thus the violence and lawlessness of the trans-Sierra frontier bear little relation to the violence and lawlessness that pervade American society today. If Bodie is at all representative of frontier towns, there is little justification for blaming contemporary American violence on our frontier heritage.

---

6. For each of the following topics/hypotheses, prepare a set of note cards based on the accompanying newspaper article. In both cases, be sure to follow the direction indicated by the hypothesis when deciding what information to record in the notes.

   Remember not to crowd information onto the cards. If you decide to quote, mark the quoted words off clearly. Then, in parentheses, state your reason for quoting — accuracy, conciseness, authority, memorable language.

   topic 1: *possible genetic basis for schizophrenia*

   hypothesis: "Recent research reveals that schizophrenia is probably caused by a defective gene."

   topic 2: *genetic bases of human behavior*

   hypothesis: "Just as research has located genetic sources of many diseases, so it will find genetic causes for behavior patterns such as addiction, schizophrenia, and criminality."

Gene Hunters Pursue Elusive and Complex Traits of Mind

By NATALIE ANGIER

It was just a handful of years ago that biologists were waving their spears, shields and pipettes in the air, boasting with full-throated glory of their success in capturing the legendary prey of molecular genetics. In a series of widely publicized discoveries, geneticists announced the isolation of the cystic fibrosis gene, the gene for Lou Gehrig's disease, the gene for Huntington's disease and a gene linked to the familial form of breast cancer.

Some of those great gene hunts had taken a decade or more, and had been a

Ninth Circle of Hell for many a graduate student and postdoctoral fellow. But molecular geneticists now look back on such triumphs, shake their heads and say, boy, did those lucky devils have it easy.

The field of genetics is moving into a new and much more difficult phase: the search for genes that may contribute in some partial and numbingly convoluted way to complex traits of the mind, the stuff of private psyche and inner life. A fat set of reports being published today in the journal *Nature Genetics* includes two studies that cover this territory.

One confirms an earlier report that had linked male sexual orientation to a spot on the X chromosome.

Another package of papers from several international teams of scientists identifies the rough location of a gene that may play a role in schizophrenia. The reports are accompanied by an editorial that tells biologists how to discriminate between a real finding in the complex field of complex traits, and an experimental coincidence no more meaningful than, say, flipping five heads in a row.

This new work in genetics is riddled with scientific, intellectual and sociocultural mine fields. Many of the straightforward disease genes have been isolated, or are on the verge of being so. These are the genes that hew to the tidy laws of Gregor Mendel, the father of modern genetics. These are the genes that almost surely cause illness in people born with defective versions of them. Inherit the cystic fibrosis mutation, for example, and you are at grave risk of chronic, debilitating lung infections. About 4,000 diseases are thought to be so-called single-gene disorders. Most are very rare in the population, but they have appealed to human geneticists because they are linked to one gene apiece, and are therefore open to molecular dissection.

Scientists are now moving on to the dread complex traits. They are looking for the genes that may predispose people to high blood pressure, heart disease, diabetes and most adult cancers. And on a far more incendiary scale, some researchers are seeking the genes that may put one at risk for a serious mental disease like manic-depressive illness,

schizophrenia or alcoholism. They are looking for genes that influence sexual orientation, or the hunger for novel experiences, or the tendency toward introversion, or a taste for nicotine. And the only thing they are sure of in their various hunts is that no single gene can explain any of the behaviors they study, and that they will spend their professional lives qualifying every claim and cautioning audiences to please, please, please, not over-interpret the results.

Nevertheless, after a long period of setbacks and missteps, the field of behavioral and psychiatric genetics is lately picking up steam and enthusiasm, reflected in the studies just published and the commentary on them. With humorous didacticism, Dr. Eric Lander of the Whitehead Institute for Biomedical Research and the Massachusetts Institute of Technology in Cambridge, and Dr. Leonid Kruglyak of the Whitehead Institute warn their fellow biologists in the *Nature Genetics* editorial that while they may often greet statistics with "glazed-eyed indifference" (and you thought scientists liked that stuff!), they are going to have to knuckle under and take statistics more seriously in this new era of mapping complex traits.

Good statistics are essential on two counts. If a disease or trait has multiple causes, including many genes and that squishy business known as "the environment," then it will take a sound use of mathematics to find an interesting genetic connection in the first place. And once that connection has been identified, a rigorous statistical analysis will assure one that it is real before one rushes it into print.

"We wrote the commentary to try to put statistics in simple terms, so people can understand why we have to have a strict threshold before declaring linkage," Dr. Lander said. "We're going to see hundreds of papers on complex traits over the next few years, and we don't want people to be crying wolf."

In fact, the field of psychiatric genetics has only begun to emerge from a slump in which a number of wolves turned out to be dogs. In the late 1980's, several research teams reported finding genes for manic depression and schizophrenia, which either were never confirmed by other researchers, or were proved wrong and had to be retracted.

But the incentive to move forward was too great to be deterred by a flub or two. For one thing, the illnesses are extremely common, each affecting about 1 percent of the population. They are devastating: for example, 30 percent of the hospital beds in the nation are occupied by schizophrenia patients, said Dr. Kenneth S. Kendler of the Medical College of Virginia in Richmond, an author with Dr. Richard E. Straub, a colleague there, of one of the schizophrenia papers appearing today. And scientists have had scant success trying to understand the illnesses through a nongenetic approach. "Psychiatry is still pretty much in the dark ages," said Dr. David Curtis of the Institute of Psychiatry in London, who contributed to the section on schizophrenia in *Nature Genetics*. "We have no idea about the basic biochemical abnormalities that occur in the course of the illnesses," and a genetic angle on the diseases may offer new insights into their cause.

Moreover, the evidence for a genetic contribution to these mental disorders is quite strong. Studies of twins, for example, showed a hereditary contribution of anywhere from 30 percent to 50 percent for schizophrenia, somewhat more for manic-depressive illness. Researchers also said that the tools they had used before in searching for genes involved in complex mental disorders were too crude for the task.

"At the beginning of using linkage analysis to study schizophrenia, we used monogenic models," like those applied to the analysis of cystic fibrosis, said Dr. Hans W. Moises of Kiel University Hospital in Germany, an author on another of today's reports. "These models are inappropriate where complex diseases are involved."

Recognizing the muddy history of their specialty, the psychiatric geneticists reporting today on their discovery of an intriguing link to schizophrenia are resolutely cautious. What the groups have found is that there appears to be a gene on the upper arm of chromosome 6 (out of the 23 pairs of chromosomes all humans have) that may play a part in some unknown percentage of cases of the disease. But every-

body involved admitted the evidence for chromosome 6p, as the region is known, is not overwhelming. Four teams found the association; and because independent replication is a benchmark for any scientific finding, the work is considered quite exciting. But in none of the individual studies was the result overwhelming, meaning that the chain of evidence is built of rather fragile links. Moreover, two other teams reported no connection at all between schizophrenia and 6p, and one of those scientists, Dr. Curtis, believes the finding will turn out to have been yet another false positive.

Dr. Ann E. Pulver of the Johns Hopkins University School of Medicine in Baltimore, who obtained one of those positive results, said that if the gene on chromosome 6 was involved in only a limited number of cases of the disease — say, 25 percent or less — there was no reason to expect every researcher to find it active in their sample of patients. She and others said the real test would come when researchers got their hands on the gene proper, rather than its approximate location; and then look to see whether the gene is mutated in patients with schizophrenia.

That will take some doing. The 6p region of the chromosome contains many hundreds of genes. Just getting to that general neighborhood had been an extraordinary task. Dr. Kendler and his colleagues, who first identified the tantalizing chromosomal association, tried to make their work tenable by going to Ireland and collaborating with researchers in Dublin and Belfast. The Irish make a good study population for a number of reasons. They have large families, making it easier to trace genetic patterns and compare one relative with another. The Irish are more genetically similar than a comparable group of, say, Americans, and that makes it easier to home in on particular genes of interest. They are also more culturally homogenized, which means most people are exposed to relatively similar environmental conditions, an important consideration for a disease thought to have some environmental component. And finally, Dr. Kendler said, the Irish use very few recreational drugs beyond alcohol, which rules out the complicating factor of

Working with Sources

those drugs thought to induce a psychosis-like state.

The scientists identified 265 families with two or more people suffering from schizophrenia. They drew blood from as many of the 1,408 individuals as they could — patients and their nonafflicted relatives alike — and extracted DNA from the blood cells. Dr. Straub then screened the DNA with 200 so-called DNA markers, bits of radioactively tagged genetic material that serve as signposts indicating a location somewhere on the 23 chromosomes. He was looking for patterns of markers that would be found in the DNA of the schizophrenics but not in their nonafflicted relatives. That broadside approach showed chromosome 6 worthy of closer examination.

Dr. Straub then coordinated a collaborative effort with other teams known to be studying the genetics of schizophrenia. He told them about the tantalizing 6p connection, and asked them to scrutinize the DNA of their family groups to see if the link held up. In some cases, it did.

Other researchers have also detected promising links to chromosomes 8 and 22. But in all cases, they are far, far from singling out the genes themselves. Moreover, even if they isolate a gene and it proves to be involved in some cases of schizophrenia, it will never be as clean an association as the Huntington's gene is with Huntington's disease. Any one gene can only tell a minor part of the somber tale of madness.

Part Four

Writing the Paper

Writing the Paper

14

Organizing and Outlining

Now that you have completed most of your research and have produced a full set of notes taken from a variety of sources, you are ready to start planning the actual writing of your paper. Of course, you may have to go back and revisit one or more sources if you suspect that you missed some useful information. Or, after you have begun to write the paper, you may hear of another relevant source and want to check it out. Research is seldom a straightforward procedure. Retracing your steps is frequently necessary.

Writing the paper is complicated by the large amount of information that must be organized into a logical sequence. In general, a research paper has three parts:

- an *introduction*, in which the topic is introduced and the thesis stated
- a *body*, in which the topic is developed and relevant information presented
- a *conclusion*, in which the paper is summed up and the thesis restated or implied

To begin to shape the core of your paper — the body — into a coherent and ordered discussion that accomplishes its purpose, you need to review the notes and the ongoing outline to gain an overview of all that your research has produced.

Organizing Your Notes

If you have used note cards, an easy way to get such an overview is to place all your note cards on a table, arranging them into groups according to subtopics. Be flexible as you experiment with different groupings and look for connections between information. Now you can see the advantage to having each note on its own card — you can easily shift a note from one logical group to another. Try to find the best way to organize the information for your paper's purpose and audience.

If you took notes in a notebook or on a computer, you can do the same thing by cutting up paper versions of your notes into sections to separate different subtopics. Alternatively, you can review the various subtopics represented in your notes on the computer screen and begin drafting a detailed outline. You can also cut and paste notes that are in a word-processing file into various arrangements, but on a computer screen it is difficult to get the kind of overview you need for organizing the essay. We recommend that you draft an outline if you use this method.

The number of subtopics you have at this stage will vary greatly from one research project to the next, but you can probably expect to find yourself faced with somewhere between ten and twenty groups of notes on the table before you. There may be as few as one or two notes within each group, or there may be several. In an effort to organize these materials, try to form a picture of the research paper as it will look at the end. In all likelihood, the paper will consist of several major divisions, each made up of several subtopics. You can use your preliminary outline (discussed in Chapter 11) as a starting point in creating these major divisions, but you should also be open to new ways of organizing.

Keep in mind that that your own interpretations, explanations, and connections related to the information will be part of the paper. In some cases, your firsthand experience with the topic will also be included in the arrangement of ideas. If this information is not reflected in the notes you have taken, you should work it in at the outline stage.

For his paper on Cotton Mather, Fred Hutchins ended up with approximately twenty subtopics. He took five of these subtopics and placed them in a major division:

> **subtopics:** the millennium's proximity; visits from an angel; the Puritan colony and the New Jerusalem; a total system — God, Devil, angels, witches; Mather's belief in his closeness to God
>
> **major division:** Mather's personal religious views

(This was not Fred's final arrangement of this information. He later broke this major division into two smaller ones: Mather's special place in God's eyes, and the Puritan colony and the Second Coming.) Fred continued to organize his other subtopics until they were all grouped into major divisions.

Refining the Outline

The preliminary outline you have been working with during the note-taking phase, and which you have gradually expanded by arranging into major divisions and subtopics, needs to be checked to ensure it logically supports your paper's hypothesis and purpose. Before you begin writing a rough draft, divide the outline further into specific points representing information from individual cards.

Checking the Major Divisions

In general, it is easier to focus on the shape of the paper's body before coming up with a plan for the introduction. For example, by arranging his notes and considering his thesis ("Cotton Mather's belief in witchcraft was based on private religious beliefs"), Fred Hutchins came up with this outline of major divisions:

Introduction

1. The cruel portrait has been updated to show Mather's humaneness.

2. Mather tried to assure fairness of the trials.

3. Mather wrote and preached against witchcraft.

4. Several theories focus on Mather's defense of the social order.

5. One writer believes Mather was antifeminist.

6. Mather's personal religious views led to his belief in witches.

Conclusion

Because he had not yet created a detailed outline, Fred could think about the shape of his paper without being confused by the details he had come across in his research. He considered the logic of the paper's major divisions and evaluated how well they supported the paper's thesis and its purpose (which was to open the minds of readers who viewed Mather as a cruel, one-dimensional persecutor).

Fred realized that point 2 was one of the examples of Mather's humaneness; that is, it fit better in support of point 1. Fred also noticed that point 3 did not require its own section because he planned to establish this point in the introduction. In addition, he knew that his sources would refer to Mather's writings against witchcraft throughout the paper, making point 3 self-evident. Fred wanted to mention Mather's influence on the Salem community, so he reworded this item to express it in terms of Mather's internal motives and effect on the course of the Salem witch hunt. Finally, point 5 referred to one aspect of the social order Mather was defending, so it belonged under point 4.

Writing the Paper

The revised short outline follows:

Introduction

1. Mather was more humane than originally portrayed. (Murdock; Hofstadter; Hansen; Levy)

2. Whatever his motives, Mather did influence the witch hunting. (Silverman; Levin)

3. Mather was deeply committed to maintaining the Puritan social order. (Hansen; Levy; Karlsen; Pestana)

4. Mather's personal religious views necessitated his belief in witches. (Levin; Silverman; Levy; Middlekauff; Miller)

Conclusion

Notice that Fred listed the sources that would support each idea in the development of his research paper. This helped ensure that he was integrating sources to expand his own ideas and not generating the major divisions of the paper based on a progression from one source to another. If you find that each major division contains only one or two sources, make sure that you are not simply reporting on each source section by section — this is a common error in poorly organized papers.

Expanding the Outline

To write an effective paper, you must organize beyond the level of major ideas. A fairly detailed outline is essential if you hope to control all the information that you have collected. Such an outline allows you to place each piece of information in its assigned slot, waiting to be incorporated into the rough draft.

Constructing a detailed outline requires a careful evaluation of your materials. A detailed outline can take one of several forms (covered in the next section). Even if your instructor does not require a formal outline, an expanded informal outline will assist you tremendously in writing your paper.

To create an expanded outline, first arrange the notes within each major division into logical groupings and sequences. Note cards simplify this process, but if you are not using note cards you can draft a detailed outline on a notebook sheet or in a word-processing file, making brief reference to the content of each note.

Next, look over your arrangement of cards or your outline draft and check it for the following aspects of organization: relevance, repetition, logical arrangement, coverage, balance, and sequencing.

Relevance. Ensure that the ideas and information relate to the major divisions and subtopics in which they are placed, and that, taken as a whole, the outline supports the hypothesis without unnecessary information. You may want to eliminate information or a subtopic that no longer seems relevant, or you may want to reassign it from one major division to another where it fits better.

Repetition. Make sure that different portions of the outline do not cover the same thing. For example, these two subtopics should probably be combined: *the effect of gender on management style,* and *differences in male and female approaches to leadership.*

Logical Arrangement. Ensure that minor ideas are listed under major ideas to which they relate. Do not leave major ideas and minor ideas listed at the same level. For example, *cellular phones* should probably be a subtopic under the major division *information technology,* not a major division itself. Fred checked for this in an earlier stage when he recognized that *Mather's antifeminism* was a subtopic under the major division about *Mather's defense of the social order.* In a more detailed outline, with more levels of information, this kind of evaluation becomes even more important.

Coverage. Make sure the elements of the outline address all points needed to complete the discussion and help the paper fulfill its purpose. You may even need to do more research on an important subtopic about which you have not uncovered enough information. A student writing on dinosaur extinction saw that she had just one brief note on a theory that is not widely held. Her research would not have been considered complete without a reasonably thorough account of that theory, which would give readers a fair chance to judge its validity. At that point, she went to the library.

Balance. Topics of equal importance should be treated fairly equally. For example, suppose you were writing about Martin Luther King Jr. and had arrived at the thesis "Martin Luther King Jr.'s success resulted from three major factors — his courage, his intelligence, and his charisma." Your outline, which determines the shape of the paper, would be strongly unbalanced if you devoted one section to "courage," one to "intelligence," and six to "charisma." If your general impression from reading the sources was that all three factors contributed equally to King's success, then you would need to return to your sources or find new sources, looking for more information about the two briefly covered factors. However, if you now realized that most of the sources had indeed emphasized charisma, you would have to revise your thesis. It might well read: "Martin Luther

Writing the Paper

King Jr.'s success depended on three factors — courage, intelligence, and charisma — of which charisma was by far the most important."

Sequencing. Each listing of outline points or sequencing of note cards reflects the potential order of ideas in the paragraphs and major sections of your paper. Experiment with this order at both the major and minor topic level to find the sequence that works best for your paper's audience and purpose. For example, if you perceive that your audience needs some background information about your topic to better understand the paper's main points, insert that information in a place beneficial to the reader (typically early in the paper if the background relates to the whole topic or at the beginnings of the sections to which it pertains if it relates to minor points). For an argument, you might want to save your most persuasive major point for last. If the information listed under a subtopic includes theoretical observations, statistics, and firsthand experience, the order of the information might make a big difference in how well a reader follows the idea once it becomes a paragraph or more in the paper. More general statements, even those from sources, typically come earlier in the paragraph or section and are followed by illustrations and concrete details that help provide support.

After checking the layout of your ideas for these aspects of organization, you are almost ready to draft the paper. If you are using note cards, put your full set of cards in the precise order you expect to follow when writing the paper. Whether you also write these points into an outline depends on your needs as a writer and your instructor's requirements.

If you are using a notebook or word processor instead of note cards, finalize your outline draft and double-check to make sure it includes all the information you want to use. You may or may not need to formalize the outline further.

Outlining is a challenging and time-consuming step, but the structure that it provides will ultimately save you time and guide your writing of the first draft.

The Traditional Outline Format

In constructing an outline, use whatever format you feel comfortable with, unless your instructor specifies a particular one. A commonly used format combines letters and numbers to designate the various levels of classification. Even if you are already familiar with this format, take time now to be sure you understand the subtle distinctions between those levels.

This list indicates the relative difference between levels:

Roman numerals (I, II) represent major divisions, each covering a large section of the paper.

Capital letters (A, B) represent subtopics, each occupying at least one, sometimes several, paragraphs.

Arabic numerals (1, 2) represent major details that support a subtopic.

Small letters (a, b) represent minor details that support a major detail.

The longer the paper you are writing, the broader the area covered by the highest category (Roman numerals) and the greater the chance that you will need a fifth set of symbols to represent the smallest details in the paper (small Roman numerals — i, ii, iii).

Many writers follow two sensible rules for constructing outlines:

Rule 1: Never break down a category into just one subdivision. To do so is illogical.

incorrect; only one detail supports subtopic A

I. Difficulties faced by Diego Rivera in early years
    A. Childhood problems
        1. Grave illness from typhus and scarlet fever
    B. Adolescent problems

At some point, childhood problems must have seemed an important subtopic, but in this outline it looks trivial. Perhaps information about another childhood problem has been assigned to a different subtopic and could be moved into this one. Or perhaps another trip to the library would produce information about a second childhood problem accidentally omitted during note taking. The outline might then look like the following:

correct

I. Difficulties faced by Diego Rivera in early years
    A. Childhood problems
        1. Grave illness from typhus and scarlet fever
        2. Dangers arising from father's radical politics
    B. Adolescent problems

However, if Rivera's only significant childhood problem had been illnesses, the outline might be revised to look like the following:

Writing the Paper

correct

    I. Difficulties faced by Diego Rivera in early years

        A. Childhood illnesses

        B. Adolescent problems

(It is not necessary to add Arabic numerals under A for the specific illnesses unless your note cards treat them extensively and you mean to discuss them in detail.)

Rule 2: Use the same grammatical form for words at the same level of classification. By doing so, you produce parallel structure — that is, a pleasing and easy-to-understand ordering of ideas.

incorrect; the subdivisions are not grammatically parallel

    A. Symptoms of senility

        1. Forgetting recent events

        2. Mistakes in simple arithmetic

        3. Occasional hallucinating

        4. Inappropriate responses in social situations

correct; each subdivision is a gerund phrase

    A. Symptoms of senility

        1. Forgetting recent events

        2. Making mistakes in simple arithmetic

        3. Hallucinating occasionally

        4. Responding inappropriately in social situations

Phrase and Sentence Outlines

The outlines presented in the previous section are examples of *phrase outlines,* in which each category is expressed in a phrase. Some instructors may require you to submit a *sentence outline,* in which each category is expressed as a complete sentence. A sentence outline usually takes more time to write than a phrase outline, but it offers you an important advantage. The sentences that make up the outline can often be used almost word for word when you start to write your paper.

Fred's outline for his Cotton Mather paper (see pages 189–90) is an example of a sentence outline. Note that in addition to using complete sentences, his outline also lists the source for each major detail at the point where it will be used.

Whichever outline form you use, be consistent. Do not mix phrases into a sentence outline or sentences into a phrase outline. (For an example of a complete phrase outline, see the sample student paper on Emily Dickinson in Chapter 22.)

Unconventional Outlines

The major reason for constructing an outline is to organize your thoughts and notes into a logical pattern before you write your research paper. The outline formats you have studied so far have been used for many years by many writers to organize their thoughts before undertaking an extensive piece of writing. However, some writers prefer to devise their own approaches to outlining that both satisfy their personal sense of organization and work well as guides to creating logical essays.

Some writers prefer to use combinations of the traditional outline formats. For example, someone might use a very precise phrase outline (including many lettered and numbered subsections) to outline a section that included many details and then switch to a sentence format to outline theoretical or explanatory sections.

While most students benefit from outlining in the order we have described (after taking notes and before drafting), you may find that outlining earlier or later in the process works better for you. If you know a lot about the topic and have a more detailed projection of the ideas it will involve, you may find that you need an outline to guide you almost as soon as you have a hypothesis — and this will certainly help you find detailed information if the outline turns out to be accurate. Or you may find that it is more beneficial to write a very rough draft of some of your paper before outlining it, to focus your ideas through drafting. In this case, preparing an outline after you draft will help you clarify the paper's organization.

You may have to do some experimenting before you find an outlining approach that best suits your particular talents for planning and writing essays. In general, if you have had problems with writing well-organized essays in the past, a tighter, more conventional form will probably serve you best. However, if you find that writing comes easily, then you might experiment with unconventional forms that allow you freer range in planning your research paper. After seeing samples of your writing in the course, your instructor can probably give good advice about which path you should take.

What kind of outlining procedure is best for you? The one that best guides you in planning an effective essay — the kind of procedure that leads to a logical expression of your ideas and knowledge in essay form. Fred Hutchins used a sentence outline whereas Shirley Macalbe and Susanna Andrews used a more conventional phrase format. David Perez used yet another approach. All four students produced successful research papers.

15

Writing the Rough Draft

After you have developed a logical outline, you are ready to begin writing the paper. This task will take a lot of time because you must plan to write at least three versions of your paper: a rough draft, a revised draft, and a polished final manuscript suitable for submission to your instructor. Many writers feel the need for even further revision, but three drafts are the absolute minimum.

In writing a draft, you are solidifying your thoughts on the topic that you have worked so hard to research. As you worked with your sources and organized your notes, you should have found yourself more and more certain about the direction your evolving hypothesis had taken. The hypothesis is now ready to act as your *thesis*, which guides you as you write and tells readers the major conclusions you reached after a thorough investigation of your topic. Of course, you may find yourself revising and refining this early thesis as you write, but by the time you finish your final draft, the statement that was once hypothetical, the hypothesis, will have become a final thesis expressing the main point of your paper.

Getting Ready to Draft

Scheduling the time to draft a long paper is the most challenging aspect for many writers. The key word here is *scheduling* as opposed to *taking* the time. If you simply try to take the time away from other activities when it is time to draft, you may find the task impossible. In many cases, drafting your research paper could take several hours or more each day over a two-week period. If you try to do all of this in the final couple of days, the results could be disastrous. You will be much better off to schedule blocks of time on several different days throughout the drafting period. Use a calendar or planning book to schedule these writing sessions far in advance. Schedule the project during times of day when you can think and write well, avoiding times when you are typically tired or unfocused, or when your attention is divided with other commitments. Keep in mind that you may need to return to the library for information or talk to your instructor as part of the drafting process, and leave some extra time scheduled for inevitable problems. Sticking to your schedule will allow you to take breaks from the project and to stop thinking about it for a while, whereas if you are working without a planned schedule you may never feel you can relax.

The environment in which you write is also an important factor in your success. If possible, use a desk or table with enough room to lay out and organize notes and sources (even if there is also a computer on the desk). Good lighting, relative quiet, and a chair you can work in comfortably all help. If such a space is not available at home, use designated study areas at your college or local library.

One good technique for maximizing the use of writing time is to make available everything you need in advance so that you are ready to write when you sit down. When it is time to draft, you don't want to have to go elsewhere to look for your notes or rough outline, not to mention for paper or a printer cartridge. Keep a dictionary, thesaurus, pen, and paper handy along with organizing tools such as folders, files, and paper clips. You may want to take ten or fifteen minutes earlier in the day or the night before your drafting session to lay out and organize all the materials you will need to begin writing.

Working on a Computer

Many people still prefer to write by hand when they are taking notes and brainstorming, and some even like to handwrite their first draft. When the time comes for revising, however, almost everyone uses a computer for changes and corrections. As we have mentioned in earlier chapters, using a computer for the note-taking and drafting stages can also make the transition from notes to complete draft much easier.

As you plan the various steps of writing your research paper, in particular drafting and revising, you should take into account whether you will have easy access to a computer. If you rely on computer labs, plan around lab access times for the several sessions you will probably need to arrive at a final draft. Even if you use a home computer, you may need to arrange access time with others in your household.

As you type the draft, stop and save your work every fifteen or twenty minutes. Because storage drives occasionally fail, save a second,

backup file once you have completed a substantial amount of work —
maybe two or more pages. For example, you can select "save" to store the
file in a hard-drive location and then choose "save as" to save another
copy on a floppy disc. If you are working in a public computer lab and
cannot save to a hard drive, you can save to two different floppy discs, or
you may be able to e-mail the document to yourself. At the end of your
session, make sure your backup file is as current as your primary file.

When drafting on a computer, you should print out your work often,
ideally at the end of every session or after each significant revision or addition. When reading a printed copy, you will notice how much easier it is
to think about the overall structure and to see the connection, or lack of
connection, between consecutive ideas or paragraphs. Mark changes on
the print copy so that you are ready to enter them when you return to the
computer.

Drafting the Introduction

The introductory paragraph or paragraphs not only state your thesis
but also establish the paper's *voice*, the personality of the writing con-
veyed by its style. The introduction may also indicate the paper's major
subdivisions and the general nature of the sources. A typical introduction
has some kind of *lead*, or attention-getting device, such as a perplexing
question, a startling fact or situation, an anecdote (small story) related to
the topic, or some background information that shows the relevance or
prevalence of the topic.

Before writing the introduction, jot down the major points you expect
it to include. In the case of Fred Hutchins's paper on Cotton Mather, the
main points were these:

topic: *Cotton Mather's belief in witchcraft*

major subtopics: modern view — humane, not cruel; defense of the
social order; possible antifeminism; personal religious views

sources: modern historians

From these materials, Fred wrote a rough draft of his introduction:

Many people today are amazed by how strongly people in colonial
New England believed in witches, and by the fact that they went so far
as to burn or hang witches out of fear. They especially wonder how
intelligent, educated ministers could be so superstitious. Why would
ministers believe witches were the agents of the Devil, and why would
they be so afraid of some people as to accuse them of being witches?

Many uneducated people might blame the Devil and witches for their bad luck, but educated religious leaders like Cotton Mather should have been setting them straight, not leading them on. No one seems to agree on the reasons why this prominent Puritan minister supported the witch hunts, but most historians today say he was not just a cruel persecutor of innocent victims. They think he saw witches as part of God's creation and that he was concerned that the trials be conducted fairly. He was mostly worried that the witches could undermine the society, for they were supposed to be the Devil's secret agents.

Fred realized that this rough paragraph would have to be made a bit more elaborate and polished, but he also saw that it achieved the basic aims of an introduction — a clear view of the ideas he wanted to present. Fred did not write the final version, which grew to three short paragraphs, until he had written the rest of the paper. Take time to note the structure of this revised introduction.

introductory paragraphs

In 1692, a series of trials held in Salem, Massachusetts, resulted in the execution of twenty people for practicing witchcraft. Over the years, many historians have tried to explain the outbreak of witchcraft hysteria at that time and in particular why certain community leaders believed in witchcraft so strongly that they played important roles in hunting down and convicting people who were considered to be witches.[1] One such leader was Cotton Mather, a prominent Puritan minister and theologian, whose complex life and voluminous writings have provided historians with ample material for attempting to understand both the man and his times.

reference to source for background information

more background material, establishing controversy over Mather

Early critics of Mather painted him as a cruel witch hunter and tormentor of innocent people. And while this negative image of Mather has not entirely disappeared, modern historians have largely ruled out the interpretation that Mather's involvement in witch hunting stemmed from a deliberate desire to inflict suffering on innocent victims. Indeed, some

Writing the Paper

historians have all but absolved Mather of any unusual responsibility for the trials. He was a person of the times, these writers argue; in late-seventeenth-century America, it was a rare person who did not believe in and fear the existence of witches. Other historians see Mather's general support of the trials growing out of his desire to defend the authority of the civil judges and protect the Puritan social system. Yet another interpretation views Mather's role as that of a champion of the patriarchal social order. This idea may explain why Mather supported the trials of accused witches, the overwhelming majority of whom were women.

narrowing of Fred's chief argument

statement of thesis

Cotton Mather was a complicated human being, and there may be some truth in all of these ideas. However, the ultimate explanation for his behavior during this fascinating if terrible moment in American history may well lie in his unique view of himself and the Puritan colony. His belief in witches, along with his need to identify and punish them, seems to have supported both his belief that he enjoyed a special, personal relationship with God and his view that the New England Puritan colony was destined to play the central role in God's plan for the future of humanity.

In the first paragraph, Fred sets up the problem he was investigating with an intriguing question: "Why did intelligent Christian ministers believe in witches to the extent of killing those accused of witchcraft?" He then provides several explanations for Mather's behavior. The first two paragraphs also establish important background for readers who may have heard of Mather but had forgotten the details. The third paragraph presents Fred's thesis: "[Cotton Mather's] belief in witches, along with his need to identify and punish them, seems to have supported both his belief that he enjoyed a special, personal relationship with God and his view that the New England Puritan colony was destined to play the central role in God's plan for the future of humanity." Thus his introduction serves as an overview of the entire paper.

Writing the Paper

Drafting the Body

Writing the rough draft of a research paper can be thought of as filling in the outline because the outline provides a structure for your own ideas and information. If you try to write your rough draft by working only from the note cards, you may find it much harder to keep in mind the relationships among them.

While writing the rough draft, you may think of a better way to present your case than you had planned. If that happens, stop writing and go back and revise your outline; if necessary, construct a new one. Remember that if you change one part of your outline, you will probably have to change other parts as well in order to maintain balance and an orderly and logical presentation of ideas.

Because the first draft is not meant to be seen by anyone but you, don't worry if you discover some weak sentences and poor word choices. Concentrate on expressing your ideas clearly. Let your ideas and sentences flow as freely as you can, getting everything down on paper in a form that reflects your thinking, however roughly. When you write the second draft, finding the right words for what you want to say will be considerably easier.

Follow these guidelines when formatting the first draft:

1. Leave plenty of space between the lines for later insertions and changes — double-spacing or more.

2. Do not slow yourself down by copying each quotation, paraphrase, or summary from your notes. When you come to a place where you need to use information from a note card, you can make a memo to yourself that says "copy from card" or "see card." However, in some cases, you may want to insert the source material right away. This can help you develop an effective voice by integrating the wording of the paraphrase, summary, or quotation into the flow of your thoughts.

3. Indicate briefly in the draft the source of each note you use in the paper, regardless of whether the note is a paraphrase, summary, or quotation. Simply note the author's name or a keyword or two from the title, plus the page number where you found the material. If you fail to make a note, you may later forget to include a source note.

Making the Draft Your Own

Your goal in the research paper is not merely to weave together information and ideas from various sources but to interpret these findings in a way that is logical and meaningful for you and your readers. Although the sources provide core support for your paper's points, what makes the paper unique is your arrangement of sources, the connections you make between them, and the conclusions you draw. Because of this, writing the first draft involves a great deal of thinking about the ideas and information in your notes in order to draw reasonable conclusions about them. It is this thinking that makes the first draft a time-consuming and challenging task.

Do not get bogged down trying to express your thoughts in exactly the right words in the first draft; experiment to find a voice and style appropriate to the paper's audience and purpose, especially in passages where you are synthesizing and interpreting information and adding explanation.

In the initial draft, one of the most important decisions you can make is your paper's *point of view* — the positioning of your voice as the author. You can write in the first-person point of view, using the pronoun "I" to present your views, or you can use the third person, a more objective voice in which you do not use the pronoun "I."

Some instructors restrict the use of first person. A third-person point of view is a more widely accepted academic voice, and many writers and readers consider it a better vehicle for presenting objective information. This does not mean, however, that you cannot include your own observations in your paper. If you can effectively use the third-person point of view to communicate both your own ideas and those of your sources, you will be well prepared for many writing tasks both in and out of academia. In the following example of third-person writing from Susanna Andrews's paper on Emily Dickinson, notice how Susanna presents her personal interpretations of source material (the shaded text) without using phrases such as *I believe* or *I conclude*.

> In suggesting that Dickinson chose obscurity after Higginson's "hesitance," Sewall does not mean to imply that she was unsure of herself as a poet because of his criticism. On the contrary, Sewall states that "in her exalted conception of herself as a poet and in her confidence in her powers, she had no . . . reason to be deferential to Higginson . . . and one cannot help feeling that she knew it" (2: 555). Thus, it was not a sense of inferiority that moved the poet to her decision. Rather, it was the realization that her poems would not be accepted in the forms she had created for them and that public recognition would require her to alter them to meet public expectations. Robert Spiller, in finding that Dickinson "failed to publish" because she would not accept compromise as a path to recognition, makes much the same point.

Some writers feel that the use of first person allows them to contribute a fuller range of their own ideas on the topic. First-person point of view may also make it easier to synthesize personal views with those of sources. First person works better to communicate field research and other information procured or observed by the author, as in this passage from Shirley Macalbe's paper on immigration:

> In presenting the following results of my interviews, I selected only those responses that related directly to the topic of this paper. In addition, I selected only those opinions that were expressed, in one way or another, by a majority of the students. Again, my purpose was not to construct a scientific study but to gather impressions from the campus that would get me started on my projected research and that might offer some chances to compare the opinions of students with the findings of experts.

This portion of the paper would have been awkward to express in third person.

If you decide to use first person in your paper, you do not need to express the "I" point of view in every paragraph. In fact, as long as you establish the point of view early in the paper, you have established the ability to break into the "I" construction in later passages, even if only in a few places. Shirley's paper, presented in Chapter 22, is a good example of this point.

If you are allowed a choice, the best way to decide on a point of view is to experiment when you draft. If you are undecided, try a few passages in first person and then rewrite them in third person. You may want to ask your instructor for help in determining which voice works better for the paper's purpose.

Integrating Your Sources

Although you are by now familiar with your notes, you are for the first time trying to blend them into a coherent whole. As you write the first draft, some situations may arise that cause special kinds of problems. The following situations occur fairly frequently.

No One Source Tells the Whole Story. Often you will have to draw details from different sources to cover a subtopic fully, so you must keep track of which facts come from which sources. If you simply combine all the details into one account, with just one source note, your readers may not realize that the picture is a composite, its parts coming from various sources. In some paragraphs, for example, you may have a citation every sentence or two, and it is possible to use information from more than one source in a single sentence.

Several Sources Disagree over a Question of Fact. When sources disagree over a question of fact, you have several options; some of them depend on the type of paper you are writing.

- Simply report the disagreement, especially if you have no basis for trusting one source more than the others. This may fit well in an analysis or a report.
- Delve into the disagreement and try to explain it or show insights related to it. For example, the disagreement may be related to bias, to information taken out of context, or to different terminology used for similar events. This approach works especially well when writing an argument or analysis.
- Choose one source, if it seems more trustworthy than the others; it may be more fully documented or the most recent. Argument papers in particular may benefit from this tactic.
- Try to verify the fact by further research.

The student writing about Emily Dickinson found that various sources gave the number of poems published during the poet's lifetime as six, seven, eight, and ten. Because the most up-to-date source, a review of three recent scholarly books about Dickinson, said the number was ten, the student simply used that number in her paper and disregarded the other sources' claims. After all, she was in no position to verify the fact herself, and the exact number was not crucial to her thesis. If the student's purpose, however, was to trace the history of Dickinson scholarship, it may have been useful to investigate and discuss the disagreement. Perhaps additional published poems had been discovered over the years, and the discoveries changed the nature of scholarship in the field.

Some Sources Disagree in Their Interpretations of a Fact or Facts. Such differences occur all the time; in fact, they help make research interesting. If the purpose of your paper is not to argue for a particular conclusion but to report the current state of knowledge on a topic, you may simply report the disagreement. Or if you are writing an analysis, you may try to understand the differences better and reveal some insights about them to the reader.

However, if your thesis states a definite position regarding your topic (an argument), you must draw your own conclusion as to which interpretation seems most soundly argued and then use the strongest supporting material in your argument. You should mention the strongest points of those who disagree with your thesis and give some of the reasoning behind these views; remember, though, that you are presenting information with the overall goal of persuading the reader to accept your thesis. The strength of your argument should demonstrate that you understand the major viewpoints on the issue, but in an argument you are not required to give balanced development to both sides.

One way to integrate information contrary to your position is to raise it as an *objection* to your thesis. In raising the objection, use language that makes it clear that you are stating a position contrary to the thesis. Phrases such as *some may say* or *those who disagree with this position* help introduce objections. If writing in first person, you might try *those who disagree with me.*

For example, if the thesis "After the age of 70, drivers should have annual driver's license tests" is placed at the end of the introductory paragraph, the following objection might become the topic sentence of the next paragraph: "Some may say that it is discriminatory to treat older drivers differently than younger ones." This paragraph could go on to briefly explain some of the reasoning behind the objection and then *counter the objection* by refuting it.

Blending Quotations into Your Draft

If you followed our advice in Chapter 11 for taking notes, many of your direct quotations should be ready to smoothly integrate into your draft. You may want to review the discussion in Chapter 12 of when to use quotations, how to indicate ellipses, and so on. Following are some additional guidelines that will help you use quoted material effectively. Note that these examples use a variety of documentation styles.

1. Quotations do not have to be full sentences. They may also be pieces of sentences or isolated phrases or words. They may occur at the beginning, middle, or end of a sentence in your paper.

   quoted term   Paul Ferlazzo, for example, infers that Higginson's response to her first letter must have included some recommendations for altering, or "regularizing," her poems, along with a request for more of her work (136).

   quoted portion of a sentence   This fact leads Thomas to conclude that Dickinson "was well aware of the world outside her little room, that in fact she used the language of this outside world to create some of her best poetry" (523).

2. Quotations should flow smoothly with the rest of the text; they should not disrupt sentence structure.

ineffective integration (run-on sentence)

However, Lacey does not agree with this perception of immigrant impact on jobs, "immigrants generally do not compete with Americans for jobs" (182).

effective integration

However, Lacey does not agree with this perception of immigrant impact on jobs. He claims that research shows that "immigrants generally do not compete with Americans for jobs" (182).

Note: It is appropriate to alter capitalization of the first word of a quotation to insert it smoothly into a sentence.

3. Use appropriate *signal phrases* to let readers know that you are about to present quoted material. To introduce quotations that are whole sentences, use a signal phrase such as *said, claims,* or *points out,* followed by a comma.

As Muller points out, "On balance, the economic benefits of immigration . . . tend to exceed private and in some areas public costs" (133).

"On balance," Muller says, "the economic benefits of immigration . . . tend to exceed private and in some areas public costs" (133).

For a more formal introduction of a quoted full sentence, use a colon.

Higginson was apparently attempting to get Dickinson to write more traditional poetry, or, as Johnson observes: "He was trying to measure a cube by the rules of plane geometry" (107).

When you use the word *that* to introduce a quotation, do not follow the signal phrase with a comma.

Perry Miller notes that "the discourse plunges into chiliastic ecstasy. The witches are signs of the times, of the death pangs of the Devil; mischievous powers prevail for the moment, but only because his rule is nearing extinction."[30]

4. When a parenthetical citation follows a quote, treat the citation as part of the sentence and place the period outside the closing parentheses.

> The ant began a "rapid expansion that was to extend its range over most of the United States by 1970" (p. 431).

When a quotation ends with a question mark or an exclamation point, the question mark or exclamation point goes inside the quotation marks. A period, however, is still included after the parentheses.

> As a result of reading this article, Dickinson sent Higginson four poems, along with a letter containing a question: "Are you too deeply occupied to say if my Verse is alive?" (*Letters* 2: 403).

Note: This parenthetical note refers to a multivolume collection of Dickinson's letters: *2: 403* means "volume 2, page 403."

5. If you quote more than four lines, indent the entire quote ten spaces or one inch (two paragraph indents) from the margin. Place the parenthetical note immediately after the *block quote,* separated by a space. No quotation marks are placed around the quote.

> Catton also suggests that Davis's attempt to lead his people to independence was somehow doomed to failure from the start:
>
> > He had done the best he could do in an impossible job, and if it is easy to show where he made grievous mistakes, it is difficult to show that any other man, given the materials available, could have done much better. He had courage, integrity, tenacity, devotion to his cause, and, like Old Testament Sisera, the stars in their courses marched against him. (279)

Integrating Visual Material

Charts, graphs, tables, maps, photographs, and other illustrations can help convey important information to your readers in a manner that is very different from written text and can help make this information more immediate, concise, and memorable. When you are deciding whether to include a visual in your paper, ask yourself the same question that you would of any other information you might incorporate into your work: "What is this visual doing to enhance my paper?" If a visual can add something significant to your paper, include it. Here are some guidelines for including specific kinds of visuals:

1. Charts and graphs illustrate relationships between different sets of data.

2. Tables contain numerical information that would be tedious to express in words. For example, see the table in Shirley Macalbe's essay (page 300).

3. Maps indicate locations and relationships between geographical and numerical information.

4. Photographs and drawings can often depict what something looks like more vividly and accurately than written description can.

These materials should be placed as close as possible to the discussion in which they are referenced, and they should be referred to in the paragraph, as in the following passage from a student paper:

excerpt from student paper   A 1999 survey found that among middle schoolers a larger percentage of Hispanic students than white or African American students smoked. By high school, however, the largest percentage of smokers was among white students (Fig. 1).

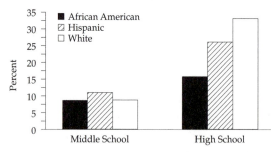

Fig.1. Cigarette smoking among middle and high school students by race and ethnicity. Data from National Youth Tobacco Survey, 1999, in *Tobacco Information and Prevention*. Centers for Disease Control and Prevention; 27 Mar. 2003; Web; 9 Feb. 2004.

In most research papers, visual materials should be used sparingly; it is rare to see more than two or three visuals in a ten-page paper, and many papers have none. Ask your instructor if you have any questions about the use of visuals as support.

As we discussed in Chapter 8, you can often save electronic images by right clicking on them and choosing "save." Insert these files into your word-processing document by placing your cursor where you want the image and using an "Insert File" command. Another method is to open the image and highlight it; select "copy" from the edit menu; and then, in your word processor, place the cursor where you want the image and select "paste."

The formats for labeling and documenting visual information in MLA style are covered on pages 265–66.

Drafting the Conclusion

Although there are many ways to end a paper, a good conclusion should accomplish two things:

1. Bring to mind the content of the paper — its thesis and main points. You can restate your thesis in terms that reflect the evidence you have presented. (If you use the same words that you used to state your thesis in your introduction, your readers may feel that you haven't taken them anywhere.) You can also allude to the paper's content without directly mentioning it again. For example, in a paper analyzing hospice choices for cancer patients, a conclusion beginning with a sentence like this might remind the reader of much of the paper's content: "Sometimes the most complex choices come along at the most difficult times in life."

2. Leave the reader with a final thought, whether it be an ultimate insight, something to further think about or act on, a prediction about the future of the topic, or a final quote. Above all, your conclusion should bring your paper to a satisfying close. The nature of the conclusion depends partly on the type of paper you are writing. An argument may have a final call to action asking the reader to do something related to the topic (such as giving up eating meat for a month). An analysis may end by asking the reader to leave with a newfound recognition of the topic's complexity.

In general, the conclusion should not introduce any new ideas or information. If you find yourself developing a new subtopic in the conclusion, try moving it to the body of the paper.

Now that you have completed a first draft of your paper, set the project aside for at least a few hours and do something else. It would be best if you could take at least a day's vacation from your paper. During the time you are not consciously working on your research project, your unconscious mind will be digesting, synthesizing, and generally working with what you have done. Then, as you tackle the second draft, you not only will feel refreshed but may also find yourself brimming with new ideas.

16

Revising the
Rough Draft

Once you have brought your outline to life by writing a rough draft, the nature of your job changes significantly. You must now become an editor of your own work. Read closely what you have written, as if for the first time, so that you can find those parts that communicate most effectively as well as those that work poorly or not at all. Then you can become the author again, rewriting, reorganizing, and adding support so that the weaker passages become as strong as the best ones. In many cases, revising will take as much time as writing the rough draft, because it is in the revising stage that you clarify what you want to say and how best to say it.

Approach your revision in an orderly way, by thinking of the task in terms of four important aspects of your paper's quality: organization, support, language, and documentation.

Revising for Organization

A good overall question for checking the organization of your paper is this: Will my reader understand how each part of the paper fits in the overall discussion? To make sure that the answer to this question is *yes*, consider the following aspects of organization.

Checking the Sequence of Ideas

No matter how hard you try to follow your outline while drafting, it is common when using multiple sources to place similar information in different locations or to repeat general points that are already established. Using a printout of your draft, make notes in the margin, describing the topics covered in each paragraph or section of the paper, and then check these notations to make sure the points are consolidated and are not repeated (of course, some of the major ideas may be repeated in the introduction or conclusion).

An even more important question is this: Does the sequence of my ideas effectively support the thesis? As you arranged your note cards and constructed your outline, you carefully thought about the best order in which to present the information and ideas that would support your thesis. Did you follow this plan? Read your paper with your outline in hand, marking any places where you veered away from the initial plan. If your draft significantly departs from your original outline, it may help to create a new outline. Looking at an outline that reflects the actual shape of your paper will help you determine whether your paper's ideas follow a clear and logical sequence.

Once you have a good overview of your paper's structure, you may find yourself dissatisfied with the way the major divisions and subtopics fit together. For example, perhaps you decided, when constructing the original outline, to present the evidence supporting your thesis first and the evidence refuting it afterward. This strategy is effective if your case is so strong that it will make the opposing arguments seem weak. On rereading your paper and reviewing your outline, however, you found that the opposing case did not seem weak; instead, it seemed to rebut much of your case point by point. One way to reverse that effect would be to switch the order of those two parts of the paper, stating the opposing case first and rebutting it with your case. Later you would revise the transitions to make the new order effective. Or you may decide to reduce the amount of coverage of the opposing argument, including only those one or two ideas that form the primary objections to your thesis. You can then use your supporting arguments, or elements of them, to answer these objections.

Rearrangements sometimes require more revision than simply switching the order of a few sections in your paper: you may occasionally find it a good idea to rewrite extensively and thereby produce a new rough draft to work with. More often, however, you will find your outline a good guide, and no major reorganization will be necessary.

Improving the Flow of Ideas

One major challenge in writing a research paper is to create a discussion that moves fluidly between ideas. The most important step in accomplishing this is to have a clear thesis, typically expressed early in the paper, and then a logical progression of relevant ideas to support that thesis, as mentioned in the previous section. However, in many parts of the discussion it is still necessary to use *transitions* — words, phrases, or sentences that help the reader understand the movement from one paragraph or major section of the paper to another.

Writing the Paper

Transitions often occur at the beginnings of paragraphs. Sometimes simple transitional words like *however* or *another* (as in *Another point to consider is . . .*) will suffice between paragraphs. Another transitional technique is to briefly remind the reader of where you have just been in the discussion and then indicate where you are going — the new topic. This kind of transition often works well as the topic sentence of a new paragraph. Here is an example from Shirley Macalbe's paper on immigration:

> In recognizing these problems related to immigration and economic pressures, we should keep in mind professor of social history Maxine Seller's point that periods of intense opposition to immigration in the United States have been "expressions of problems within the nation as a whole" (199).

The first part of the topic sentence, "In recognizing these problems related to immigration and economic pressures," recalls the ideas developed in the paper just before the new paragraph, while the rest of the sentence introduces the new idea. This is not just a language trick to make ideas glide along. In crafting the language of such a transition you will force yourself to *recognize the relationship between your ideas* and pass along this recognition to the reader. Shirley introduces Maxine Seller's point in her paper to add another level of analysis to the discussion. She wants us to redefine "these problems" (competition with immigrants for jobs and the related social friction) as not just immigration problems but as a symptom of larger underlying issues. The transition leads us from the foreground of the discussion to the deeper background.

If you study the transitions in the sample essays in Chapter 22, you will notice that not every paragraph includes a transitional device. Sometimes ideas flow together without explicit transitions if the thesis is clear and the sequence of ideas makes sense, and, in some cases, if you simply satisfy the reader's expectations. After the introduction, for example, most readers expect either the first major point of the paper's body or a bit more background information on the topic before the body begins. Either section could be introduced without transitioning as long as its content indicated the structural role. Similarly, it is not necessary to signal a conclusion with "In conclusion." Instead, use general, summary-level language and content that indicates to the reader that he or she is reading a conclusion. See page 209 for more on what a conclusion should accomplish.

Sometimes it takes more than a sentence to transition between ideas. When you are leaving behind a major section of the paper, or when a lot of information has been presented that leads to an important conclusion or needs to be analyzed, an entire paragraph may be necessary to help the reader understand the flow of discussion. For an example, turn to Susanna Andrews's paper on Emily Dickinson (Chapter 22). On page 323, the paragraph that begins "For Emily Dickinson, then . . ." is largely transitional, summarizing the previous discussion of Dickinson's attitude toward fame and then moving into the evidence of this attitude in her poetry.

Using Section Headings to Organize

In some fields, particularly in business and some social sciences, it may be appropriate to indicate the main topics and subtopics of the discussion with section headings. This book is an example of material organized with headings, which signal shifts in subject matter and help readers find information quickly. Often headings can be generated from the main divisions of the outline. See Chapter 21 for guidelines on formatting headings.

Revising Paragraphs for Organization

After you have checked the paper's organization at the global level, check it at the ground level, too: the paragraph. Paragraphs are the building blocks of a paper's organization. Think of a paragraph as a group of sentences that work together to support a controlling idea — the idea expressed in the *topic* (or *main idea*) sentence. Ask yourself if a reader would be able to understand easily the controlling ideas in your paragraphs, either because you have provided clear topic sentences or because you have so carefully constructed your paragraphs that the controlling ideas can be inferred readily from all the sentences taken together. Although you should not feel that you must impose a single rigid concept of paragraph structure on your writing, you should be certain that your paragraphs contribute to a logical progression of ideas in your paper. To the extent that they do not, you must revise.

If you think that one or more of your paragraphs might be confusing to a reader, the first thing to do is to see if the rewriting (or addition) of a topic sentence will clarify your thoughts. Make sure you and your readers can understand the topic sentence's relation to the overall discussion. If a paragraph remains confusing even after you have improved its topic sentence or created a new topic sentence for it, try focusing on the following additional features of paragraph structure:

- *The relevance of the sentences to the paragraph's controlling idea.* In the same way that you checked the overall structural elements for relevance, check the sentences of each paragraph. Do they all support the topic sentence?
- *The order of information in the paragraph.* Will the reader know why one sentence follows another, or how the ideas or information relate? Be sure you understand why the ideas appear in this particular order and then make sure the reader will understand as well. Also, keep in mind your reader's expectations: interpretive statements,

for example, often follow factual information, and details follow the topic sentence.

- *The smoothness with which you have moved from one idea to the next within the paragraph.* After you are sure that your ideas are in a logical order, check that the sentences flow smoothly throughout the paragraph. Transitional words and phrases such as *however, similarly,* and *for example* can help (but don't overuse them).

- *The integration of source material.* If you are integrating more than one source into one paragraph, try to indicate the relationship between the various pieces of source information. The following paragraph from Shirley Macalbe's essay on immigration provides a good example of this. Language that helps position the source information is highlighted:

> Lacey and Isbister may be accurate in a general sense, and the AFL-CIO may be right in pointing out abuses and contributions of immigrant workers, but other research shows that immigrant impact on jobs is more severe than these sources seem to imply, even if the impact is rather limited. Thomas Muller, for example, has found that immigrants do compare with some "unskilled workers" in certain areas and with "some low-skilled native-born workers unable to improve their occupational status and unwilling (or unable) to move from areas with large numbers of low-skill, low-wage immigrants to other areas" (133). Walter Fogel, a professor of industrial relations, supports Muller's contention. He tells us that late-nineteenth- and early-twentieth-century immigrants joined the oversupply of unskilled laborers in the United States, causing additional economic hardship for Americans who were already doing poorly (98).

As you review your work, try to read each paragraph as though you were a reader unaware of what the writer intended to say. Do you follow the paragraph's point? Try to get a second reader, preferably a writing center tutor or, if possible, your instructor, to read parts of your draft and comment on whether the organization makes sense.

Revising for Support

Support is the heart of good writing. The draft is merely a skeleton if not expanded with details, explanation, and interpretation to bring the discussion alive. As you revise your draft, consider the following questions:

Have you used concrete, clear, and accurate support? The use of concrete, clear, and accurate support is critical in writing at any level. Good writing contains names, numbers, events, strong verbs, detailed observations, and other concrete information. If you make the claim that "government policies have damaged the environment," you must back it up with accurate, concrete detail: "the policies have added millions of tons of carbon monoxide to the air because of low fuel-efficiency requirements for light trucks and SUVs."

Have you provided the right amount of support to make the point? How much detail is enough? The answer to this question depends on the thesis, the audience, and the scope of the writing project. In general, even minor points need at least two or three pieces of credible detail to be accepted and understood by the reader. However, a long list of details to make a point may not be necessary. Major points may need two to three pages or more of organized and detailed subtopics. The audience also needs explanatory and interpretive language to be able to understand the information and relate it to the paper's overall purpose.

Avoid relying on general statements from source material to stand alone as support. For example, the quote "Young people are unduly influenced by advertising" does not in itself prove the point to your audience, even if you are convinced of the source's credibility. Your audience deserves to know some of the reasons and details that support the point, whether they come from the same source as the quote or from other sources. The fact that a source made a general statement does not necessarily make the point understandable for the reader.

Have you included a variety of detail? Use detail not only from different sources but also of different types: facts and statistics from primary and secondary research; theories, ideas, and analysis from experts; and quotations from experts or people with firsthand experience. You may also want to offer examples and anecdotes of real events and experiences, as well as visual and multimedia information when appropriate. Keep in mind that you will also need to include your own explanations and interpretations.

Revising for Language

Writing effective sentences is primarily a matter of style, and style develops only through a great deal of attention to specific sentences. Even when you recognize that a sentence calls for improvement, you may have trouble deciding just what changes would make it better. As you revise your paper, you can help yourself by being alert to a few common weaknesses in sentence construction. Pay particular attention to sentences in your rough draft that may be either too complex or too simple and to patterns of construction that may be monotonously repetitive.

216 CHAPTER 16 • REVISING THE ROUGH DRAFT

Fixing Overly Long Sentences

Some sentences may be too long and complicated for readers to follow comfortably. Usually such sentences can be broken down into more easily digested sentences, as the following example illustrates:

overly long sentence	Throughout the war, many Southerners came to think of Lincoln as a power-hungry autocrat, who, in spite of the public speeches in which he advocated peace and reconciliation, was in reality determined to destroy anyone, in the North or South, who stood in the way of his gaining absolute control of the nation he had been elected to govern.
improvement	Throughout the war, many Southerners came to think of Lincoln as a power-hungry autocrat, in spite of the public speeches in which he advocated peace and reconciliation. They believed that he was in reality determined to destroy anyone, in the North or South, who stood in the way of his gaining absolute control of the nation he had been elected to govern.

Fixing Overly Short Sentences

Short sentences are easy to understand, but a series of five or six very short, choppy sentences actually may be more difficult to read than two or three sentences of average length. When you find such a series in your draft, consider combining several of them into longer sentences. Save your short sentences until they can be used most effectively — for example, when emphasizing a particularly important point.

too many short sentences	Throughout the war, many people detested Lincoln. They considered him to be power-hungry. His speeches called for peace and reconciliation. But these people did not believe him. They included Northerners as well as Southerners. They believed that he intended to destroy anyone who opposed him. They thought he desired to gain absolute control of the country. They saw his election as part of his plan to rule as a dictator.

Writing the Paper

improvement   Throughout the war, many people detested Lincoln, whom they considered power-hungry. Although his speeches called for peace and reconciliation, these people did not believe him. Both Northerners and Southerners thought that he intended to destroy anyone who opposed him as he sought dictatorial control of the country he had been elected to govern.

Fixing Repetitious Sentence Patterns

Check the patterns of your sentences to see if you have repeated one pattern monotonously. Such repetition may needlessly bore your readers.

repetitious pattern   Hartman says that ... Anna Freud states that ... Mahler claims that ... Recently, Kohut stated that ...

improvement   Hartman says that ... This idea gained support from Anna Freud, who believes ... Mahler agrees, for the most part, claiming that ... Recently, Kohut added further support to this idea when he stated ...

The second example is an improvement over the first not only because it is more varied but also because the writer has taken a set of ideas from different sources and blended them into a smoothly flowing passage that shows how these ideas relate to each other.

Revising Word Choice

When you revise your word choice, keep in mind the following suggestions:

- *Find variety.*   Use appropriate synonyms for words that appear often (except for technical terms, which do not allow substitutes). The terms are highlighted in the following examples:

lacking variety   A young, idealistic anthropologist, on first venturing into a tribal society, is likely to suffer severe disillusionment. For one thing, most such societies live under physical conditions that no one coming from American society can possibly anticipate. Far more surprising, however, is that these societies often practice customs radically different from the ideal life in nature that naive students like to imagine.

improvement A young, idealistic anthropologist, on first venturing into a tribal society, is likely to suffer severe disillusionment. For one thing, most such people live under physical conditions that no one coming from America can possibly anticipate. Far more surprising, however, is that these communities often practice customs radically different from the ideal life in nature that naive students like to imagine.

- *Achieve accuracy.* Avoid vague, loose terms that may be misinterpreted. Here are some examples of revising to eliminate the emptiness of vague words:

vague Einstein's work affected the world.

Oedipus Rex is a first-rate play.

improved Einstein's theories reshaped the world of modern physics.

The play Oedipus Rex provides profound insights into human behavior.

Of course, you cannot entirely avoid vague terms, but you can keep them to a minimum and use with care. In short, say exactly what you mean, or at least come as close as possible.

- *Eliminate slang.* Avoid words that are not appropriate to the formal context of a research paper.

inappropriate The CIA has been blasted recently for failing to perform its duties with sufficient restraint.

The prosecutor called on a well-known shrink to testify that the defendant was not really crazy.

improved The CIA has been sharply criticized recently for failing to perform its duties with sufficient restraint.

> The prosecutor called on a well-known psychiatrist to
> testify that the defendant was not legally insane.

If you decide to use a thesaurus when revising word choice, use it carefully. Books of synonyms or the thesaurus function on your word processor can be valuable in helping you remember a word whose meaning you know well; they can be dangerous if you use them to select high-sounding words that are unfamiliar to you. The connotations of such words may not be appropriate to the contexts in which you place them. You may find a dictionary of synonyms more useful than a thesaurus because the former defines and illustrates the different shades of meaning between synonyms.

Most word-processing programs offer a spell-check feature. While these can be helpful, you should not rely on them entirely. These programs cannot differentiate between the correct spelling of *their* and *there* or *mail* and *male,* and they will not find the word *wheat* misspelled as *heat.* Some programs also contain grammar checkers, but these work even less well than spell checkers. Although grammar checkers catch some mistakes, they miss many more. Even worse, they label as wrong many sentences that are perfectly acceptable, or they sometimes make inappropriate suggestions for revision. Use these tools cautiously, and learn how to proofread.

Avoiding Sexist Language

Over the last few decades, many people have come to realize that some fairly familiar words and phrases are biased against women. Common examples of sexist nouns include *policeman, businessman, congressman, spokesman, cleaning lady, stewardess,* and *housewife.* You may feel that as long as you use words such as *chairwoman, congresswoman,* and *policewoman* when appropriate, you are not being sexist. That, however, is not the case because you are likely to end up using the male formations much more often, leaving the subtle impression that these positions belong in the male domain. Usually an inoffensive substitute can be easily called to mind. In some cases, a little reflection is required. Follow the general idea behind this partial list, and you will have no problems.

TV anchorman	anchor (*Anchorperson* is a bit cumbersome.)
chairman	chair, chairperson
fireman	firefighter
policeman	police officer
spokesman	representative, spokesperson
weatherman	meteorologist
congressman	representative, legislator, member of Congress
stewardess	flight attendant

Writing the Paper

The common sentence construction that uses single-sex pronouns when referring to a group that includes both men and women presents a somewhat greater challenge to you as a writer. Examine the following sentences:

A doctor needs to consider his patients' feelings before presenting his diagnoses.

When a teacher reads a student's essay on a controversial issue, she should try to be objective.

You can, of course, substitute *his or her* or *he or she,* but this construction may detract from the smoothness of your sentences. You may find these remedies more artful:

switch to plural	Doctors need to consider their patients' feelings before presenting their diagnoses.
	When teachers read their students' essays on a controversial topic, they should try to be objective.
avoid using any pronouns	Doctors need to consider patients' feelings before presenting diagnoses.
	When reading a student's essay on a controversial issue, a teacher should try to be objective.

Avoiding Other Forms of Insensitive Language

Prejudice in language can extend beyond gender discrimination. As you revise, look for wording that may misrepresent or offend any group or individual. Use sensitivity when writing for audiences in our diverse society. The following are only a few examples of the kind of insensitive language you should avoid:

- Negative references to darkness or blackness — for example, *dark times, a black mood.*
- Characterizations of normalcy that exclude — for example, do not refer to marriage with children as a *normal* lifestyle; that depiction is inaccurate for many.
- References such as *nonwhite* that describe people by what they are not. Use more accurate terms such as Asian American, African American, and so on.

Writing the Paper

- Potentially offensive terms for a group of people. For example, use *Native American* instead of *Indian*. Because acceptable terms change over time, the name that the group currently uses to describe itself is usually best.

Revising for Documentation

When you begin revising your final draft, look ahead to Part Five to understand the format requirements for the documentation style you are using. Insert the in-text citations in the exact form they will appear in the final version of your paper. Don't make the mistake, for example, of switching from APA style for the citations (Burstrom, 2004) to MLA style (Burstrom 44).

It is also very important to confirm that you have documented all appropriate material. Paraphrases, summaries, and quotations must be documented unless they are considered general knowledge for your audience. Read your paper to ensure that all information taken from sources has been documented. Keep in mind that misrepresentation of source material as your own or failure to indicate direct quotation, even if the passage is otherwise documented, constitutes plagiarism.

Two Examples of Revision

Revising for Support

Sometimes you will find that you need to go back to the library and search for a few more details to make a point. One student, for example, drafted a paper supporting this thesis:

Advertising affects different segments of the population in different ways, often preying on those with less developed defenses.

The student found that one interesting aspect of this discussion had to do with varying rates of smoking among different age, race, and socioeconomic categories. The following paragraph is his first draft of this part of the paper. His comments on the weaknesses he noticed after rereading the first draft are also shown.

first draft

Smoking affects different segments of the population in different ways, and this may be related to advertising. In 1999, about 35% of all high school seniors smoked, a rise of 7% among seniors since 1992 (Silber). "Each day more than 2,000 persons under age 18 become daily smokers" ("Cigarette

no information about the norm

Writing the Paper

lack of support and analysis

too heavy with statistics

unclear focus; possible irrelevant information

works cited entries

Smoking Statistics"). Ninety percent of adult smokers first started as teens (Cross). This is because smoking ads prey on teenagers (Silber). Also, people with lower education have a higher chance of smoking. Those with more than 16 years of education have only an 11.6% chance of smoking. Smoking rates among Native Americans are over 40%, and one third of people living in poverty smoke ("Cigarette Smoking Statistics").

"Cigarette Smoking Statistics." *American Heart Association.* 20 Nov. 2003. Web. 2 May 2010.

Cross, Gary. "Valves of Desire: A Historian's Perspective on Parents, Children, and Marketing." *Journal of Consumer Research* 29 (2002): 441-47. Print.

Silber, Judy. "Youths Smoke Out Truth in Advertising." *Los Angeles Times* 22 Feb. 2000, record ed.: 3. *ProQuest Newspapers.* ProQuest. Shoreline Community College Lib. Web. 22 Nov. 2003.

The student then expanded the revision notes into the following, more detailed plan of action:

- no information about the norm—contains statistics about smoking rates in different categories, but gives nothing to compare to such as average statistics for the entire population.
  ACTION: find and add appropriate statistics for the norm.
- lack of support and analysis—"smoking ads prey on teenagers" needs support.
  ACTION: add more information about how ads influence youth (shift information from earlier paragraph on ads targeting youth to here).
- too heavy with statistics—lacking examples, observed detail, etc.

Writing the Paper

ACTION: indicate the effects of some of the statistics in more human terms; do primary research analyzing ad content? Joe Camel? • <u>unclear focus; possible irrelevant information</u>—contains a lot of information about smoking and youth, then shifts into other demographics
ACTION: revise to focus one paragraph or more on smoking and youth; use the other material elsewhere or cut.

With these information needs in mind, the student engaged in some focused research and was able to add relevant information that gave different dimensions to the discussion.

second draft

Advertising may partly explain why smoking rates vary among different segments of the population. In particular, teenagers appear to be lured into smoking at disproportionate rates. In 1999, about 35% of all high school seniors smoked (Silber). By contrast, at around the same time period (2001) only about 23% of the adult population smoked ("Cigarette Smoking Among Adults"). Ninety percent of adult smokers first started as teens, and many started as early as 12 or 13 years old (Cross 443; "Cumulative Age"). Teens probably smoke more than the general population because smoking ads prey on their insecurities. These ads show thin models, rugged outdoor types like the Marlboro Man, and (ironically) athletic-looking people engaged in smoking (Silber). With these techniques, tobacco companies exploit the fact that teens will naturally pay more attention to the imagistic and emotional aspects of the ads than the health facts related to smoking (Cross 443-444). This probably explains why adult smoking rates are dropping, but teen rates are rising ("Cigarette Smoking"; Silber). Of course, the motivation for the tobacco companies is that once teens are hooked, they are likely to be lifetime consumers of tobacco.

The rise and fall of the suave but goofy Joe Camel is an interesting study in advertising aimed at creating these lifelong addicts. . . .

new works cited entries

"Cigarette Smoking Among Adults — United States, 2001." *Morbidity and Mortality Weekly Report* 10 Oct. 2003 (52): 953-56. *Centers for Disease Control and Prevention.* 9 Oct. 2003. Web. 13 Dec. 2003.

"Cumulative Age of Initiation of Cigarette Smoking — United States, 1991." *Tobacco Information and Prevention Source. Centers for Disease Control and Prevention.* 30 Oct. 2000. Web. 13 Dec. 2003.

The student went on to develop two additional paragraphs using the Joe Camel character as a case study, paragraphs that included both researched information, and firsthand analysis of ads featuring Joe Camel. After the discussion of Joe Camel, the student provided information about the dire effects these ads have on teenagers, not only in terms of addiction and possible health problems later in life but also in the correlation between teen mental-health problems and smoking habits. Finally, the student added a brief passage in which he speculated about similar causes for different smoking rates between other segments of the population. By investing two to three hours to revise the original passage, the student transformed just over one hundred words of unfocused material into a much longer and more effective passage full of excellent support.

Revising for Language

After revising for organization and support, here is how one student, Anita, took a closer look at her sentences and her word use to see if the writing itself could be improved. Her self-evaluation, along with some advice from her instructor, led her to make the following changes to her draft:

quotation marks added to express irony

a bit more accurate — Ponce de Leon did not want to be restored to childhood

sentence combining for variety and to lessen repetition of *fountain*

***unfortunately* works better than *but* to prepare reader for following sentence**

potentially offensive term "Indian" replaced; more accurate description of events added

***silly* isn't a fair word to describe the explorer's search — in his day, many people believed that nature held the secret to extended life**

again, combining for variety and to clarify *it* as referring to *dream*

unnecessary and wordy

vague word in this context

more precise

rewritten to improve clarity and style of thesis

wordy and repetitious

unclear pronoun reference

Many American schoolchildren are told that Juan Ponce de Leon "discovered" Florida in 1513 while searching for the Fountain of Youth, whose waters, ~~He believed the~~ he believed, ~~waters of the fountain would~~ ~~make him young again.~~ restore him to youthful manhood. Unfortunately, ~~But~~ he never found the fountain. Instead, he found death at the hands of Native Americans protecting their homeland. ~~by an Indian arrow.~~ Today, we ~~know how~~ smile at the naivete of ~~silly~~ Ponce de Leon ~~was~~ for believing in a fountain of youth provided by a beneficent nature. But his dream of extending his life span was one that many people have had throughout the ages, and it is a dream that is ~~It is~~ still very much with us today.

By now we have pretty much given up hope ~~that somewhere in nature we may discover~~ of discovering the Fountain of Youth or a marvelous herb that can relieve us of the ~~problems~~ anxieties and debilities associated with the process of aging. Instead, our hopes of extending life expectancy are in the hands of scientists. Gerontologists (~~people~~ scientists who study aging) are attempting to slow down — and perhaps even overcome — nature's timetable for human aging. Although not all scientists think that increasing the life span is possible ~~Not all scientists think that it is possible. But many~~ in the near future, many ~~do. Many~~ gerontologists and knowledgeable commentators are optimistic about our chances ~~for increasing the life span. Gerontological researchers are optimistic~~ because of the promising results ~~they~~ researchers have obtained from experiments with animals and cell cultures. These experiments might well lead us to a "fountain" of extended, healthy life, if not to eternal youth.

Writing the Polished, Final Draft

Equipped with a carefully revised draft, you are ready to produce the polished, final version of your research paper. As you write the final version, you may continue to make changes in wording to improve the clarity of your paper. You may also make minor alterations in your paragraphs and sentences to improve the flow of thought. However, if at this time you find yourself making major changes in the organization or the content of your paper, you have embarked on the final draft without being fully prepared. If this is the case, consider this draft as another revision and work out your problems before again attempting to produce the final draft.

There are two more jobs you must do before you begin to prepare the manuscript of your paper. You must finalize the in-text citations, acknowledging the source of each quotation or paraphrase in the paper, and you must ready a final version of your works cited or references. Chapters 17 through 20 discuss the form and placement of these source citations.

Reviewing Part Four

The following questions and exercises will help you reinforce and practice the skills covered in Part Four. For additional practice, visit **<bedfordstmartins.com/writingresearch>**.

Questions

1. Why should you review all your note cards before beginning to write? What problems might you discover at this stage, and how might you deal with them?
2. A thesis is a far more comprehensive statement than the hypothesis you started with. What additional features go into the thesis to make it more inclusive?
3. What are the usual objectives of an introductory section?
4. What is the function of an outline? What are some problems that you might encounter when constructing an outline?
5. At least how many versions of a research paper must you write? Why?
6. What should you do when your sources disagree about factual matters?
7. Briefly outline the steps in revising a rough draft.

Exercises

1. Read the following introductions, keeping in mind that an effective introduction should state the thesis, point out the major questions addressed by the research, and indicate the kinds of evidence used in reaching the paper's conclusions (thesis). Which introduction best fulfills these objectives? Explain your choice.

title: Jefferson Davis as President: A Confederate Asset

Version I

Jefferson Davis became president of the Confederate States of America in 1861, shortly after the Civil War began, and remained its leader until 1865, when the war ended and he was imprisoned, only to be released two years later. Davis, as senator from Mississippi before the war, had staunchly advocated the states' rights movement, which had arisen largely as a defense of slavery. A graduate of West Point, Davis had served in the Mexican War and as secretary of war under Franklin Pierce. His background made him a strong candidate for the Confederate presidency once the war was underway.

At the beginning of the Civil War, the two sides seemed evenly matched. The North enjoyed a seeming advantage in numbers and a definite industrial superiority. The South, on the other hand, was better able to mobilize its soldiers, since much of the work back home was being performed by slaves, and its military leaders far outshone those of the North. Eventually, the North's material edge and the emergence of General Ulysses S. Grant were able to wear the South down, but some people blamed the defeat on the South's leader, Jefferson Davis, who they believed had mishandled his responsibility as commander in chief. Other observers defend Davis as an intelligent man fated by history to a tragic end.

Version 2

As a new millennium dawned, the Stars and Bars of the Old South still flew over the state capitol of South Carolina, in memory of the heroic although doomed struggle for a people's right to choose its own economic and social system. Bloodier than all other American wars, producing more dead than all of them combined, the Civil War has fascinated later generations of Americans in both the North and the South.

For the South, humiliated in defeat, no explanation for its devastating loss, given the brilliance of its field officers, especially General Robert E. Lee, could salve its wounds. For the North, its superior moral position sufficed as explanation, but survivors in the South looked to more concrete scapegoats, and Jefferson Davis, its president, stood out like a sore thumb among the crowd at the Confederacy's funeral. His vice president later wrote a scathing account of the debacle, placing full blame on Davis, and many historians thereafter have placed much, if not all, of the blame on his shoulders. But maybe they were wrong.

Version 3

For many years after Robert E. Lee surrendered at Appomattox, historians tended to lay much of the blame for the South's crushing defeat on the president of the Confederacy, Jefferson Davis. One writer, however, in comparing Davis to Abraham Lincoln, claims that Davis's reputation would have been quite different if he had been on the winning side. When a leader fails to achieve victory, even if his cause is doomed from the start, his "errors and defects and limitations of character . . . stand out as do a few spots of ink on a white sheet of paper" (Patrick 44-45). This does not mean that Davis had no faults. Almost all historians agree that the man suffered from character flaws. He spent far too much time on administrative details; he often interfered in military matters; and he allowed himself to be drawn into bitter controversies with other political leaders.

The question all Civil War analysts must answer is this: To what extent did Davis's failings contribute to the defeat of the Confederacy? A survey of modern studies of Davis and the Civil War reveals a softening in the historical judgment of Davis as a leader. Most historians today conclude that Jefferson Davis was probably the most capable president the South could have chosen. Indeed, given the enormous problems the Confederacy faced, Davis was a definite asset in the struggle to secede from the Union.

2. Read through a printout of your entire draft and note, by writing in the margins, the topics covered in each major section and paragraph. Check the order of these topics to see if they match your outline. Then, check them for repetition, coverage, and overall support of the thesis. Note the results of your analysis.

3. Identify a one- or two-paragraph passage in your paper that seems well supported because of the variety and relevance of its details. Explain why you think it is well supported. Find another passage that you feel is less well supported and compare it to the first passage. Discuss the difference.

4. Read at least two pages of your draft out loud, and record the reading if possible. Listen to it for clarity, for fluidity as it moves between various ideas, and for consistency of style and voice.

Alternatively, read it aloud to someone else and ask that person to comment on these aspects. Report the results of what you hear.

5. Identify at least three sentences in your draft that you feel use language very effectively, and explain why. Then identify three sentences that use language less effectively. Revise these sentences until you feel more satisfied, and explain what you changed.

6. Revise three consecutive paragraphs in your rough draft until you are satisfied with the entire sequence. Check for organization, support, language, and documentation. Show every stage of your revision, and explain your reasons for making each change.

Part Five

Documenting Sources

17

Understanding Documentation Requirements

After you have written, revised, and polished your research paper, one essential step remains: finalizing the documentation. Although the specific formats for documenting sources depend on the documentation style being used (these are covered in Chapters 18 through 20), they all involve two elements:

1. citations within the text of the paper to tell readers where you found the various ideas and information that form the content of your essay
2. a list at the end of the paper — titled *Works Cited*, *References*, or *Bibliography*, depending on the documentation style — of all the sources of material you have used in your essay

The following excerpts from Shirley Macalbe's paper show the relationship between in-text citations and end-of-text documentation.

excerpt from student essay

Throughout U.S. history, opponents of immigration have raised racial, religious, and nationalistic objections or questions about large-scale immigration to the United States (Jones 247-

in-text citation directs readers to works cited entry for Jones

305). Naturally, since the September 11, 2001, terrorist attacks against the United States, commentators such as Michelle Malkin have raised security concerns related to immigration policies (30).

However, much opposition to immigration is also expressed in economic terms. For example, Dan Lacey, a workplace consultant, business journalist, and editor, found that "research on immigration attitudes" shows that many Americans who oppose immigration fear losing their jobs to immigrants (41).

when author's name is included in signal phrase, only page number is listed in parentheses

excerpt from works cited list

Jones, Maldwyn Allen. *American Immigration*. Chicago: U of Chicago P, 1960. Print.

Lacey, Dan. *The Essential Immigrant*. New York: Hippocrene, 1990. Print.

Malkin, Michelle. *Invasion: How America Still Welcomes Terrorists, Criminals, and Other Foreign Menaces to Our Shores*. Washington, DC: Regnery, 2002. Print.

Although citation of sources can be tedious, it serves several important purposes, and you should take it as seriously as you do the work of researching and writing the paper. As we discussed in Chapter 13, these purposes include the following (see pages 171–72 for more on each of these points):

- Give credit where credit is due.
- Tell your readers where to find more information about your topic.
- Give knowledgeable readers some idea of how authoritative a particular statement is.
- Provide the date of initial publication.
- Give an overall sense of how thoroughly you carried out your research.

Types of Material That Require Source Notes

While writing the rough draft, you noted the sources of all ideas and information that came from your notes. Now you must formally incorporate citations into your text, clearly indicating those sources for your reader. Before we discuss how to prepare these citations, we must answer an important question: Is it necessary to indicate the source of every piece of information that goes into your paper? For instance, you might wonder whether it is essential to state where you found simple facts such as the following:

The Battle of Gettysburg was fought in Pennsylvania in 1863.

Nitrogen makes up 78 percent of Earth's atmosphere.

Traffic jams are almost constant in Los Angeles.

There are nine U.S. Supreme Court Justices.

Depending on the nature of your research topic, identifying the source of every such fact could clutter the paper with distracting and unhelpful citations. To prevent this, it is generally agreed that you do not have to document information that is considered general knowledge for your paper's audience. For most adults, the facts listed here are good examples of general knowledge. Most people who read your paper will either know these facts already or could easily look them up in the reference section of any library, even a small one.

However, if you are writing for a more focused audience, such as experts in a particular field, what is considered general knowledge becomes more specific. Someone with a background in literature probably knows that *Don Quixote* is considered the world's first novel. An audience knowledgeable about audio recording would know that *delay, distortion, flange,* and *reverb* are common effects applied to music.

Naturally you will sometimes be unsure whether a particular fact is general knowledge. In that case, insert a note. Before you begin any research paper, however, it is best to ask your instructor what kinds of information do not call for documentation.

Looking at the problem the other way around, we can say that documentation is required for any information that falls into one of the following categories:

- opinions, judgments, theories, and personal explanations
- "facts" that are open to dispute, and virtually all statistics
- factual information that is not general knowledge (for example, the results of a recent scientific test)

Opinions, Judgments, Theories, and Personal Explanations

Encyclopedias contain a lot of general information, but that does not mean that all information found in an encyclopedia can be considered general knowledge. In the following encyclopedia entry, the annotated passages constitute opinions. If you used them in your paper, they would require notes.

"influenced by her ... French contempo-raries" is an inference; "greatly" indicates a judgment

"refreshing simplic-ity," "vigorous treatment," and "pleasing color" reflect personal observations and judgments

CASSATT, Mary (1845–1926). American figure painter and etcher, b. Pittsburgh. Most of her life was spent in France, where she was greatly influenced by her great French contemporaries, particularly Manet and Degas, whose friendship and esteem she enjoyed. She allied her-self with the impressionists early in her career. Mother-hood was Cassatt's most frequent subject. Her pictures are notable for their refreshing simplicity, vigorous treat-ment, and pleasing color. She excelled also as a pastelist and etcher, and her drypoints and color prints are greatly admired. She is well represented in public and private galleries in the United States. Her best-known pictures include several versions of *Mother and Child* (Metropoli-tan Mus.; Mus. of Fine Arts, Boston; Worcester, Mass., Art Mus.); *Lady at the Tea-Table* (Metropolitan Mus.); *Modern Women,* a mural painted for the Women's Building of the Chicago exposition; and a portrait of the artist's mother. See catalog by A. D. Breeskin (1970, rev. ed. 1980); N. M. Mathews, ed., *Cassatt and Her Circle: Selected Letters* (1984); N. Hale, *Mary Cassatt* (1987); N. M. Mathews, *Mary Cas-satt: A Life* (1994).

"Facts" Open to Dispute

This category includes commonly accepted "facts" based largely on inference. When new evidence is discovered, new inferences may have to be made. For example, the significance of a particular fossil bone is defi-nitely a matter of judgment, and the nature of the astronomical phenome-non known as a "black hole" has not by any means been as definitively established as many popular accounts suggest. Much of the work done by behavioral scientists consists of collecting statistical information (the average number of children in Chinese American families, the rate of ju-venile crime in Boston, and so on). Although the statistics you encounter in your research may seem to be hard facts, these so-called facts can be disputed. Indeed, theories and conclusions based on such facts are contin-ually debated by the experts. Therefore, almost all information in the be-havioral sciences must be documented except historical facts about indi-vidual persons and events in the field.

Similarly, information gathered by observation and experimentation is often subject to dispute. The results of similar experiments may vary, or different researchers may interpret identical results differently. New in-formation may contradict or confuse earlier findings. Accordingly, such information should be documented so that your readers know its source.

For example, you might read in a newspaper or magazine this week that "scientists at the Murphy-Weiss Laboratories in Ipswich, Mass., have shown that cola drinks cause liver cancer in rats and monkeys." The headline might even have read: "Soda Pop Causes Cancer." The experiment may have been honestly and carefully executed, and the information may eventually be accepted as fact. However, until other scientists have duplicated these scientists' work and arrived at the same results, this information is just a "possible" fact and therefore needs to be documented.

Factual Information That Is Not General Knowledge

Be sure to take your audience into consideration when deciding what you can safely consider to be general knowledge. If a fact is stated without documentation by several authors and can be easily looked up within a variety of reference sources, it is probably general knowledge within the field. However, if you are writing for a nonexpert audience, you should cite information that is very specific or may seem obscure to your readers. The following documented information from Susanna Andrews's paper on Emily Dickinson may be well known by Dickinson experts, but for the paper's audience it is not general knowledge:

documented fact in student paper	Upon the poet's death at fifty-six, her sister discovered over one thousand poems and initiated an effort to publish them. Beginning four years later, in 1890, these poems finally appeared in print (Sewall 1: 4-11).

Some of the experts you consult in your research will provide evolving information that is not yet general knowledge. For example, in November 2003, scientists discovered the closest known galaxy to the Milky Way, the Canis Major dwarf galaxy. This new information may spread quickly to astronomers, but to others it is not considered general knowledge. In some cases, new information may not even be widely known in the field. You may need to ask your instructor or, if possible, an expert in the field to determine whether new research findings should be documented for your particular audience.

One last question: Is it necessary to provide source notes for ideas and information that you were already aware of before undertaking the research paper? If the information falls into one of the three categories just discussed, you must take the time to locate a source for it. Readers have a right as well as a need to know of a reliable source for the information in question. Furthermore, finding a source protects you against remembering incorrectly what you have previously heard or read. Thus it is always wise when reading sources to take notes on everything that is relevant to your hypothesis, even when you are familiar with the information.

General Information about In-Text Citations

In-text citations can take one of two forms: parenthetical citations or numbered notes. Many of the examples and discussions in this book follow the Modern Language Association's preferred format, which uses parenthetical citations. For examples of this system, which is used by most instructors of language, literature, and other humanities courses, see Chapter 18 and the papers "The New Immigrants: Asset or Burden?" and "Emily Dickinson's Reluctance to Publish" in Chapter 22. A second system, devised by the American Psychological Association (APA) and used in most of the social sciences, is discussed in Chapter 19 and exemplified by David Perez's paper on fire ants ("*Solenopsis invicta:* Destroyer of Ecosystems"), also in Chapter 22. *Chicago* style, a traditional numbered endnote/footnote format, which many history instructors prefer, is briefly explained in Chapter 20 and then illustrated in the paper "Cotton Mather's Necessary Witches" in Chapter 22. Yet another system, the number system used for scientific research, is briefly explained in Chapter 20.

For every paper you are assigned, be sure to ask your instructor which system of citation you should use. Then consult a guidebook such as this one for the proper format.

General Information about the List of Sources

A list of all your sources must appear at the end of your paper in a section titled *Works Cited, References,* or *Bibliography,* depending on which citation system you use. Arrange the items alphabetically according to the authors' last names. If a source has no known author, list it alphabetically according to the first word of its title (ignoring *A, An,* and *The*). The sample papers in Chapter 22 show that all the major citation systems alphabetize the list of sources.

Do not inflate your list of sources by including items that were not direct sources of the information in your paper. This means that, as a rule, no item should appear among your sources unless at least one citation in the paper refers to it. To be useful to your reader, a list of sources must answer several basic questions about each source.

- What is its full title?
- Who wrote or created it?
- Where and when was it published? By what publisher?
- If the source is an article in a periodical or an essay in a book, on what pages can it be found?

Occasionally other kinds of information will have to be added. For books, there may be translators, editors, or volume numbers; for periodicals, the handling of dates and of volume and issue numbers varies according to the type of periodical (annual, monthly, weekly, daily); and for nonprint sources, such as films, recordings, television programs, and online sources, yet other kinds of information must be included. The exact information required in the sources list and the format of it will vary between different documentation systems, so make sure you know which system you should use. Chapters 18 through 20 cover each of the major systems.

Abbreviations for Bibliographical Terms

The following list presents standard abbreviations for common bibliographical terms.

chapter	chap.
edition/edited by	ed.
editor	ed.
no date	n.d.
no place of publication/no publisher	n.p.
number	no.
part	pt.
reprint	rpt.
revised edition	rev. ed.
supplement	supp. (MLA); suppl. (APA)
translator	trans.
volume	vol.

In most cases, these abbreviated forms should be used only within parentheses, figures and tables, and documentation. Note that APA style capitalizes some of the abbreviations in certain situations (Ed. for editor, Rev. ed. for revised edition, 4 vols. but Vol. 4).

u. – university
p. – publish or pres

18

Using the MLA Parenthetical System

In general, the MLA's main documentation system requires that you identify the source of any idea, information, or borrowed language that you use in your paper. This system comprises two corresponding parts, each of which is described extensively in this chapter.

1. A brief **parenthetical citation** placed in the text of the paper after the use of source material contains basic information that the reader can use to find the source in the list of works cited.

2. The **works cited section,** an alphabetized list of all the sources you cite, appears at the end of your paper and contains publication information on each source.

Following is a cited passage from Shirley Macalbe's essay and the corresponding works cited entry:

excerpt from student paper

Throughout U.S. history, opponents of immigration have raised racial, religious, and nationalistic objections or questions about large-scale immigration to the United States (Jones 247-305).

works cited entry

Jones, Maldwyn Allen. *American Immigration.* Chicago: U of Chicago P, 1960. Print.

General Guidelines for Parenthetical Citations

Basic Format

- The parenthetical citation is typically placed at the end of the sentence in which the source material is used (as in the example from Shirley's paper) if it does not cause confusion about what is being documented. For clarity the citation may also be placed in other locations in the sentence.

  Since nuclear power plants are safer now than in the past (Tillson 77), they may be used more effectively in the future.

- If you have mentioned the author's name in the passage that contains the source material, the citation usually consists of just the page number(s) on which the information was located (if the source is paginated).

  This fact leads [the critic Owen Thomas] to conclude that Emily Dickinson "was well aware of the world outside her little room, that in fact she used the language of this outside world to create some of her best poetry" (523).

  If the source is not paginated, mentioning the author's name in the sentence would suffice.

- If you have not mentioned the author's name, the citation must include that information.

  paginated source   But an economist who predicted the recession of the early 1990s a year in advance fears the price of gold will decline slowly for at least ten years (Goodserve 143).

  electronic source with no pagination   U.S. schools place too much value on computers in education (Oppenheimer).

- If the author has written more than one of the sources in your works cited list, your citation must include a shortened form of the particular title unless it is already mentioned in the passage.

Chomsky claims that all humans inherit the same basic linguistic structural framework on which their community's particular language is fitted (*Language* 29-41).

The works cited list in this case also includes Chomsky's *Syntactic Structures*.

• If the author is not listed, as in many newspaper articles or Web pages, the title must appear in the note, if not mentioned in the documented passage. (Titles may be shortened.)

Throughout her life, Essie Mae Washington-Williams often met secretly with her father, Strom Thurmond, and received considerable financial assistance from him ("Thurmond's" A13).

The following is the works cited entry for this source:

"Thurmond's Mixed-Race Daughter Steps into Spotlight." *The Seattle Times* 18 Dec. 2003, Metro ed.: A13. Print.

Spacing and Punctuation

• Leave a space before the opening parenthesis. If a punctuation mark follows the citation, place it *outside* the closing parenthesis and leave a space after the punctuation mark.

Morgan believes the whale stands for God (132), whereas Kay claims it "embodies all that is evil" (19-20). This controversy derives largely from . . .

• The parentheses are placed *inside* a sentence, directly following the quotation or paraphrase they refer to, and *outside* quotation marks. (See previous example.)

• If a quotation ends with a question mark or an exclamation point, the mark is placed within the quotes, and a period is still used after the parenthetical citation.

In *Stories from a New Ireland*, editor Carolyn Walsh asks, "What, for instance, constitutes Irishness in 2002? . . . Are there stratas of Irishness, or is it now more a perspective, a state of mind?" (vii).

• If you quote more than four lines from a source, set off the quotation from the rest of the text by indenting ten spaces or one inch (or two paragraph indents) from the margin. Place the parenthetical note after the final mark of punctuation, separated by a space.

Catton also suggests that Davis's attempt to lead his people to independence was somehow doomed to failure from the start.

> He had done the best he could do in an impossible job, and if it is easy to show where he made grievous mistakes, it is difficult to show that any other man, given the materials available, could have done much better. He had courage, integrity, tenacity, devotion to his cause, and, like Old Testament Sisera, the stars in their courses marched against him. (279)

Sample Parenthetical Citations

Sources with More Than One Author. If a source has more than one author, a parenthetical citation should give the last names of all the writers. If there are more than three authors, you can use the first author's last name followed by "et al." — Latin for "and others" — but this form of citation diminishes the importance of the other authors. Whichever method you choose, you should consistently use the same method in text references as you do in the works cited list.

Davis took the position that "the President was entrusted with military leadership, and he must exercise it" (Randall and Donald 271).

An investigation of iridium levels in the Dolomites revealed traces insufficient to justify Alvarez's hypothesis (Sapperstein et al. 12).

The works cited list would show:

Randall, J. G., and David Donald. *The Divided Union*. Boston: Little, 1961. Print.

Sapperstein, M. L., et al. "Iridium Levels in the Dolomites." *Astronomy Today* Sept. 1983: 12-15. Print.

Two or More Sources for One Citation. Sometimes a piece of information or an idea will appear in more than one of your sources. Usually, especially with purely factual information, you choose one of the sources and refer only to it. Occasionally, however, when each source offers some interesting additional commentary that a curious reader might enjoy investigating, you should mention each of them in your citation, separating them with semicolons.

> Many of Davis's personal troubles grew out of his ill health (Catton
> 121-22; Nevins 3: 86-89).

Indirect Source: A Source Quotes Another Writer. Frequently, your source will quote another writer's work, and you may want to quote that second writer. When this happens, you must make every reasonable effort to find the original source in order to verify the accuracy of the quotation. You should check to be certain it was not quoted out of context (see page 151). When you have seen that source, you can add it to your list of works cited and refer directly to it in a parenthetical citation.

Sometimes, however, you will find it impossible to locate the original source. In that case, you will be forced to rely on your first source, but your parenthetical reference must indicate, with the abbreviation "qtd." (for *quoted*), that you got the quote from an indirect source.

In this example, the author was quoting from an out-of-print book, *Criminal Man*, that was written in Italian.

> Lambroso's racism becomes apparent in his remark that "[criminals']
> physical insensibility well recalls that of savage peoples who can bear,
> in rites of puberty, torture that a white man could never endure. All
> travelers know the indifference of Negroes and American savages to
> pain: the former cut their hands and laugh in order to avoid work; the
> latter, tied to the torture post, gaily sing the praises of their tribe while
> they are slowly burnt" (qtd. in Gould 18).

The works cited entry would show the following:

> Gould, Stephen Jay. "*Criminal Man* Revived." *Natural History* Mar. 1976:
> 16-18. Print.

Reference to an Entire Work. If you refer to an entire source — whether it is a book, an essay, a film, or another work — you do not need a parenthetical citation as long as you mention the author (or the editor, director, performer, etc.) in the passage.

> Gore Vidal's *Lincoln* presents a very readable reconstruction of the
> president's approach to problems, both personal and political.

> Gould settled the perplexing question as to whether a Portuguese man-of-war is an organism or a colony by approaching the problem from a new point of view, that of overlapping, evolving categories rather than rigidly fixed definitions.

The author's name is enough to lead a reader to the right source in your works cited list.

> Vidal, Gore. *Lincoln*. New York: Random House, 1984. Print.
>
> Gould, Stephen Jay. "A Most Ingenious Paradox." *Natural History* Dec.
> 1984: 20-29. Print.

Summary of a Chapter. Occasionally you will make a statement that summarizes a major idea from a chapter in a book. For a chapter, you may use the chapter number instead of page numbers.

> Chomsky claims that all humans inherit the same basic linguistic structural framework on which their community's particular language is fitted (*Language* ch. 2).

Quotation from a Literary Work. When writing on literary topics, you will usually quote from the plays, poems, or prose works under discussion. For works of prose reprinted in many editions (novels, short stories, and most plays), indicate the page numbers, as with other sources, but also include chapter, book, act, or scene number so that readers can locate the quoted material in any edition. For poems, indicate the quoted material not by page numbers but by line numbers. For long poems, like *The Iliad*, give the canto or book number plus the line number(s), separated by a period. When citing poems that are not divided into parts, use the word *line(s)* in the first reference: (lines 4-8). In later references, use just the numbers: (9-10). For verse drama, give the act, scene, and line number(s), separated by periods.

novel

> It would seem that Captain Ahab has forever
> rejected God as he commences his final soliloquy
> in *Moby-Dick* with "I turn my body from the sun . . ."
> (468; ch. 135).

poetry

> Along the same lines, given her deliberate decision
> to forgo publication rather than compromise her art,
> the first lines of another poem become significantly

clear: "Publication--is the Auction / Of the Mind of Man" (1-2). And there can be no doubt that when she wrote the following stanza, Emily Dickinson had accepted the fact that true fame would not be hers in her lifetime.

> Some--Work for Immortality--
> The Chiefer part, for Time--
> He--Compensates--immediately
> The former--Checks--On Fame--
> (1-4)

drama (reference to Othello)

Once again, Shakespeare deftly shifts images, this time in Othello's speech over the sleeping Desdemona, from lightness of color (Desdemona as compared to Othello) to light as a symbol of life (5.2.3-13).

If you do not mention the title of the verse drama or long poetic work in your text, add the title — which you may abbreviate — to the citation. Italicize the abbreviation as you would a full title.

quotation from Doctor Faustus

> I see there's virtue in my heavenly words;
> Who would not be proficient in this art?
> How pliant is this Mephistophilis,
> Full of obedience and humility!
> Such is the force of magic and my spells:
> Now, Faustus, thou art conjuror laureate,
> That canst command great Mephistophilis.
> (*Faustus* 1.3.30-36)

long poetic work (quotation from Paradise Lost)

> Thus Adam to himself lamented loud
>   . . . on the ground
> Outstretcht he lay, on the cold ground, and oft
> Curs'd his Creation, Death as oft accus'd
> Of tardy execution, since denounc't
> The day of his offence. Why comes not Death,
> Said he, with one thrice acceptable stroke
> To end me? (*PL* 10.845-56)

Notice the difference between the punctuation of this citation and the punctuation for volume and page numbers: 10.845-56 reads "book ten, lines 845-56"; 3:203 reads "volume 3, page 203."

Quotation from a Sacred Text. If you are citing a sacred text, give the title, the book, and the chapter and verse. In text, spell out the names of books mentioned. In a parenthetical citation, use an abbreviation for books with names of five or more letters.

She ignored the admonition "Pride goes before destruction, and a
haughty spirit before a fall" (*New Oxford Annotated Bible*, Prov. 16.18).

Blending Notes into Your Text Smoothly

This system of documentation encourages you to name your sources as you refer to them in the essay and to put as little information as possible in the parenthetical notes. Keep in mind that your notes should avoid, as far as possible, breaking a reader's concentration. This example shows how an obtrusive parenthetical citation can be made less obtrusive.

obtrusive   Certainly, then, the woman who has been called "one
                       of the greatest lyric poets of all time" (Winters 40)
                       was all but unknown as a poet during her lifetime.

less obtrusive   Certainly, then, the woman Yvor Winters has called
                       "one of the greatest lyric poets of all time" (40) was
                       all but unknown as a poet during her lifetime.

Notice that the parenthetical citation was placed directly after the quoted phrase. If it had been put at the end of the sentence (to reduce the interruptive effect), the citation would seem to cover the whole idea, not just the part that belonged to Yvor Winters.

When paraphrasing, you will sometimes find it difficult to slip the source author's name into the passage, especially when the paraphrase presents factual matter rather than a judgment, as in the following example. In these cases, a parenthetical citation alone at the end of the paraphrased passage can be used to identify the author.

During her later years, Emily Dickinson had virtually no direct contact
with anyone outside her immediate family. While she was still
connected to her circle of friends, the poet made at least one tentative
attempt to find an audience for her poetry. But only a handful of verses

were published anonymously, most of them in a local newspaper, and these were subjected to considerable editing. On the poet's death at fifty-six, her sister discovered more than a thousand poems and initiated an effort to publish them. Beginning four years later, in 1890, these poems finally appeared in print (Sewall 1:4-11).

Here you would have had no reason to introduce Sewall's name in the text because the information is both factual and very general; nothing seems to be particularly the work of a specific biographer. (*Note:* Some instructors may prefer that you introduce all paraphrases with a signal phrase at the beginning of the passage.)

This example also demonstrates that it is not necessary to document every single sentence in a passage summarized or paraphrased from one source. As long as the beginning of the cited passage is reasonably clear to a reader, a few sentences in a row that all come from one source can be cited at the end of the passage.

Both of the following examples are well-constructed passages using the same sources; both make good use of the parenthetical-citation format. The differences are a result of a shift of purpose by the writer. The comments that follow the examples explain the effect of the variation.

Example 1

Recent studies show that anorexia can be successfully treated by psychotherapy (Evans et al.; Kline; Yaster and Korman). These studies dealt mostly with young persons who came to therapy voluntarily and continued treatment for at least six weeks. The authors of the studies concluded that anorexia is a "socially induced disorder" (Kline 214) and not a biologically caused illness.

Example 2

Recent studies show that anorexia can be treated successfully by psychotherapy. Kline achieved an 85 percent cure for twenty cases in adolescent women. A group of Illinois therapists found that "most victims underwent marked improvement following four sessions" (Evans et al. 35). In California, Oscar Yaster and T. G. Korman, working with a population of males and females ages 16-30, produced "significant remission rates" among those completing five sessions or more of group and individual treatment (17-18).

Notice that in Example 1 the writer did not intend to make a specific statement about each of the sources. Therefore, she cited all three of them after the introductory sentence of the paragraph. However, when she decided to quote a phrase from one of the three sources, which she felt spoke for all three, she then cited that one study.

If the writer had wanted to say something about each source, however, she might have constructed Example 2, in which she would delay citing the sources until she referred to each one individually. No special citation was needed for Kline because the writer was summarizing the full study. With Evans et al., she introduced a quotation, and that called for a citation indicating the page number. Although the last of the three sources was quoted very briefly, a citation was still needed to show where the phrase could be found. (Putting that citation directly after the quoted phrase would have created an unnecessary interruption.)

Numbered Notes for Special Purposes

Once in a while, you will find something that might interest your readers but is not essential to whatever idea you are developing in the paper at that point. If that happens, insert a citation number directing readers to an informational footnote or endnote. Endnotes, if you use them, are placed on a separate page between the end of the paper and the works cited section. Insert the citation number immediately after the final mark of punctuation for the sentence that led you to think of adding the additional information. Raise the number half a line.

> Literary critics, serious biographers, and writers of fictionalized accounts of her life created an image of Emily Dickinson as a timid, reclusive, mystical thinker who was too absorbed in personal sorrows and ecstasies to be concerned with literary recognition. And this image persists, to a great extent, in the public mind today.[1]

The endnote or footnote would read as following:

> [1]For a full discussion of sources leading to the "Emily myth," see Ferlazzo 13-21.

This citation offers readers more information than they could get from the simple parenthetical citation "Ferlazzo 13–21." Numbered notes should be used in rare cases when you need to comment on a source or offer additional explanatory information. They are not a substitute for normal parenthetical citations.

Guidelines for Works Cited

A list of all your sources must appear at the end of your paper, in a section titled *Works Cited*. Following are some guidelines that apply to most works cited entries:

Basic Format

- Arrange the items alphabetically, according to the authors' last names or, for sources with no listed author, the first word of the title (ignoring *A, An*, and *The*). See the works cited lists for the papers on the new immigrants and Emily Dickinson in Chapter 22.
- The first line of each entry starts flush with the left margin; each subsequent line indents five spaces or one-half inch.

Punctuation and Capitalization

- Periods separate the main parts of an entry: Author. Title. Place of publication: Publisher, date. Medium. Each period is followed by one space.
- The first letters of all major words in titles are capitalized even if they are not capitalized in the original.
- Titles of major works such as books or periodicals (not articles) are italicized.
- Titles of articles, essays, and other short works are placed in quotation marks. (Exception: See "Critical Review," page 258.)
- Standard abbreviations can be used for many terms. See page 239 for a list of abbreviations commonly used in source citations.
- If some publication information is not available, use "N.p." for "no publisher," "n.d." for "no date," or "n. pag." for "no pagination." Terms such as *anonymous* or *unavailable* are not used.

In the sections that follow, more detailed information is given for the most common types of sources, dividing them into four categories: books, periodicals, electronic sources, and other kinds of materials. Later in your college career, advanced research may lead you to rarer kinds of publications. At such times, you may need to check the *MLA Handbook for Writers of Research Papers,* Seventh Edition, for the correct format.

Directory to MLA Style for Works Cited

Sample Entries for Books

1. Basic Format

Author. *Title of Book*. City of Publication: Publisher, Year of Publication. Medium.

Publishers' names are shortened; terms such as *Inc., Co., Publishers,* and *Press* are dropped. Only the first surname is used when the publisher's name is made up of one or more individuals' names: *Norton* for *W. W. Norton and Company, Farrar* for *Farrar, Straus and Giroux. University* and *Press* are abbreviated for university presses: *Oxford UP, U of Chicago P*. If the book was published by an imprint of a publisher, hyphenate the name: "Anchor-Doubleday."

2. Single Author

note punctuation and indentation; *Graphics* is a shortened form of *The Graphics Press*

Tufte, Edward R. *Envisioning Information*. Cheshire: Graphics, 1990. Print.

3. Two or More Authors

list authors' names in the order in which they appear on title page of source; for two or three authors, list all names; for four or more authors, either list all names or list just the first author followed by the abbreviation "et al."

Stebbins, Robert C., and Nathan W. Cohen. *A Natural History of Amphibians*. Princeton: Princeton UP, 1995. Print.

Dugan, James, Robert C. Cohen, Bill Barada, and Richard M. Crum. *World beneath the Sea*. Washington: Natl. Geographic Soc., 1967. Print.

Dugan, James, et al. *World beneath the Sea*. Washington: Natl. Geographic Soc., 1967. Print.

4. Author of an Essay in a Collection

"Ed." stands for edited by; pages on which full essay appears are shown, even if only a page or two are used as sources

Brooks, Gwendolyn. "The Rise of Maud Martha." *Invented Lives: Narratives of Black Women 1860-1960*. Ed. Mary Helen Washington. New York: Anchor-Doubleday, 1987. 429-32. Print.

If all the essays in a collection are by the same author, you do not need to include the individual essay title in the works cited entry. If the collection contains essays by various authors — as in the preceding example — the essay title should be cited.

If you use more than one essay from the same collection, you do not need to repeat the full information for the collection with each essay.

Make a works cited entry for the book and then create additional entries that list the author and title of the essay followed by a brief reference to the book. End the entry with the page numbers that the essay appears on.

entry for the collection

Sullivan, Patricia A., and Donna J. Qualley, eds. *Pedagogy in the Age of Politics: Writing and Reading (in) the Academy.* Urbana: NCTE, 1994. Print.

entries for individual essays in the collection; note that the medium is omitted

Bleich, David. "The 'Kinds of Language' Curriculum." Sullivan and Qualley 195-213.

Reagan, Daniel. "Naming Harlem: Teaching the Dynamics of Diversity." Sullivan and Qualley 43-55.

5. Two or More Sources with the Same Author

line of three hyphens is used in place of author's name for all entries after the first; works listed alphabetically by title

Gitlin, Todd. *Inside Prime Time.* Berkeley: U of California P, 2000. Print.

---. *Media Unlimited: How the Torrent of Images and Sounds Overwhelms Our Lives.* New York: Metropolitan, 2001. Print.

6. Author of Several Sources Having Different Coauthors

coauthored books follow singly authored books alphabetically by coauthor; repeat the first author's name in each entry

Chomsky, Noam. *Language and Problems of Knowledge.* Cambridge: MIT P, 1988. Print.

Chomsky, Noam, and Morris Halle. *The Sound Pattern of English.* New York: Harper, 1968. Print.

Chomsky, Noam, and George A. Miller. *Analyse formelle des langues naturelles.* The Hague: Mouton, 1971. Print. No. 8 of *Mathematiques et sciences de l'homme.*

7. Anonymous Author

anonymous work of classic literature

Beowulf. Trans. Seamus Heaney. New York: Farrar, 2000. Print.

unsigned book or pamphlet; both writer and publisher unknown

Latchkey Kids. Huntingdon: n.p., 1989. Print.

8. Corporation as Author

Phillips Petroleum. *66 Ways to Save Energy.* Bartlesville: Phillips Petroleum, 1978. Print.

9. Editor

editor's ideas are cited

Gardner, Martin, ed. *The Annotated Alice. Alice's Adventures in Wonderland and Through the Looking Glass.* By Lewis Carroll. New York: Potter, 1960. Print.

the work itself is cited

Carroll, Lewis. *The Annotated Alice. Alice's Adventures in Wonderland and Through the Looking Glass.* Ed. Martin Gardner. New York: Potter, 1960. Print.

10. Encyclopedia Article

form for unsigned article; although article's title is "Isaac Newton," it is entered under "Newton," under which a reader would look it up

"Isaac Newton." *New Encyclopaedia Britannica.* 2002 ed. Print.

form for signed article; publisher's name is not necessary for well-known encyclopedias

Rudnytsky, Peter L. "John Milton." *World Book Encyclopedia.* 2002 ed. Print.

11. Enlarged Edition

See "Revised or Enlarged Edition," page 255.

12. Government Agency as Author

note abbreviations Cong. (Congress), House (House of Representatives), sess. (session); Lib. of Cong. (Library of Congress); GPO (Government Printing Office), publisher for many federal documents

United States. Lib. of Cong. Copyright Office. *Report on Copyright and Digital Distance Education.* Washington: Copyright Office, 1999. Print.

United States. Cong. House. Committee on Ways and Means. *Background Material and Data on Programs within the Jurisdiction of the Committee on Ways and Means.* 102nd Cong., 2nd sess. Washington: GPO, 1992. Print.

United Nations. Centre on Transnational
Corporations. *World Investment Report*. New
York: United Nations, 1991. Print.

13. Introduction, Preface, Foreword, or Afterword

reference here is to
Edel's rather than
Wilson's writing; had
Wilson's text also
been cited, book
would be entered
twice, once under
each author's name

Edel, Leon. Foreword. *The Thirties*. By Edmund
Wilson. New York: Farrar, 1980. vii. Print.

14. Reprint

note distinction
between reprint and
revised edition:
revision means that
changes were made,
and only new version's
publication date is
given; reprint includes
no changes, and both
dates are given (date
of first printing follows
title, reprint date
follows publisher)

Boys, C. V. *Soap Bubbles and the Forces Which Mould
Them*. 1916. New York: Doubleday, 1959. Print.

15. Revised or Enlarged Edition

editions other than
first must be
identified by number
(2nd ed., 3rd ed., etc.),
by name (rev. ed., enl.
ed., etc.) or by year
(2003 ed., etc.) —
whatever information
is shown in book

MLA Handbook for Writers of Research Papers. 7th ed.
New York: MLA, 2009. Print.

Chomsky, Noam. *Language and Mind*. Enl. ed. New
York: Harcourt, 1972. Print.

See also "Encyclopedia Article," page 254.

16. Title within a Title

Especially in the field of literary criticism, titles of books and essays often contain titles of other works. When a book's title includes the title of another book, do not italicize the interior title.

The Theological Underpinning of Moby-Dick.

When a book's title includes the title of a poem or an essay, italicize the interior title and place it within quotation marks.

The Anthropological Background of "The Waste Land"
of T. S. Eliot.

17. Translation

translator's ideas are cited

Fitzgerald, Robert, trans. *The Iliad.* By Homer. Garden
City: Anchor, 1974. Print.

only the work itself is cited

Homer. *The Iliad.* Trans. Robert Fitzgerald. Garden
City: Anchor, 1974. Print.

18. Volume Numbers

For works that are published in more than one volume, you must
indicate which volume(s) you used in your paper.

entry indicates that all three volumes have been used

Dickinson, Emily. *The Poems of Emily Dickinson.* Ed.
Thomas H. Johnson. 3 vols. Cambridge:
Belknap-Harvard UP, 1955. Print.

entry indicates that only one volume has been used

Manchester, William. *The Last Lion: Winston Spencer
Churchill.* Vol. 2. Boston: Little, 1988. Print.

a volume will often have its own title; if so, it is cited first

Nevins, Allan. *The Organized War, 1863-64.* New York:
Scribner's, 1971. Print. Vol. 3 of *The War for the
Union.* 4 vols.

Sample Entries for Print Periodicals

19. Basic Format

newspaper or magazine article

Author. "Article title." *Periodical Title* Date: Page(s) of
the article. Medium.

journal article

Author. "Article title." *Periodical Title* Volume number.
Issue number (Year): Page(s) of the article. Medium.

- A periodical entry contains two titles: that of the article (within quotation marks) and that of the periodical (italicized, like the title of a
  book).
- For periodicals that do not carry specific dates — month, or day
  and month — volume numbers are needed. Academic journals are
  especially likely to go by volume and issue rather than by date.

- MLA requires the use of volume and issue number for all scholarly journals, whether the journal begins each issue on page 1 or numbers the pages consecutively throughout the volume.

- Include the medium ("Print") at the end of the entry.

- Page numbers of the full article (not just the pages cited) are placed at the end of the entry. If the article appears on consecutive pages, express the page numbers as a range (49–57, for example). If the article is not printed consecutively, use the number of the first page followed by a plus sign (26+).

For electronic periodical articles, see the sample entries on pages 260–62. See the "Guidelines for Works Cited" on page 250 for further formatting information.

20. Article in a Journal

> Flynn, Elizabeth A. "Feminism and Scientism."
>
> *College Composition and Communication* 46.3
>
> (1995): 353-68. Print.

when author's name is not given, source is listed by title

> "Do Cities Change the Weather?" *Mosaic* 5.3 (1974):
>
> 29-34. Print.

21. Article in a Monthly Periodical

do not give volume or issue number

> Damasio, Antonio R., and Hanna Damasio. "Brain
>
> and Language." *Scientific American* Sept. 1992:
>
> 88-109. Print.

> Wallach, Amei. "Beacon of Light." *Smithsonian* Sept.
>
> 2003: 66-72. Print.

22. Article in a Weekly Periodical

issue is identified by date, month, and year

> Holson, Laura M. "A Franchise Fantasy." *New York*
>
> *Times Magazine* 9 Nov. 2003: 28-36. Print.

> "Risking It All." *U.S. News and World Report* 3 Nov.
>
> 2003: 19. Print.

23. Article in a Daily Newspaper

when only a writer's initials are known, do not reverse their order

> J. K. "Explodes an Illusion." *Daily Worker* 30 Dec. 1936:
>
> 7-8. Print.

Documenting Sources

include the paper's edition (if designated) after the date; include section number or letter with the page number, if there is one

"Defiant Chief Justice Ousted in Alabama." *New York Times* 14 Nov. 2003, late ed.: A1+. Print.

when paper's title does not include name of city, that information is shown in brackets (for national newspapers, like *The Daily Worker*, do not list a city)

Sullivan, Kevin, and Mary Jordan. "Earnings Trump Education for Many Mexican Children." *The Sunday Oregonian* [Portland, OR] 30 Nov. 2003, 1st ed: A13. Print.

24. Critical Review of Another Work

"Rev. of" is neither italicized nor enclosed in quotation marks; if the review has its own title, list it in quotation marks before "Rev. of"

Yorke, Edmund. "Introducing the African Past." Rev. of *History of Africa*, by Kevin Shillington. *Journal of African History* 32.2 (1991): 339-40. Print.

25. Issue Numbers

if no volume number is included, treat an issue number exactly as you would a volume number

Pritchard, Allan. "West of the Great Divide: A View of the Literature of British Columbia." *Canadian Literature* 94 (1982): 96-112. Print.

26. Reprint of a Journal Article

Mazzeo, Joseph A. "A Critique of Some Modern Theories of Metaphysical Poetry." *Modern Philology* 50.2 (1952): 88-96. Rpt. in *Seventeenth-Century English Poetry*. Ed. William R. Keast. New York: Oxford UP, 1962. 63-74. Print.

27. Title within a Title

Italicize the titles of books, plays, and long poems.

"Hawthorne's Reaction to *Moby-Dick*."

Place single quotation marks around the title of an essay, short story, or short poem.

"A Psychoanalytic Interpretation of 'America.'"

Sample Entries for Electronic Sources

Electronic sources fall under the same general documentation requirements as any other source material, and the formats for citing these sources are similar to print media. However, because electronic sources are not referenced as systematically as print media and because the contents or URLs of such documents can be changed at any time, you need to provide the reader more information when documenting these sources.

Most formats follow this general pattern:

> Author. Title(s). Publication information (both print, if applicable, and electronic). Access information.

There is such variety in the area of electronic publication that you should consult the relevant formats and examples mentioned in the following subsections. Here are some additional guidelines for documenting electronic sources.

- If some citation information is unavailable, as is common, simply omit the information.
- Some electronic sources are available in several formats — for example, a popular magazine might be available on CD-ROM, through an online subscription service, and on a World Wide Web site. To cite such a source, cite the format in which you found the source.

See "Guidelines for Works Cited" (page 250) for further formatting information.

Web Sites

28. Basic Format

> Author. "Title of Page." *Title of Web Site*. Sponsor or publisher, date of electronic publication or last update. Medium. Date of access.

- Look for the name of the site's author or editor at the bottom of the page as well as the top. List any editors immediately after the title of the site in the works cited entry: Ed. John Smith.
- Web page titles are placed in quotation marks; Web site titles are italicized.

- The sponsor or publisher of the Web site follows the title of the site. This information is usually found at the bottom of the homepage, near the copyright. Use "N.p." if no publisher or sponsor is listed.
- If listed, the date of electronic publication or last revision is usually found at the bottom of the Web page. Use "n.d." if no date is listed.

29. Document from a Nonperiodical Web Site

> Smith, Martha Nell, and Lara Vetter. "Emily Dickinson Writing a Poem." *Dickinson Electronic Archives.* Martha Nell Smith, 1999. Web. 20 May 2010.

begin with the document's title if no author is listed

> "Overview of Canterbury Tales." *Chaucer Metapage.* Ed. Larry D. Benson et al. N.p., n.d. Web. 19 Dec. 2009.
>
> "Workers' Stories of Abuse, Exploitation Point to Need for Immigration Reform." *AFL-CIO: America's Union Movement.* AFL-CIO, 6 Sep. 2001. Web. 27 Nov. 2009.

30. An Entire Web Site

specific documents or pages are not listed when summarizing or commenting on an entire Web site

> *NBA.* NBA Media Ventures, 2010. Web. 2 June 2010.

Electronic Periodical Articles

31. Basic Format

article from an electronic database

> Author. "Title of Article." *Title of Periodical* Print Publication Information. *Database.* Medium. Date of Access.

article from an online periodical

> Author. "Title of Article." *Name of Magazine* Publication Information. Medium. Date of Access.

The latter format is used for online versions of print periodicals (such as the *New York Times*) as well as for periodicals that publish solely online (such as *Salon.com*).

32. Article or Abstract from an Electronic Database

> Epstein, Robert. "Examining the Nation's Psyche."
>> *Psychology Today* Mar. 1999: 20. *Academic*
>> *OneFile*. Web. 11 May 2010.
>
> Gorman, James. "When Fish Fluoresce, Can
>> Teenagers Be Far Behind?" *New York Times*
>> 2 Dec. 2003, late ed: F3. *ProQuest Newspapers*.
>> Web. 28 Dec. 2009.

If you are citing an abstract instead of the full text of an article, insert the word *Abstract* followed by a period after the publication information (just before the database information).

33. Article from a Personal Subscription Service

list the name of the service

> "Romanticism." *Compton's Encyclopedia Online*.
>> Vers. 3.0. 1998. *America Online*. Web. 17 Mar.
>> 2000.

34. Article from an Online Journal

document the source as you would an article from a print periodical; then add the medium and date of access

> Bostock, William W. "The Global Corporatisation of
>> Universities: Causes and Consequences."
>> *AntePodium* 3 (1999): n. pag. Web. 27 Jan. 2010.
>
> Goodrick, Glyn, and Graeme Earl. "A Manufactured
>> Past: Virtual Reality in Archaeology." *Internet*
>> *Archeology* 15 (2004): n. pag. Web. 5 Feb. 2010.

35. Article from an Online Magazine

> Worth, Robert. "A Model Prison." *The Atlantic Online*.
>> Atlantic Monthly Group, Nov. 1995. Web. 22 Mar.
>> 2010.

36. Article from an Online Newspaper

> Uchitelle, Louis. "Productivity Gains Help Keep
>> Economy on a Roll." *New York Times*. New York
>> Times, 22 Mar. 1999. Web. 25 Nov. 2009.

37. Article from an Online Newswire

"Libya Pledge: Victims' Families Angry." *CNN.com*. Cable News Network, 21 Dec. 2003. Web. 25 Feb. 2009.

Other Electronic Sources

38. CD-ROM

The Future of Higher Education: The Best Way to Predict the Future Is to Create It. Washington: National Education Association, 2002. CD-ROM.

for a book on CD-ROM, include the print publication information, adding "CD-ROM" as the medium

The Oxford English Dictionary. 2nd ed. Oxford: Oxford UP, 2000. CD-ROM.

39. Periodically Revised Database

print publication information is given first; then the medium and database name; then the vendor's name and the date of electronic publication

Natchez, Gladys. "Frida Kahlo and Diego Rivera: The Transformation of Catastrophe to Creativity." *Psychotherapy-Patient* 4.1 (1987): 153-74. CD-ROM. *PsycLIT*. SilverPlatter. Nov. 1998.

40. Scholarly Project

Victorian Web. Ed. George P. Landow. N.p., 2010. Web. 26 Aug. 2010.

for a short work within a scholarly project, list the author of the work followed by the title in quotations

Pyle, Forest. "'Frail Spells': Shelley and the Ironies of Exile." *Romantic Circles Praxis Series*. Ed. Orrin N. C. Wang. U of Maryland, 1999. Web. 27 Jan. 2010.

41. Complete Online Book

include information about original print publication

Chomsky, Noam. *Deterring Democracy*. Cambridge, MA: South End Press, 1992. *Znet*. Z Communications, n.d. Web. 5 Jan. 2009.

42. Short Work within an Online Book

include information
about the original
print book

Dickinson, Emily. "The Farthest Thunder That I
Heard." *The Complete Poems of Emily
Dickinson*. Boston: Little, 1924. N. pag.
Bartleby.com: Great Books Online. Web. 5 Dec.
2009.

43. Online Reference Work

"Zeugma." *A Handbook of Rhetorical Devices*. Ed.
Robert Harris. *VirtualSalt*. Robert Harris, 24 Dec.
2009. Web. 3 Mar. 2010.

44. Mailing List (listserv) Posting

Sherwood, Matthew. "Writing Process and Self
Discipline." *CompLit Listserv*. 15 Feb. 1995. Web.
19 Feb. 1995.

45. Newsgroup Posting

include the subject
line, the date of the
posting, and the date
of access

Otto, Santy. "Muslim Women in These Days." *Google
Groups: soc.feminism*. Google, 13 Nov. 2003.
Web. 14 Oct. 2009.

46. Real-Time Communication

if you are citing a
specific posting, start
with the name of the
speaker

Fosmire, Michael. "Chat with the Pocket PC
Development Team." *Microsoft Developer
Network*. Microsoft Corp., 27 Sept. 2002. Web.
25 Nov. 2009.

47. E-Mail Message

if e-mail was sent to
someone other than
you, substitute that
person's name for
"the author"

Garretson, Kate. "CUNY Proficiency Exam." Message
to the author. 22 Feb. 1999. E-mail.

48. Electronic Image of a Work of Art

> Picasso, Pablo. *Woman Seated in an Armchair*. 1938. Detroit Institute of Arts. *dia.org*. Web. 28 Dec. 2009.

49. Online Interview

> Cheney, Dick. Interview by Tim Russert. *MSNBC.com*. MSNBC.com, 14 Sept. 2003. Web. 20 Oct. 2009.

Sample Entries for Other Material

50. Film or Video Recording

when studying the film itself (as art form or as adaptation of a novel) title is listed first

> *Howard's End*. Dir. James Ivory. Sony, 1992. Film.

when studying the work of a director, list director's name first

> Miyazaki, Hayao, dir. *Spirited Away*. Buena Vista, 2001. DVD.

51. Interview

a private interview

> Boxer, Barbara, Sen. Personal interview. 17 Mar. 2000.

a broadcast interview

> Cruz, Nilo. Interview by Tony Cox. *The Tavis Smiley Show*. Natl. Public Radio. KUOW, Seattle. 22 Dec. 2003. Radio.

52. Lecture

> Barker, Cara. "Living on the Edge." C. G. Jung Society, Seattle. 21 Sept. 2003. Lecture.

53. Letter

use "MS" for manuscript or handwritten letters and "TS" for typed letters

> Entwhistle, Jacob, M.D. Letter to the author. 28 May 2000. TS.

54. Microform

> Sharpe, Lora. "A Quilter's Tribute." *Boston Globe*. 25 Mar. 1989. Microform. *NewsBank: Social Relations* (1989): fiche 6, grids B4-6.

55. Sound Recording

> Ford, Richard. "Jealous." *Women with Men*. Random
> House Audio, 1997. Audiocassette.
>
> Radiohead. *Kid A*. Capitol, 2000. CD.

56. Television Program

> "McLaughlin Group." PBS. KCTS, Seattle. 27 Dec.
> 2003. Television.

57. Podcast

for a podcast downloaded from a Web site, list the medium "MP3 file" at the end of the entry

> Goldston, David. "Will New Congress Take on Global
> Warming?" *Talk of the Nation Science Friday*.
> Narr. Ira Flatow. NPR, 19 Jan. 2007. MP3 file.

How to Cite Sources of Illustrative Materials

A final matter regarding documentation concerns the layout and labeling of graphs, tables, and other illustrative materials. In general, these items should be placed as close as possible to the text to which they relate. For tables, place a label and title over the table and a source note below it; for figures, place the label, title, and source note below. If a useful title is already included with the table or figure, you may use that title. Double space all of the text. (See the following examples.)

Table 1

Curbside Recycling Programs--Number Served, by Region: 1995-2001

Region	1995	1997	1999	2000	2001
Total	**7,375**	**8,969**	**9,349**	**9,247**	**9,704**
Northeast	2,210	3,406	3,414	3,459	3,421
South	1,281	1,344	1,581	1,427	1,677
Midwest	2,985	3,357	3,477	3,582	3,572
West	899	862	877	779	1,034

Source: United States, Bureau of the Census; *Statistical Abstract of the United States: 2003*; Washington: GPO, 2003; 220; Print.

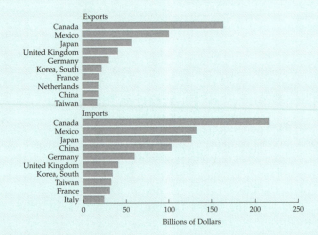

Fig. 1. Top Purchasers of U.S. Exports and Suppliers of U.S. General Imports: 2001, from: U.S. Bureau of the Census, *Statistical Abstract of the United States: 2003* (Washington: GPO, 2003) 800. Print.

Tables are referred to as "Tables," but graphs, pictures, diagrams, and other kinds of illustration are all referred to as "Figures" (usually abbreviated "Fig."). Each kind of item is numbered consecutively throughout the paper with Arabic numerals (Table 1, Table 2; Fig. 1, Fig. 2, Fig. 3). In addition to the source note that accompanies the table or figure itself, do not forget to include a citation in the works cited list. The citation for either the sample table or figure would be as follows:

United States. Bureau of the Census. *Statistical Abstract of the United States: 2003*. Washington: GPO, 2003. Print.

19

Using the APA (Author/Year) System

Many behavioral science instructors will ask you to follow the system devised by the American Psychological Association (APA), which uses parenthetical citations in the text that correspond to sources listed at the end of the paper under *References*. The APA system is similar in form to the MLA parenthetical-citation system; the major difference lies in the contents of the parenthetical citations.

- In the APA system, you generally give the year of publication in the parenthetical citation, whereas in the MLA system, you never put the date in the parentheses.
- In the APA system, you include the page numbers only for a quotation, not for paraphrases or summaries, as in MLA.

These differences are not trivial. The APA believes the most important information is the time the idea was presented to the world; the MLA is primarily concerned with precisely locating the information within the source.

The APA system is a variant on a general approach called the *author/year* system. (Some disciplines within the behavioral sciences have arrived at their own slightly different versions of the author/year system. Several of them are briefly illustrated in Chapter 20.)

Guidelines for Parenthetical Citations

Basic Format

- Insert the parenthetical note immediately after the last name of the author. You are strongly encouraged to mention the author's name in your text rather than in the parenthetical note. The note contains just the year of publication.

  Robinson (1986) asserted that child abuse in upper-middle-class homes manifests itself in subtler ways.

- If a source has two authors, mention both in all references.

  Martin and Elder (1969) demonstrated that abusive parents were usually themselves abused.

- If, for stylistic reasons, you do not mention the authors' names in your text, place them inside the note.

  It was shown in the late 1960s (Martin & Elder, 1969) that abusive parents were usually themselves abused.

- You can avoid using a parenthetical note by mentioning both author and date in your text.

  In 1969, Martin and Elder demonstrated that abusive parents . . .

- When you quote a source directly, use a note to indicate the page number as well as the date and author if they are not already clear in the text. For electronic or other works without page numbers, paragraph numbers may be used instead, preceded by the symbol ¶ or "para."

  Rogers (1984) believed that "virtually all female abusers suffered from primary splitting" (p. 67).
  One theorist believed that "virtually all female abusers suffered from primary splitting" (Rogers, 1984, p. 67).
  Denes (1980, ¶1) claimed that psychotherapy is an art that is "volatile, unpredictable, standardless in its outcome, subjective in its worth."

Punctuation

- As in the MLA system, parenthetical citations are included within the sentences to which they refer.
- Commas separate name from date when both appear inside a note.
- An ampersand (&) is used instead of *and* between authors' names when more than one name appears in a note (but use *and* when you mention coauthors in your text).
- The abbreviations "p." and "pp." are used to indicate page and pages, except after volume and issue numbers.

Sample Parenthetical Citations

A Source with More Than One Author. When a source has three, four, or five authors, cite all of the authors' names in the first reference; in later citations, use the first author's name and "et al." If a source has six or more authors, use the first author's surname and "et al." for the first and subsequent citations. If two of your sources have several authors with the same person or people heading both series of names, include as many of the names as necessary to distinguish the sources. In the following example, the lead author is the same in the third and fourth entries, but other authors are different; therefore, later references to either work must list the second author as well as the first.

> Gold, Bache, Cohen, and Arnach (1978) found that . . .
>
> Gold et al. (1978) were not so sure that . . .
>
> Marx, Walcott, Blau, and Johanssen (1985) said . . .
>
> Marx, Martin, and Schuster (1980) were convinced that . . .
>
> A study of college students (Marx, Walcott, et al., 1985) concluded that . . .

Authors with the Same Last Name. If two authors have the same last name, use initials to distinguish them, both in notes and within the text.

> J. Prescott (2001) tried testing infants . . .
>
> A later study (D. Prescott, 2003) could find no . . .

An Organization or a Government Agency as Author. If the author is an organization or a government agency, place the full name in the first note and the abbreviation in brackets; abbreviate thereafter.

An international agency (Organization for Economic Cooperation and Development [OECD], 2003) took a strong interest in . . .

A hotly contested survey by an international agency (OECD, 2003) came to the conclusion that . . .

Two or More Sources by the Same Author. If an author contributed more than one source to your list, and two of them were published in the same year, lowercase letters are added to the years.

Freud (1923a) first announced . . .

In a now-famous essay (Freud, 1923b), the idea of . . .

A Source with No Author Listed. When a source lists no author, use a short form of the title in the parenthetical note.

One source ("New Therapies," 2003) predicted that . . .

The references page would list this article as follows. Note that the article is listed without quotation marks, and only the first word is capitalized.

New therapies emerging for autoimmune skin disorder. (2003, Nov. 26). *Immunotherapy Weekly*, p. 105.

Indirect Source: A Source Quotes Another Writer. If one of your sources mentions the work of another author, and you want to refer to that other work, use this form:

Ashkenazi's work (cited in Beatty, 1992) showed . . .

Be sure to list Beatty's work, not Ashkenazi's, in your list of references because that is where you found the information.

An Entire Web Site. If you need to cite an entire Web site, not a specific document on the site, simply give the URL of the site as a parenthetical note. You need not list the site in the list of references.

Results of recent polls are available on the organization's home page (http://www.gallup.com).

Personal Communications. Letters, memos, phone conversations, e-mail messages, and postings to online discussion forums like newsgroups and mailing lists (listservs) are considered personal communications and are generally cited only in text, not in the references list.

S. A. Hatem (personal communication, May 5, 1996) . . .

However, if a posting is archived, include the source in the list of references.

Guidelines for a List of References

Basic Format

- Sources are listed alphabetically by their authors' last names or, when the author is not known, by the first word of the title, ignoring *A*, *An*, and *The*.
- No first names are given for authors, just initials (unless two people have the same last names and initials).
- When a source has more than one author, all authors' names are entered by last name, followed by initial(s). (This rule applies even to six or more authors.)
- The year of publication (inside parentheses) follows the author's name. When two or more sources have the same author, list the sources chronologically. If two or more articles appeared in the same year, use letters (a, b, c) to distinguish them, and list them alphabetically. Repeat the author's name in each case.
- Include the state of publication only if the city is not well known or could be confused with another city, and use postal state abbreviations.
- The first line of each entry starts at the left margin. Remaining lines indent five spaces (or one tab) from the margin.

Punctuation and Capitalization

- Book titles and periodical names and volume numbers are italicized.
- Titles of essays and periodical articles are not placed in quotation marks or italicized.
- Only the first word, proper nouns, and proper adjectives in book, essay, and article titles are capitalized. All main words in names of periodicals are capitalized, as is the first letter of the first word of a subtitle.
- Commas are used between authors' surnames and initials and between authors. With more than one author, an ampersand (&) is used before the last author's name.
- Periods separate the main parts of an entry: Author. (Date). Title. Publisher.

Documenting Sources

The following sample list will help you understand these points. (Only authors and titles are shown in this example so that you can concentrate on the basic guidelines.)

Freud, A. (1951). *An experiment in group upbringing.*

Freud, S. (1905). *Three essays on the theory of sexuality.*

Freud, S. (1910a). *Five lectures on psychoanalysis.*

Freud, S. (1910b). *Leonardo da Vinci and a memory of his childhood.*

Freud, S. (1931). *Female sexuality.*

Goldstein, J., Freud, A., & Solnit, A. J. (1979). *Before the best interests of the child.*

Klein, M. (1961). *Narrative of a child analysis.*

See page 239 for a list of standard abbreviations for bibliographical terms.

Directory to APA Style for References

Sample Entries for Books

1. One Author

omit *Publishers, Co.,* and *Inc.* in publisher names, but do not omit or abbreviate *University, Books,* or *Press*

Frydenberg, E. (1999). *Learning to cope: Developing as a person in complex societies.* New York, NY: Oxford University Press.

2. Two or More Authors

Zigler, E., & Muenchow, S. (1992). *Head Start: The inside story of America's most successful educational experiment.* New York, NY: Basic Books.

3. Editor

Sternberg, R. J., & Wagner, R. K. (Eds.). (1999). *Readings in cognitive psychology.* Fort Worth, TX: Harcourt.

4. Essay in a Collection

Giamatti, A. B. (1998). The green fields of the mind. In N. Dawidoff (Ed.), *Baseball: A literary anthology* (pp. 490-493). New York, NY: Library of America.

Sample Entries for Print Periodicals

(For electronic periodical articles, see the sample entries on page 275.)

5. Article in a Newspaper

Herbert, B. (2004, January 23). The other America. *The New York Times,* p. A23.

6. Article in a Magazine

For magazines published monthly, list the year and month. For weekly magazines, include the day. If a volume number is readily available, include it (in italics) after the title.

Bower, A. (2003, February 17). Sharing family values. *Time 161*(7), pp. 62-63.

pp. is not used when a volume number is listed

> Watkins, D. (2003, November). Brain not inflamed? Alzheimer's may not be an inflammation after all. *Scientific American, 289*(5), 24-26.

7. Article in a Journal

If the issues of a journal are continuously paginated over the course of the year, you do not need to include the issue number.

volume number is italicized; *pp.* is not included when a volume number is given

> Dunlosky, J., Kubat-Silman, A. K., & Hertzog, C. (2003). Effects of aging on the magnitude and accuracy of quality-of-encoding judgments. *American Journal of Psychology, 116*, 431-432.

When a journal is paginated by issue, include the issue number in parentheses after the volume number.

the volume number, but not the issue number, is italicized

> Scruton, R. (1996). The eclipse of listening. *The New Criterion, 15*(3), 5-13.

Sample Entries for Electronic Sources

For electronic sources in the list of references, APA style requires much of the same information as for print sources. The purpose of a citation for both types of sources is to give your reader the necessary information to retrieve the source. For electronic sources, the minimum information needed is the author and the title of the document; the date it was published or posted (if available) and the URL of the home page of the publication. Include the date of retrieval only if the content is likely to change.

If you need to break the URL because it will not fit on one line, do so only after a slash or before a period. Do not add a hyphen at the break, and remove a hyphen added by your word-processing program. The APA also recommends omitting sources that no longer exist on the Internet at the time you complete your work.

8. Document from a Nonperiodical Web Site

italicize title of document; if no author is listed, begin entry with title of document; do not include title of site

> *ACLU student drug testing cases across the nation.* (2002, March 15). Retrieved from http://www.aclu .org/DrugPolicy/DrugPolicy.cfm?ID=11001&c=79

if no date is given, type *n.d.* in parentheses where the date would normally appear.

Greenberg, D. L. (n.d.). *Urban girls and sports.* Retrieved from http://www.womenssports foundation.org

9. Article from an Online Periodical

Hyde, J. S., DeLamater, J. D., & Hewitt, E. C. (1998). Sexuality and the dual-earner couple: Multiple roles and sexual functioning. *Journal of Family Psychology, 12*(3), 354-368. Retrieved from http://www.apa.org/pubs/journals/fam/

an article from an online periodical with no print version

Lithwick, D. (2002, September 5). 9/11 and the law. *Slate.* Retrieved from http://slate.com

10. Article or Abstract from an Electronic Database

References for articles and abstracts found on electronic databases, such as LexisNexis or PsycARTICLES, should follow the format for the particular kind of print document, such as a newspaper article, an abstract, or a government report. Some online articles have a "digital object identifier" or DOI. Use the DOI at the end of the entry in place of the URL. If an article does not have a DOI, after the publication information add the URL of the home page of the journal.

an abstract of a journal article

Isaacs, K. T. (2003). Reality check: A look at the disturbing growth of violence in books for teens. *School Library Journal, 49*(10), 50-52. A110075844.

11. Document from a University Web Site

Oi, D. H., & Koehler, P. (1996). *Imported fire ants on lawns and turf.* Retrieved from University of Florida, Institute of Food and Agricultural Sciences website: http://edis.ifas.ufl.edu/LH059

12. Online Government Report

United States Food and Drug Administration. (2003, January). *FDA actions on new bioterrorism*

legislation. Retrieved from http://www.cfsan.fda
.gov/~dms/fsbtact5.html

13. E-Mail Message or Discussion-Group Posting

The APA suggests that you omit online sources such as e-mail and
postings to newsgroups and mailing lists (listservs) from your work because they are not connected with recognized scholarly organizations
as other sources usually are. If you do cite an e-mail or a posting from a
newsgroup or mailing list that does not archive its messages, do not include that source in your list of references: cite it only in the text, as a personal communication, as shown on pages 270–71.

**an archived
newsgroup posting**

Conrad, E. (1996, July 8). Proof of life after death
[Electronic mailing list message]. Retrieved
from news://sci.archeology

**an archived electronic
mailing-list (listserv)
posting**

Freed, A. (2001, February 24). Language use,
feminism, and economics [Electronic mailing
list message]. Retrieved from Feminists in
Linguistics electronic mailing list: http://
listservlinguistlist.org/archives/fling.html

Sample Entries for Other Kinds of Sources

14. Film or Video Recording

Ritchie, M. (Director). (1972). *The candidate* [Motion
picture]. United States: Warner.

15. Interview

**interview recorded on
tape or transcript (if
contents of interview
are not recoverable,
see discussion of per-
sonal communications,
pages 270–71)**

Schickele, P. (1996, June 2). [Interview by Margaret
Juntwait]. *Weekend around New York*. New York,
NY: WNYC Radio.

16. Review

review of a book

Mantel, H. (2001, March 29). The monster we know.
[Review of the book *Interpreter of maladies*, by
Jhumpa Lahiri]. *The New York Review of Books*,
48(5), 22-23.

APA

review of a motion picture (retrieved from an online periodical)

O'Hehir, A. (2002). Who's afraid of Virginia Woolf? [Review of the motion picture *The Hours*, 2003]. *Salon.com*. Retrieved from http://salon.com

17. Sound Recording

include recording artist in brackets if different from songwriter or composer; list recording date at end of entry if different from copyright date

Colvin, S. (1991). I don't know why. [Recorded by A. Krauss & Union Station]. On *Every time you say goodbye* [Cassette]. Cambridge, MA: Rounder Records. (1992)

18. Television Program

single episode

Kuttner, P. K., Moran, C., & Scholl, E. (Writers), & Chamberlain, W. (Executive Director). (1994, July 19). Passin' it on [Television series episode]. In D. Zaccardi (Executive Producer), *P.O.V.* New York, NY: WNET.

television series

Zaccardi, D. (Executive Producer). (1994). *P.O.V.* [Television series]. New York, NY: WNET.

20

Using Other Documentation Systems

Instructors in fields other than English or the social sciences will often require that you document sources using a system other than the MLA or APA systems explained in Chapters 18 and 19. This chapter explains two other systems that are widely used and then discusses the preferred system in each academic discipline and any distinctive features of that system as it is used in that discipline.

The *Chicago* (Endnote/Footnote) System

Some instructors, particularly those in the fields of history, philosophy, and religion, may prefer that you document your sources by inserting numbers in your text to refer to notations on a separate page of endnotes (called simply *Notes*) or at the foot of each page. The following guidelines pertain to one such documentation system, known as *Chicago* Style because it is based on the *Chicago Manual of Style,* 15th edition (Chicago: University of Chicago Press, 2003).

If you are using this system, insert a superscript (raised) number at all points where you would have used a parenthetical note. These numbers must run in sequence throughout the paper: 1, 2, 3, and so on. If you find you have left out a note after inserting all the numbers within the text, you must change all the succeeding numbers. Do not create "5a," for instance, when inserting an entry between 5 and 6.

After all the numbers have been placed within the text, make a list of notes at the end of the paper. Next to each number, enter the bibliographic information that precisely identifies the source of the quotation, paraphrase, or summary. Occasionally an instructor may ask you to place footnotes at the bottom of each page rather than compile a list of endnotes. The rules for punctuating footnotes are the same as those for endnotes, and both should be single-spaced with a blank line between each note (however, some instructors prefer double-spacing throughout the notes).

Insertion of Numbers within the Text

- Type each number half a space above the line (many word-processing programs place superscript numbers on command), and directly (no space) after the final punctuation of the sentence it refers to.
- For quotations that end in the middle of a sentence, place the number directly after the final quotation mark.

Here are examples in which numbers replaced parenthetical notes in Susanna Andrews's paper on Emily Dickinson.

Dickinson sent Higginson four poems, along with a letter containing this question: "Are you too deeply occupied to say if my Verse is alive?"[8] This . . .

Certainly, then, the woman Yvor Winters called "one of the greatest lyric poets of all time"[2] was all but unknown as a poet during her lifetime.

Paul Ferlazzo, for example, infers that Higginson's response to her first letter must have included some recommendations for altering, or "regularizing," her poems, along with a request for more of her work.[9]

When you quote from a literary work, use a note for the first reference, identifying the specific edition you used and informing your readers that all subsequent notes will be in-text parenthetical notes. After the first note, simply insert the pages or, as in the following quotation from *Paradise Lost*, the book and line numbers.

> Evil into the mind of God or Man
> May come and go, so unapprov'd, and leave
> No spot or blame behind: Which gives me hope
> That what in sleep thou didst abhor to dream,
> Waking thou never wilt consent to do. (*PL* 5.117-21)

Basic Endnote Format

This format differs from that of entries in the works cited list in the MLA parenthetical system, although the same basic questions are answered: Who? What? Where? When?

works cited   Cook, Blanche Wiesen. *Eleanor Roosevelt*. New York:
                         Viking, 1992.

endnote   1. Blanche Wiesen Cook, *Eleanor Roosevelt*
                         (New York: Viking, 1992), 79.

Here is the basic endnote format:

- The first line of each note indents five spaces to the note number; each subsequent line is typed flush with the left margin.
- Author's name is given in normal (not reverse) order.
- Commas replace the periods used in works cited. No comma is used before parentheses. No comma follows a title that ends with a question mark or an exclamation point.
- Parentheses surround publishing information.
- Page number(s) are added at the end. Do not use "p." or "pp." A comma comes between parentheses and page number(s).

A few samples of the most common situations should give you an idea of how to handle this system.

1. Editor or Translator

    1. Martin Gardner, ed., *The Annotated Alice: Alice's Adventures in Wonderland and Through the Looking Glass*, by Lewis Carroll (New York: Potter, 1960), iv-vi.

    2. Feodor Dostoevsky, *Crime and Punishment*, ed. George Gibian, trans. Jessie Coulson (New York: Norton, 1964), 142.

2. Essay in a Collection

    3. Gwendolyn Brooks, "The Rise of Maud Martha," in *Invented Lives: Narratives of Black Women 1860-1960*, ed. Mary Helen Washington, 430 (New York: Anchor-Doubleday, 1987).

3. Introduction, Preface, Foreword, or Afterword

> 4. Leon Edel, foreword to *The Thirties*, by Edmund Wilson, vii (New York: Farrar, 1980).

4. Article in a Journal

note the colon between date and page number, unlike the format for books

> 5. Lucinda Becker, "Presenting Gender: Changing Sex in Early Modern Culture," *Modern Language Review* 98, no. 1 (January 2003): 183.

5. Article in a Magazine or Newspaper

a comma rather than a colon separates the date and page numbers

> 6. Stephen Jay Gould, "A Most Ingenious Paradox," *Natural History*, December 1984, 20.

no comma follows a title that ends with a question mark or an exclamation point

> 7. Vaclav Smil, "The Future: Perfect or Posthuman?" *Natural History*, September 2002, 83.

enclose a quotation within a quotation in single quotation marks

> 8. "Presidential Panel Holds Hearings on 'Right to Die,'" *New York Times*, April 12, 1981, late edition, sec. 1.

6. Document from a Nonperiodical Web Site

For nonperiodical Web documents, include as much of the following as possible: author, title of the document, title of the Web site (italicized), name of the site's sponsor, and URL.

> 9. Henry Louis Gates Jr., "Are We Better Off," *The Two Nations of Black America*, PBS Online, http://www.pbs.org/wgbh/pages/frontline/shows/race/etc/gates.html.

when no specific author is named, list the site's sponsor as the author

> 10. The American Heart Association, "Healthy Lifestyle," http://www.americanheart.org/presenter.jhtml?identifier=1200009.

7. Article from an Online Periodical

If the work is an electronic reprint, include print publication information followed by the URL. Date of access is not necessary unless the content is likely to change.

online article also available in print

> 11. Junko Mori, "Task Design, Plan, and Development of Talk-in-Interaction: An Analysis of a

Small Group Activity in a Japanese Language Classroom," *Applied Linguistics* 23, no. 3 (September 2002): 325, http://www3.oup.co.uk/applij/hdb/Volume_23/Issue_03/230323.sgm.abs.html.

online article with no print version; no page references are included because article is unpaginated

12. Katharine Mieszkowski, "What's Labor Going to Do about Offshoring?" *Salon*, January 27, 2004, http://www.salon.com/tech/feature/2004/01/27/amy_dean/index_np.html.

8. Article from an Electronic Database

URL refers to the home page of the database service

13. Ewald Engelen, "How to Combine Openness and Protection? Citizenship, Migration, and Welfare Regimes," *Politics and Society* 31, no. 4 (December 2003), http://proquest.com.

Shortened Form for Second and Further References to Same Source

After you have produced one complete note for a particular source, you can use a shorter form for all subsequent references to the same source. The shortened form includes the author's last name, a shortened form (usually four words or fewer) of the title, and the page number. In this example, earlier notes would have given the complete bibliographic information for Freud's *Interpretation of Dreams* and his *Moses and Monotheism*. A comma goes between the author and title.

16. Freud, *Dreams*, 303.

17. Freud, *Moses*, 68.

In this system, as in the MLA parenthetical system, mentioning the source or the author in the text affects the amount of information that appears in the note.

Jehovah was originally the god of a local volcano, according to Freud.[19]

19. *Moses*, 23.

Don't carry this too far, however. Never give just the page number(s) in the shortened notes. Always mention either the author or the title unless a note refers to the same source as the previous one, in which case you can often simply use the Latin abbreviation *Ibid*.

17. Freud, *Moses*, 68.

18. Ibid.

19. Ibid., 23.

Do not overuse *Ibid.*, though, because it forces the reader to look back at a previous note to identify the reference. If an extended series of notes all refer to the same source, it is better to make the second and subsequent ones into parenthetical page citations in the text.

> Jehovah was originally the god of a local volcano, according to Freud (ibid., 23).

If you use the endnote system, you may not need to include a works cited page or bibliography with your paper. However, find out your instructor's preference. For a full example of the endnote system of documentation (including a bibliography), see the sample paper by Fred Hutchins in Chapter 22.

The Number System

A fourth system, sometimes called the *number system*, is used primarily in mathematics, computer sciences, chemistry, physics, and engineering. Each source is assigned a number in the list of references, and these numbers — shown in parentheses or as superscripts — are what readers see in text references, instead of page numbers or years. Sources are listed by the order in which they are used in the paper, not alphabetically.

numbers appear in parentheses

Widlow (1) discovered that cells injected with . . .

Breitenstein and Forester (2) attempted to convert . . .

Morgan (3) and Stanley (4) both argued that stress . . .

numbers appear as superscript

Widlow[1] discovered that cells injected with . . .

Even if you do not mention the author in the text of your paper, place only the number assigned to the material in the text. If you refer to more than one source at the same time, include the number assigned to each source.

> Recent experimentation (5, 6, 7) seems to indicate . . .

In these sciences, writers rarely quote their sources directly; however, if you quote, the page number must be included in the note.

> As Johnstone stated (2, p. 18), "The outcome depended on . . ."

Format Preferences for Various Academic Disciplines

Most disciplines use variations of either the APA (author/year) or the number system of citation. In-text citation styles resemble rather closely the models we have described in this text; there is more variation among different disciplines' approach to listing references. Find out your instructor's preference or consult one of the discipline-specific style guides mentioned later in this section.

When comparing citation styles for listing references in various fields, expect to see differences in these areas:

- placement of publication date
- use of underlining and quotation marks and capitalization for titles
- abbreviation of periodical names
- treatment of publisher's location and name

Sciences

As we mentioned in the preceding section, the physical and applied sciences generally use the number system. The biological and earth sciences (including biology, botany, geology, and zoology) mainly use the author/year system, except for the biomedical sciences (medicine, nursing, and health), which use the number system. For a complete description of the CSE [Council of Science Editors] style, see *Scientific Style and Format: The CSE Manual for Authors, Editors, and Publishers,* 7th edition (2006).

Consider the following examples of citation styles of some specific sciences.

- *Biology, botany,* and *zoology* use the author/year system and list references in alphabetical order. These examples follow basic CSE style for author/year citation.

all author names are inverted; no periods follow abbreviations; initial letters of first words of titles and proper nouns are capitalized; titles of articles are not placed in quotation marks; titles of books and periodicals are not underlined or italicized; page count is given for books

Hairston NG, Smith FE, Slobodkin LB. 1960. Community structure, population control, and competition. American Naturalist 94:421-25.

Ross C. 1995. Writing nature. New York: St Martin's. 650 p.

- *Chemistry* uses the number system and lists references in the order in which they are cited in the paper.

note omission of titles for periodical articles and use of underlining for book titles; journal years of publication are in bold type

(1) Raptolinsky, T. Chemists and the New Technology; Mills Ltd.: Manchester, **1976**; pp 102-109.

(2) McQuarrie, D.; Simon, J. D. Molecular Thermodynamics. **1999,** 42, 505-511.

- *Engineering* follows the same general format as physics (see below).
- *Mathematics* uses the number system and lists references in alphabetical order. For more information, see the American Mathematical Society's *The AMS Author Handbook: General Instructions for Preparing Manuscripts,* revised edition (Providence: AMS, 1996).

note that all titles are underlined

[1.] Paul Bennacerraf, God, the Devil, and Goedel, Monist 51 (1967), 9.

[2.] John Allen Paulos, Beyond Numeracy, New York, Vintage, 1991.

- *Physics* uses the number system and lists references in the order in which they are cited. For more information, see the American Institute of Physics' *Style Manual: Instructions to Authors and Volume Editors for the Preparation of AIP Book Manuscripts,* 5th edition (New York: AIP, 1995).

page numbers for books tell which pages are relevant to paper

[1]J. O. Hirschfelder, R. E. Wyatt, and R. D. Coalson, Lasers, Quanta, and Molecules (Wiley, New York, 1989), pp. 801-22, 867-90.

titles of articles are not given; titles of periodicals are not underlined

[2]J. M. Jauch, Are Quanta Real? A Galilean Dialogue (Indiana University Press, Bloomington, 1973), pp. 72-77.

[3]D. R. Hofstadter, Physical Review B, 14, no. 6, 45-64 (1976).

Social Sciences

The social sciences (business, economics, education, geography, physical education, political science, psychology, sociology, etc.) generally follow

APA style, except for history, which follows the *Chicago* endnote/footnote system or MLA style.

- *Business* and *economics* use the author/year system and list references in alphabetical order; a similar alternate style is shown here. See the American Management Association's *AMA Style Guide for Business Writing* (New York: AMACOM, 1996).

note that last item, although numbered like a periodical, is a pamphlet or small book, and no page numbers are given

Bloomfield, C. L., and Fairley, I. R. (1991). Business Communication: A Process Approach. San Diego: Harcourt Brace Jovanovich.

Easterlin, R. (1973). "Does Money Buy Happiness?" The Public Interest, 30, 1-17.

United States Department of Commerce. (1979). Survey of Current Business, 59, no. 7.

- *Education* generally uses APA format. MLA format is sometimes used for research in humanities education.
- *History* follows the *Chicago* endnote/footnote system or MLA format.
- *Political science* usually follows the APA format.
- *Psychology* uses the APA author/year system, but some journals use the number system. Both systems follow alphabetical order when listing references. Ask your instructor which to use.
- *Sociology* uses the author/year system and lists references in alphabetical order. Book and journal titles are not underlined, and article titles are not capitalized (after the first word) or enclosed in quotation marks. Your instructor's preferences may vary somewhat from this.

preferred form

Inglehart, Ronald. 1991. Culture shift in advanced industrial society. Princeton, NJ: Princeton University Press.

Reider, Noriko T. 2003. "Tranformation of the Oni." Asian Folklore Studies 84:133-158.

Reviewing Part Five

The following questions and exercises will help you reinforce and practice the skills covered in Part Five. For additional practice, visit <bedfordstmartins.com/writingresearch>.

Questions

1. Why do research papers include parenthetical citations? Is the answer the same for all disciplines?

2. When might you use a traditional footnote number while working with the MLA system of parenthetical documentation?

3. Explain why you would or would not cite a source for each of the following pieces of information. If the audience of your paper affects whether you would cite the source, explain why.

   - the definition of *palindrome*
   - the names of Emily Dickinson's father and mother
   - the latest census data about the size of the average American household
   - the poet T. S. Eliot's interpretation of the river in *Huckleberry Finn*
   - Dr. Elizabeth Kübler-Ross's concept of the appropriate attitudes toward dying patients
   - author Willa Cather's date and place of birth
   - results of a recent study of caffeine's effect on the heart
   - American patriot Nathan Hale's last words, "I regret that I have but one life to give for my country."

4. What are some similarities in the way that electronic sources and print sources are documented in the MLA system? What are some differences? Explain why there are different requirements for electronic sources.

Exercises

Construct a works cited page for the following sources, putting all of the information in the correct order, according to the MLA format. If you need help getting started, note that the first five of the following items appear in the bibliography for the Dickinson paper in Chapter 22.

1. Your research led you to a book titled Emily Dickinson: A Collection of Critical Essays, in which you found an essay called Emily

Dickinson and the Limits of Judgment. The book was edited by Richard B. Sewall, and the essay was the work of Yvor Winters. The essay begins on page 38 and ends on page 56. The book was published in 1963 by Prentice-Hall, the location of which was shown as Englewood Cliffs, New Jersey.

2. Your research uncovered an essay, Father and Daughter: Edward and Emily Dickinson, which was published in a journal, American Literature, in January 1960. This is volume 40, and the essay covers pages 510 to 523. The writer is Owen Thomas.

3. When quoting Emily Dickinson's poetry, you used a collection called The Complete Poems of Emily Dickinson, which you found online at a site titled Bartleby.com: Great Books Online. The URL for the book is http://www.bartleby.com/113, and it was published electronically in June 2000. You accessed the site on July 15, 2000. The book was originally published in 1924 by Little, Brown and Company, located in Boston, Massachusetts.

4. When quoting the poet's letters, you used a three-volume collection called The Letters of Emily Dickinson, which was published in Cambridge, Massachusetts, by the Harvard University Press in 1958. The editors were Thomas H. Johnson and Theodora Ward.

5. You read a book written by the critic Paul J. Ferlazzo in 1976. The book is titled Emily Dickinson and was published by Twayne Publishers, which is located in Boston, Massachusetts.

6. You read a tribute to the poet, called The First Lady of Mt. Holyoke, which appeared in the South Hadley (Massachusetts) Gazette on December 10, 1984. This unsigned essay appeared on the second and third pages of the second section of the newspaper.

7. You wrote a letter to a professor at Mt. Holyoke College, Joanna Caldwell, who is an authority on the poet and her works. You quote a remark from her reply to you, which was written on November 4, 2003.

8. You read an article in the magazine Psychology Today, written by John Forsyte, Joanna Caldwell, and Edgar Polishook. The article, titled Emily Dickinson: Inhibited Genius?, appeared in the July 1979 issue on pages 68 to 80.

9. You read a review of Ferlazzo's book (see item 5), written by Joanna Caldwell, which was published in PMLA, volume 65, pages 343 to 345. This issue was published in May 1980.

10. You find an article about Dickinson on the ProQuest periodical database called "I'm Nobody! Who are you? Are you — Nobody — Too?" However, you have lost your notes on everything but its title. Use a periodical database to find the article and construct a works cited entry for it.

Part Six

Preparing the Manuscript

21

Following Format Requirements

As you may already know, presentation is an important part of any research paper. The style in which you communicate strongly influences how well your readers understand what you are trying to say or how willingly they accept your argument.

The first rule in preparing a paper to be turned in is to read it over carefully for spelling, mechanical, or grammatical errors (see Chapter 16). Corrections should be made before the final copy is printed or completed rather than immediately before you turn it in. Written corrections on your work are usually not acceptable.

College research papers should be printed using a good-quality printer. (In some cases you may be allowed to submit an electronic version of your paper.) Be sure to save at least one electronic file of your paper and a backup printed copy.

Papers should follow specific formatting rules and guidelines. Your instructor will likely review the format he or she prefers. If not, however, the rules listed here are standard for all academic and professional writing and should serve as basic guidelines for you.

Basic Formatting

1. Use 8½-by-11-inch, high-quality white paper.
2. Leave 1-inch margins on all four sides: top, bottom, left, and right.
3. Double space the lines of your paper.
4. Print the paper with a high-quality print setting. Use a laser printer if possible.

Abiding by these rules will result in professional-looking written work that will be easy for your readers to follow and comprehend. Specific kinds of research papers may call for more specific formatting decisions, but this is something that you will need to discuss with your instructor.

Following a Particular Format

Your instructor will usually tell you if he or she wants you to follow a particular formatting style such as MLA or APA. The format that you work with can determine such decisions as how you list information on a works cited or references page and whether you use footnotes or endnotes. Make certain, then, that before you complete your paper you have worked with the format that your instructor recommends.

Creating a Title Page

A separate title page can be useful and pleasing to the eye because it sets off information that is more important to the identification than the content of the paper. In addition to the title of your paper, information that typically appears on the title page includes your name, the class the paper was written for, your instructor's name, and the date on which the paper was handed in, in that order. The title should be centered on the page, and the other information should appear on separate lines, ending 1 inch from the bottom of the page. The sample papers in Chapter 22 show example title pages.

Understanding Abstracts

Some instructors require students to write abstracts for their research papers. An abstract is a concise summary that allows a reader to grasp the purpose and major ideas of a paper without having to delve into all the details.

Abstracts are more commonly encountered in science papers and are usually required for papers using the APA documentation format.

The idea behind the use of abstracts is simple: an abstract saves time for other researchers who want to determine quickly whether an article will be useful for their own research project. Thus, an abstract must present a complete picture of what the article covers but be brief enough to let readers know quickly whether reading all of it will be worthwhile.

The research paper on the fire ant, *Solenopsis invicta*, is preceded by an abstract (see page 330). When you read the paper (in Chapter 22), take time to consider how well its writer summarized his work in his abstract.

Paginating Your Paper

Except for the title page, all pages of your research paper should be numbered, including the pages containing the list of sources at the end. Unless your instructor tells you differently, page numbers should appear in the upper right corner. If you are using MLA format, precede your page numbers with your last name in case any pages accidentally become separated from the rest of the document. If you are working in APA format, instead of your name, use the first two major words of the title of your paper. You can follow either of these styles automatically by using a header function on many word-processing programs. Headers or page numbers should appear ½ inch from the top of the paper and flush with the right margin, 1 inch from the right side of the page.

Selecting an Appropriate Font

Though your word-processing program may afford you a large selection of fonts, many of them are not acceptable for academic writing. When selecting a font, use the following guidelines:

1. Use a 12-point type size.
2. Choose a font that is as simple and professional looking as possible. In general, use a serif font, in which the characters have fine lines projecting from their ends, rather than a sans serif font like this.
3. Avoid fonts that look like handwriting and *ornate* fonts. They can be difficult to read and will not give your work the seriousness that it deserves.
4. If your word-processing program allows you to use *italics,* check with your instructor to make sure that he or she does not prefer underlining.
5. Keep your font consistent throughout your work unless you have a strong reason for doing otherwise.

Using Color

If you have access to a color printer, you may want to use color to draw attention to important elements in your paper, such as visuals. Keep in mind, though, that color works much like variation in fonts: it can easily become too much of a good thing. When deciding whether to use color, consider the following guidelines:

1. Color can draw the reader's eye to specific details and can make images more lively, distinct, and easy to read.

2. Overusing color looks confusing and unprofessional. In general, use italics or underlining rather than color for highlighting important words in the text, and do not print the main text of your document in a color other than black.

3. If you are using color for anything other than reproducing a visual, the fewer and more consistent colors you use, the better.

22

Four Sample Research Papers

This chapter contains four sample student research papers. These papers were chosen as samples not only because they demonstrate competence in the research techniques described in this book but also because the students were writing for different academic disciplines and therefore used slightly different approaches to their projects.

The first paper, "The New Immigrants: Asset or Burden?" and the second paper, "Emily Dickinson's Reluctance to Publish," illustrate MLA documentation style and procedures. The third paper, *"Solenopsis invicta:* Destroyer of Ecosystems," illustrates APA style, a system used by researchers in various scientific and social-science disciplines. The fourth paper, "Cotton Mather's Necessary Witches," illustrates the *Chicago Manual of Style* endnote/footnote method of documentation.

The New Immigrants: Asset or Burden?

by

Shirley Macalbe

Professor Alan Sandalt

Humanities 1101

December 11, 2003

Macalbe ii

Outline

THESIS: From the findings of experts on immigration, we can conclude that if the new immigrants have economic effects on the United States similar to those that earlier immigrants have had, then they will prove to be, for the most part, an asset rather than a burden.

Introduction

   I. Background

      A. Immigration as historically controversial issue in the United States

      B. Immigration as current issue of controversy

      C. Economic issues as principal reasons for resistance to immigration

  II. Consideration of "asset vs. burden" question

      A. Past history of immigration as possible predictor of value of new immigrants

      B. Agreement among many experts that past history bodes well for success of most new immigrants

 III. Student interviews

      A. Purpose

      B. Selection of interviewees

      C. Selection of interviews for analysis

      D. Analysis of interviews

 IV. Controversies on impact of immigrants

      A. Lacey and Isbister: little or no competition between immigrants and Americans for jobs

      B. Muller and Fogel: evidence of some competition

Macalbe iii

    C. Miles: immigrant pressure as one major cause of the Los Angeles riot in 1992

    D. Question of whether immigrants cause problems or intensify already existing problems

V. Encouraging patterns of immigrant economic history

    A. Fogel: despite some negative effects on low-skill workers, overall impact of immigration strongly positive

    B. Isbister: based on models and other evidence, optimistic outlook for success of new immigrants

    C. Lacey: immigrants a benefit and "essential" to continued economic health of America

VI. Challenges to claim that immigrants are economic burden on society

    A. Muller on relationship between taxes and immigrants

    B. Isbister on immigrant taxes vs. services

    C. Lacey on theory that immigrants "overwhelm" public assistance programs

    D. Seller on growth of self-help organizations in immigrant communities of the past

Conclusion

Macalbe 1

The New Immigrants: Asset or Burden?

The ideal image of the United States, symbolized
by the Statue of Liberty, is of a country that welcomes
immigrants and provides them with opportunities to
succeed in their new surroundings. It is certainly true
that millions of people from foreign lands have come
here and have improved their lives. But a study of the
history of immigration to the United States also shows
that periods of heavy immigration have caused
controversy in this country about the desirability of
allowing so many foreigners to enter. And in the midst of
such controversy, as Elizabeth Midgley notes, many
Americans who voiced opposition to immigration have,
from time to time, succeeded in forcing legislation to
limit the flow of newcomers to America.

Immigration has once again become a
controversial issue in the United States because large
numbers of foreigners have been entering the country
in recent years. Most of these new immigrants, unlike
the great waves of immigrants in the past, are not from
Europe. According to the U.S. Citizenship and
Immigration Services, of the more than thirteen million
people to enter the United States as legal immigrants
between 1989 and 2002, the overwhelming number were
from developing countries. More specifically, the INS
reports, all of the ten countries that were the largest
sources of immigrants during this period were in Latin
America, the Caribbean, and Asia. (See Table 1.) In

Introductory background paragraph

Reference to entire work

Controversial nature of subject offers reason for research

Preparing the Manuscript

Macalbe 2

Table 1

Immigrants Admitted, by Top 10 Countries of Birth, 1989-2002

All Countries	13,850,874
Mexico	3,761,410
Philippines	730,805
China	606,368
India	586,541
Vietnam	576,817
Dominican Republic	453,774
El Salvador	417,885
Korea	279,609
Haiti	263,135
Cuba	263,135

Source: United States, Dept. of Homeland Security,
U.S. Citizenship and Immigration Services; *2002 Yearbook of Immigration Statistics* (Washington: GPO, 2003) 16-19. *uscis.gov.* Web. 21 Nov. 2003.

assessing the effect of these numbers, Nathan Glazer, a professor of sociology, explains that the American public is undecided about whether these new immigrants will make the United States a stronger nation or a weaker one (3).

Question behind this research

Throughout U.S. history, opponents of immigration have raised racial, religious, and nationalistic objections or questions about large-scale immigration to the United

Macalbe 3

States (Jones 247-305). Naturally, since the September 11, 2001, terrorist attacks against the United States, commentators such as Michelle Malkin have raised security concerns related to immigration policies (30). However, much opposition to immigration is also expressed in economic terms. For example, Dan Lacey, a workplace consultant, business journalist, and editor, found that "research on immigration attitudes" shows that many Americans who oppose immigration fear losing their jobs to immigrants (41). In the same economic vein, Thomas Muller, an economist with the Urban Institute, points out the widespread concern among Americans that the new immigrants use welfare and other public aid programs to such an extent that they are a "financial burden" on government and, therefore, a financial burden on American taxpayers (126-27).

It is, of course, impossible to predict with certainty what permanent economic effects the new immigrants will have on the United States. But sociologists, economists, journalists, consultants, and other experts on immigration affairs have investigated the economic effects of past immigration. From their findings, we can conclude that if the new immigrants have similar economic effects on the United States as earlier immigrants have had, then they will prove to be, for the most part, assets rather than burdens.

As part of the background for my research, I took the opportunity to conduct informal interviews on my

Mixture of quotation and paraphrase

Two sources connected

Nature of sources

Thesis statement

Preparing the Manuscript

Macalbe 4

Preparing the Manuscript

Explanation for interview portion of paper—note use of first person when researcher refers to herself

campus with selected students. The purpose was to gather firsthand impressions about what economic effects the students perceived the new immigrants have had, or might have, on the country. And since I attend a community college in New York City--a city with a large population of new immigrants--I had the chance to talk to students for whom the new immigrants were real people, and not just textbook statistics.

Explanation for interviewee selection

In selecting potential students to interview, I looked for U.S.-born American citizens with no direct ties to the developing countries that make up the great majority of new immigrants. I did this because I wanted to gather impressions and opinions that could be offered with as few preconceptions as possible. From thirty-five attempted interviews, I selected the twenty in which students spoke at some length to the topic and produced fairly complete expressions of how they thought the new immigrants were affecting, or might affect, the economic status and future of the United States. Of the group, six were native-born African Americans; seven were native-born Americans with immigrant roots in northern Europe; seven were native-born Americans with immigrant roots in southern Europe. Twelve of the students were male, and eight were female.

Explanation for selection of interviews used in analysis of results

Specific identification of selected interviewees

Criteria for presenting data from interviews

In presenting the following results of my interviews, I selected only those responses that related directly to the topic of this paper. In addition, I selected only those opinions that were expressed, in

Macalbe 5

one way or another, by a majority of the students.   **Presentation of findings from interviews**
Again, my purpose was not to construct a scientific study
but to gather impressions from the campus that
would get me started on my projected research and that
might offer some chances to compare the opinions of
students with the findings of experts.

1. None of the students expressed a definite
   opinion in answering the question "Do you think
   the new immigrants will be an economic asset
   or an economic burden to the country?" Some
   said they had trouble thinking of people as
   "assets" or "burdens" in an economic sense and
   did not think they could evaluate the
   immigrants in that way. A majority (eleven)
   responded much as one student, Joseph Verano,
   did: "Everybody here except the native
   Americans, maybe, came from someplace else.
   Most of us did OK, so I guess these new people
   have a chance to do OK."

2. When asked about problems they thought the
   new immigrants were causing, seventeen were   **"Problem" identified through interviews**
   of the opinion that the immigrants were taking
   away jobs from native-born Americans because
   the immigrants were willing to work for less
   money than Americans would accept. Eight
   complained that the immigrants were even
   competing with Americans for part-time jobs,
   such as waiting on tables and pumping gas, the

Preparing the Manuscript

Macalbe 6

kinds of jobs students look for to earn money
while attending school.

Second "problem" identified through interviews

3. Another problem that a majority (seventeen)
brought up had to do with what they called
welfare. They claimed that too many immigrants
were getting money from the government,
causing Americans to pay higher taxes to
support them. When asked if they thought the
immigrants were only interested in getting
welfare and not in getting jobs, seven of the
seventeen said they thought that was the case.
For these students, welfare was a permanent
way of life for many immigrants.

Transition paragraph, including restatement of thesis

With information and impressions from my
interviews, I turned to see what the experts had to say
about the economic effects the immigrants were having
on the United States. As previously stated, my research
led me to conclude that the experts generally agreed
that, based on the past history of immigration, the
newcomers should be a benefit to the economic growth
of the United States.

Relationship between interviews and library sources

Interestingly, but not surprisingly, the students
brought up a number of points that the experts discuss in
their studies of immigration. Lacey, as was shown, points
to the fear that immigrants may take away jobs from

Subtopic: economic issues as principal cause of resistance to immigration

Americans as the major reason for opposition to the new
immigration. However, Lacey does not agree with this
perception of immigrant impact on jobs. He claims that

Preparing the Manuscript

Macalbe 7

research shows "that immigrants generally do not compete with Americans for jobs." Instead, Lacey continues, the record shows that while immigrants take over low-paying jobs, other Americans move into better-paying jobs and improve their lives (182). Professor John Isbister of the University of California, Santa Cruz, also points out that immigrants may take jobs that Americans generally refuse to do. By "performing the most unpleasant tasks in the marketplace," immigrant workers help increase the country's productivity (147).

Another indication that immigrant workers do not pose significant threats for job competition is the fact that the AFL-CIO, the nation's largest labor union, is working for the rights of immigrant workers, even those who are undocumented. Rather than calling for deportation, the AFL-CIO has undertaken a campaign to remedy the labor abuses these workers suffer and "to make the public aware of the important role undocumented immigrant workers play in the nation's workforce" ("Workers' Stories"). It seems reasonable that if the AFL-CIO supports the rights and praises the contributions of undocumented immigrant workers, there is at least a strong perception that these workers do not take away jobs.

Lacey and Isbister may be accurate in a general sense, and the AFL-CIO may be right in pointing out abuses and contributions of immigrant workers, but other research shows that immigrant impact on jobs is

Note refers to quoted and paraphrased passage

Preparing the Manuscript

Transition to subtopic: possible problems caused by immigration

Macalbe 8

more severe than these sources seem to imply, even if
the impact is rather limited. Thomas Muller, for example,
has found that immigrants do compete with some
"unskilled workers" in certain areas and with "some low-
skilled native-born workers unable to improve their
occupational status and unwilling (or unable) to move
from areas with large numbers of low-skill, low-wage
immigrants to other areas" (133). Walter Fogel, a
Use of one source to support another professor of industrial relations, supports Muller's
contention. He tells us that late-nineteenth- and early-
twentieth-century immigrants joined the oversupply of
unskilled laborers in the United States, causing
additional economic hardship for Americans who were
already doing poorly (98).

    Jack Miles, a journalist for the *Los Angeles Times*,
discusses an important event in relation to the effect of
immigration on the lives of underprivileged Americans.
Periodical mentioned to clarify source of journalist's essay In an *Atlantic Monthly* article, he argues that
immigration played a large role in the riot that enflamed
Los Angeles in July 1992. Miles contends that the "black
rage" unleashed by African Americans during that riot
was not just the result of the acquittal of a number of
Partial summary of periodical article in relation to subtopic white police officers who had been charged with use of
excessive force in what seemed to be--according to most
people who saw parts of a videotape of the incident--a
brutal beating of an African-American motorist, Rodney
King. For Miles, behind the outbreak of violence was the
desperation of "fifteenth-generation African Americans"

Preparing the Manuscript

Macalbe 9

who were being forced to compete for low-wage jobs and limited community resources with "first-generation Latin Americans and Asian Americans" (51). Miles's article is really aimed at questioning U.S. immigration policies. He fears that the country may be forced to choose between its humane tendency to admit people who are desperately seeking a new life in America and the obligation to improve the lives of many African Americans who have suffered from a long history of prejudice and neglect.

 In recognizing these problems related to immigration and economic pressures, we should keep in mind professor of social history Maxine Seller's point that periods of intense opposition to immigration in the United States have been "expressions of problems within the nation as a whole" (199). So, we might ask whether immigrants are the cause of the problems we have been discussing, or whether they intensify certain problems that have been simmering within the United States. In concluding his article, Miles makes clear that in regard to the Los Angeles riot and the conditions that fostered it, the nation as a whole may well be responsible. He talks of "that old and still unpaid debt" that goes back to the Civil War. He is referring, of course, to the promise of a nation in which African Americans are finally afforded their rightful place in a society where prejudice and fear do not set one group against another (68).

Presentation of the cause-and-effect question in relation to immigration problems

Macalbe 10

Transition to subtopic: "encouraging patterns" in support of thesis

When we go beyond the particular problems in which immigration may play a part, however, the history of immigration in the United States shows encouraging patterns. Thus even though Fogel summarizes the negative effects of immigration on low-skill workers in the past, his overall assessment of the immigrants' impact on the nation's economic health is strongly positive:

Direct quotation with ellipsis

"The economic growth to which immigrants contributed mightily brought . . . opportunities for millions of Americans and much of the basis for the high standard of living that most enjoy today" (98). In addition, Isbister uses theoretical models to show

Summary of findings that offer additional support

positive economic impacts that the new immigrants will have on U.S. society. Immigrant labor adds to the economy's overall production, increasing capital. In turn, this capital may create more jobs and increase wages for all (147).

Continued support of thesis

In a strong defense of immigration, Lacey denounces those who would restrict the flow of newcomers, going so far as to say that immigration is not only beneficial to America but also essential to its future economic growth. He berates what he calls the "standard wisdom" that says that whenever a new wave of immigrants arrives, the economic wealth of those who are already here will go down.

Indented long quotation used to preserve tone and wording of the passage

> Standard wisdom notwithstanding, those who study the American economy scientifically know that both consumption

Macalbe 11

and immigration *add* to America's affluence,
rather than subtract from it. In a consumption-
based economy such as America's, ever-rising
consumption has always been the seemingly
magical force that makes wonderful things
rise from the bare earth. (171)

The second major economic point that my student
interviewees showed concern about, and that a number
of the experts I consulted commented on, was the
perception that immigrants cause financial burdens **Second major**
to Americans because immigrants have a great **objection to**
immigration
dependence on welfare and other government aid **challenged**
programs. On this point, evidence from the past and
some present indications tend to show that new
immigrants do, initially, put some financial stress on
communities where they are represented in large
numbers. In most cases, however, the stress is usually
temporary, and immigrants, by and large, return more
economic assets to such communities than they received
initially.

Muller, using past evidence and more recent data, **Specific support**
for challenge
explains that taxes will be "somewhat above average" **in previous**
for established residents in areas where new **paragraph**
immigrants decide to live in numbers. He adds,
however, that the tax money is usually made up for by
the profits the community gets from the economic
activity of the immigrants. "On balance," Muller says,
"the economic benefits of immigration . . . tend to exceed

private and in some areas public costs" (133). Isbister points out that immigrants are paying taxes in the areas where they live. "Most work for employers who are required by law to deduct anticipated income taxes . . . , and they have no way of avoiding the sales, property, and excise taxes that Americans pay" (154). At the same time, because of legal and cultural barriers, immigrants tend to have less access to government services such as education, health care, and welfare. Therefore, they may "absorb less government spending than demographically comparable natives" (153). And Lacey, again attacking standard wisdom, claims that the idea that "impoverished immigrants" will overwhelm the welfare system is false. He says that "a number of studies have discredited that theory" and have found, instead, that a good number of the new immigrants have cultural "aversions" to seeking public assistance (185). If Lacey is correct, we might expect to see a growing number of self-help organizations in ethnic communities where new immigrant groups have gathered. In the past, Seller explains, these organizations and communities served not only groups of immigrants but also the country as a whole by providing financial assistance and a sense of security for great numbers of desperate people in a period when the United States offered little economic security to anyone (171). If the future is similar to the past in this regard, the growth of such self-help activities should further reduce any possible

Preparing the Manuscript

Speculation on future based on pattern of the past

Macalbe 13

financial burden the new immigrants might place on Americans.

It is worth keeping in mind that the past does not always accurately predict the future. However, if most of the immigrants who have come to the United States in **Conclusion** the recent past follow patterns of economic upward mobility similar to those of immigrants who came to America in the more distant past, then, at the least, the new immigrants will--in the words of one of my interviewees--"probably have a chance to do OK." At best, they may provide the impetus for a new age of economic prosperity and growth in the United States.

Macalbe 14

Works Cited

Fogel, Walter. "Nonimmigrant Labor Policy: Future Trend or Aberration?" Papademetriou and Miller 93-122.

Glazer, Nathan, ed. *Clamor at the Gates: The New American Immigration*. San Francisco: Inst. for Contemporary Studies, 1985. Print.

Isbister, John. *The Immigration Debate: Remaking America*. West Hartford: Kumarian, 1996. Print.

Jones, Maldwyn Allen. *American Immigration*. Chicago: U of Chicago P, 1960. Print.

Lacey, Dan. *The Essential Immigrant*. New York: Hippocrene, 1990. Print.

Malkin, Michelle. *Invasion: How America Still Welcomes Terrorists, Criminals, and Other Foreign Menaces to Our Shores*. Washington: Regnery, 2002. Print.

Midgley, Elizabeth. "Comings and Goings in U.S. Immigration Policy." Papademetriou and Miller 41-69.

Miles, Jack. "Blacks vs. Browns." *Atlantic Monthly* Oct. 1992: 41+. Print.

Muller, Thomas. "Economic Effects of Immigration." *Glazer* 109-33.

Papademetriou, Demetrios G., and Mark J. Miller, eds. *The Unavoidable Issue: U.S. Immigration Policy in the 1980s*. Philadelphia: Inst. for the Study of Human Issues, 1983. Print.

Macalbe 15

Seller, Maxine. *To Seek America: A History of Ethnic Life
in the United States.* Englewood: Ozer, 1977. Print.
United States. Dept. of Homeland Security. U.S.
Citizenship and Immigration Services. *2002
Yearbook of Immigration Statistics.* Washington:
GPO, 2003. 16-19. *uscis.gov.* Web. 21 Nov. 2003.
Verano, Joseph. Personal interview. 15 Nov. 2003.
"Workers' Stories of Abuse, Exploitation Point to Need for
Immigration Reform." *AFL-CIO: America's Union
Movement.* AFL-CIO, 6 Sep. 2001. Web. 27 Nov. 2009.

Preparing the Manuscript

Emily Dickinson's Reluctance to Publish

by

Susanna Andrews

English 102: American Literature

Section 3c

Professor Ann Leigh

August 2, 2000

Andrews ii

Outline

Introductory paragraph, including thesis statement

I. Background of the "myth of tragic Emily"

   A. Life in brief

      1. Retreat from social life

      2. Tentative effort to find an audience

      3. Eventual publication of her work

   B. First biographies

      1. The myth's genesis

      2. Its revision in recent years

   C. Refutation of "unworldly" image through analysis of poems

      1. The vocabulary (Thomas; Howard)

      2. The content (Griffith)

II. The correspondence between Dickinson and Higginson

   A. The beginnings of their dialogue

      1. Higginson's article

      2. Dickinson's approach

   B. Higginson's first letter to the poet

      1. "Surgery" advised

      2. Request to see more poems

   C. Higginson's second letter

      1. Further revision advised

      2. Dickinson's response--disavowal of ambition

   D. Interpretations of Dickinson's reaction

      1. Disavowal questioned

      2. Higginson's blindness noted

Andrews iii

III. Dickinson's view of herself as an artist
  A. Her state of mind
    1. Self-confidence
    2. Realization that the world was not ready
    3. Refusal to compromise
  B. Dickinson's real reason for approaching Higginson
    1. Need for special kind of advice
    2. The painful first publications
  C. Higginson's effect on Emily Dickinson
    1. His limitations recognized
    2. His confusion in face of genius
    3. Her rejection of his advice
IV. Evidence from Dickinson's poetry
  A. Choice between fame and popular recognition
    1. Kher's interpretation of poem
    2. Poem's suggestion of her choice
  B. Choice between publication and artistic integrity
    1. Dickinson's decision to forgo publication
    2. Opposition of immortality and time
Conclusion

Andrews 1

Emily Dickinson's Reluctance to Publish

At her death in 1886, Emily Dickinson left behind
over seventeen hundred poems. Of this number,
only ten were published while she was alive, and
all of these through the initiatives of others (Benfey 4).
Certainly, then, the woman Yvor Winters called "one
of the greatest lyric poets of all time" (40) was all but
unknown as a poet during her lifetime. For many
years after her poems first appeared in 1890, her
reluctance to publish was attributed to a supposed
unconcern for worldly matters, including literary
fame. Literary critics, serious biographers, and writers
of fictionalized accounts of her life created an image
of Emily Dickinson as a timid, reclusive, mystical
thinker who was too absorbed in personal sorrows
and ecstasies to be concerned with literary recognition.
And this image persists, to a great extent, in the public
mind today.[1]

Since the late 1950s, however, a new view of the poet
has been emerging. This view, based on close studies of
Dickinson's life, letters, and poetry, reveals an artist well
aware of her worth, who deliberately chose to withhold
her poems from the world until they could be valued as
unique artistic creations, even if this meant postponing
fame until after her death.

Beginning in her mid-twenties, Emily Dickinson
gradually retreated from the many stimulating personal
relationships that had filled her early life. By her late

Introduction

Note includes page number given onscreen

Question behind this research

The traditional view

Extra information offered in an endnote

Nature of sources

Thesis statement

Subtopic: background of the myth

Preparing the Manuscript

Andrews 2

thirties, her retirement was complete; she passed the rest
of her days living with her parents and her younger
sister, who managed the household. During her later
years, Emily Dickinson had virtually no direct contact
with anyone outside her immediate family. While she
was still connected to her circle of friends, Dickinson
made at least one tentative attempt to find an audience
for her poetry, but only a handful of verses were
published anonymously, most of them in a local
newspaper, and these were subjected to considerable
editing. Upon the poet's death at fifty-six, her sister
discovered over one thousand poems and initiated an
effort to publish them. Beginning four years later, in
1890, these poems finally appeared in print (Sewall 1:
4-11).

Over the years, as her following grew, Emily
Dickinson became the subject of a number of highly
romanticized biographies. Her admirers were trying to
establish a connection between her cloistered existence
and the powerful passions that course through much of her
finest poetry. Only after scholarly editions of her letters
and poetry appeared in the 1950s were literary critics in a
good position to produce an accurate picture of the poet's
life and her attitude toward her art. Even so, a good deal of
the mystery remains with us.

The idea that Emily Dickinson knew very little of
the real world has been disputed by recent studies of her

Preparing the Manuscript

Note refers to the entire paragraph, summarizing source

Subtopic: refutation of myth

Andrews 3

life and works. One biographer and critic, Owen Thomas, finds a remarkable number of legal, political, and financial words and expressions in her poetry. This fact leads him to conclude that Dickinson "was well aware of the world outside her little room, that in fact she used the language of this outside world to create some of her best poetry" (523). In the same vein, William Howard points out that the largest group of specialized words in Dickinson's poems reflects the scientific and technological discussions of her day (230). Further disagreement with the image of the poet as a shy, unworldly creature comes from Clark Griffith, who sees her as a person whose sensibility was "responsive to the brutalities which life imposes on the individual, and acutely aware of the nothingness with which existence seems surrounded" (5-6). If we reject the image of Emily Dickinson as a mystical recluse who had little interest in the real world, we must also question the theory that she did not publish her poems out of the same lack of interest.

Perhaps the most substantial evidence regarding Dickinson's reluctance to publish can be found in her letters to a professional writer and social reformer, Thomas Wentworth Higginson. This correspondence began in 1862, after Higginson published an article in the April issue of the *Atlantic Monthly*, entitled "Letter to a Young Contributor," which offered some practical advice for beginning writers seeking to publish. As a result of reading this article, Dickinson sent Higginson four

Note clearly refers to Thomas's work

New source identified in text

Connection of subtopic with thesis

Subtopic: correspondence with Higginson

Preparing the Manuscript

Andrews 4

poems, along with a letter containing this question: "Are you too deeply occupied to say if my Verse is alive?" (*Letters* 2: 403). This and other early letters in their correspondence reveal the poet's interest in gaining recognition. Later correspondence with Higginson seems, however, to have dampened her hope of achieving critical praise.

Unfortunately, almost all of Higginson's letters to Dickinson have been lost. Nevertheless, the main points of his answers to her early letters have been inferred by numerous critics, using the poet's replies to Higginson as the basis for these conclusions. Paul Ferlazzo, for example, infers that Higginson's response to her first letter must have included some recommendations for altering, or "regularizing," her poems, along with a request for more of her work (136). Ferlazzo bases this judgment on Dickinson's second letter to Higginson, which says, in part, "Thank you for the surgery--it was not so painful as I supposed. I bring you others--as you ask--though they might not differ--" (*Letters* 2: 404). The "surgery" surely refers to some changes recommended by Higginson, and Ferlazzo thinks it is significant that the poet admits that she was sending him more of the same kind, for this indicates that she did not intend to follow his advice (137).

In a second letter to Dickinson, Higginson must have recommended that she not try to publish for the present time, perhaps suggesting that she rewrite her poems

---

Reference to primary source; *Letters* are clearly Dickinson's; note includes title because Dickinson is author of two of the works cited

Quotation from *Letters* interrupts reference to Ferlazzo; otherwise, one note at end of paragraph [(136-37)] would be sufficient

Support for thesis

Preparing the Manuscript

Andrews 5

along the lines he had prescribed. This can be inferred from her reply to this letter, which reads, in part:

> I smile when you suggest that I delay "to
> publish"--that being foreign to my thought,
> as Firmament to Fin--If Fame belonged
> to me, I could not escape her--if she did not,
> the longest day would pass me on the
> chase--. . . My Barefoot--Rank is better.
> (*Letters* 2: 408)

Those critics who believe that Dickinson's reluctance to publish was a deliberate choice on her part do not take at face value her avowal to Higginson that publishing was "foreign" to her. Instead, they see Higginson's inability to recognize the genius in her work as a major factor in her decision to renounce her desire to publish. As Richard Sewall says it, Dickinson's

> disavowal about publishing can hardly be
> taken literally. After all, she had sent him
> [Higginson] the poems in response to his
> article on how young writers could get their
> work published. . . . What she said . . . about
> publishing and fame could perhaps mean
> that, in view of Higginson's hesitance, she
> was renouncing her ambition to be a public
> poet, . . . perhaps in the hope that some
> far-off Tribunal would render different and
> unequivocal judgment. . . . (2: 555)

Note referring to long, indented quotation comes *after* concluding punctuation

Extended quotation; student felt it was necessary to identify "him" in brackets

Preparing the Manuscript

Andrews 6

Subtopic: Dickinson's view of herself as an artist

Support for thesis

Two sources connected

Readers could be confused because Sewall's name precedes quotation, so Spiller's name is added to the note

In suggesting that Dickinson chose obscurity after Higginson's "hesitance," Sewall does not mean to imply that she was unsure of herself as a poet because of his criticism. On the contrary, Sewall states that "in her exalted conception of herself as a poet and in her confidence in her powers, she had no . . . reason to be deferential to Higginson . . . and one cannot help feeling that she knew it" (2: 555). Thus, it was not a sense of inferiority that moved the poet to her decision. Rather, it was the realization that her poems would not be accepted in the forms she had created for them and that public recognition would require her to alter them to meet public expectations. Robert Spiller, in finding that Dickinson "failed to publish" because she would not accept compromise as a path to recognition, makes much the same point as Sewall:

> The general reading public that asked for meter that is smooth, rhythm that is easy, and words that are limited to only one obvious meaning interested her not at all. She was willing to wait. (Spiller 127)

In this same regard, Thomas Johnson remarks that, although Dickinson's early letters to Higginson do indicate an interest in publication, she is also asking for a special kind of advice. "At the time she wrote Higginson," Johnson explains in his biography of the poet, "she does not seem to be trying to avoid publication as such; she is inquiring how one can publish and at the same time preserve the integrity of

Andrews 7

one's art" (11). This inquiry, Johnson continues, was a real concern for Dickinson because, prior to her writing to Higginson, two of her poems had been published anonymously in the *Springfield Daily Republican*, an influential newspaper at that time, and both poems had been altered radically by editors to suit their sense of regularity.

Mixture of paraphrase and quotation

Modern critics and biographers are in almost universal agreement that she was disappointed in Higginson's response to her poetry. They also agree that, as Ferlazzo puts it, the man "lacked discernment as to her purpose as an artist" (139). Johnson, in his appraisal of their correspondence, concludes that Higginson, though somewhat impressed by the working and thoughts in Dickinson's poems, "literally did not understand what he was reading" (111). By this, Johnson means that Higginson was confronted with the work of an "original genius" and was bewildered as to what to make of it. Throughout his correspondence with her, Higginson was apparently attempting to get Dickinson to write more traditional poetry, or, as Johnson observes: "He was trying to measure a cube by the rules of plane geometry" (107). There is no evidence, however, that she ever followed any of Higginson's suggestions, despite the fact that she maintained a friendly correspondence with him for many years.

For Emily Dickinson, then, the idea of revising her creations for the sake of achieving quick--and probably

Subtopic: evidence from poetry

Preparing the Manuscript

Andrews 8

fleeting--recognition was what was "foreign" to her, not
recognition based on acceptance of her poems as unique
works of art. This conviction comes through clearly in several of her poems; for example:

**Reference
to primary
source**

> Fame is the one that does not stay--
>
> Its occupant must die
>
> Or out of sight of estimate
>
> Ascend incessantly--
>
> Or be that most insolvent thing
>
> A Lightning in the Germ--
>
> Electrical the embryo
>
> But we demand the Flame. (lines 1-8)

**Support for
thesis**

In commenting on this poem, Inder Nath Kher
says that it does not mean that Dickinson is "averse to
genuine fame." It means, he continues, "that she does
not wish to be considered as writing simply for the sake
of some cheap glory" (128). Reinforced by this poem--
assuming "we" in the last line refers to the poet--is the
conclusion that Dickinson would rather have had "the
Flame" of her artistic integrity than the "insolvent thing"
called popular recognition.

**References to
primary sources**

Along the same lines, given the deliberate decision
to forgo publication rather than compromise her art, the
first lines of another poem become significantly clear:
"Publication--is the Auction/Of the Mind of Man" (lines
1-2). And there can be no doubt that when she wrote the

**Support for
thesis**

following stanza, Emily Dickinson had accepted the fact
that true fame would not be hers in her lifetime.

Andrews 9

Some--Work for Immortality--
The Chiefer part, for Time--
He--Compensates--immediately
The former--Checks--on Fame--
(lines 1-4)

She chose to maintain her artistic integrity and await
that immortality.

      The personality of Emily Dickinson will continue to
fascinate those who enjoy speculating about brilliant
artists whose lives were cloaked in privacy. Since she
said so little about herself outside of her somewhat
enigmatic poetry and her letters, the popular image of a
mystical, romantic Emily Dickinson is likely to coexist for
many years with scholarly appraisals of her life and
work. Her poetry, however, does more than create an
aura of mystery about its author; it reveals a dedicated
genius moved by deep, religious reverence for her craft.
Yet Emily Dickinson, gifted with the power to create
extraordinary works of art, also felt compelled to
preserve the uniqueness of her creations by refusing to
compromise in order to attain public recognition. She
was willing to trust that future generations of readers
would award her the fame her work deserved.

Conclusion

**Restatement
of thesis**

Preparing the Manuscript

Andrews 10

Note

[1]For a discussion of the sources of the "Emily myth," see Ferlazzo 13-21.

Andrews 11

Works Cited

Benfey, Christopher. "The Mystery of Emily Dickinson."
    Rev. of *The Poems of Emily Dickinson: Variorum
    Edition*, ed. R. W. Franklin; *Open Me Carefully:
    Emily Dickinson's Intimate Letters to Susan
    Huntington Dickinson*, ed. Ellen Louise Hart and
    Martha Nell Smith; and *The Emily Dickinson
    Handbook*, ed. Gudrun Grabher, Roland
    Hagenbüchle, and Cristanne Miller. *New York
    Review of Books*. NYREV, 8 Apr. 1999. Web. 14 May
    2000.

Dickinson, Emily. *The Complete Poems of Emily
    Dickinson*. Boston: Little, 1924. *Bartleby.com: Great
    Books Online*. Web. 15 July 2000.

---. *The Letters of Emily Dickinson*. Ed. Thomas H.
    Johnson and Theodora Ward. 3 vols. Cambridge:
    Harvard UP, 1958. Print.

Ferlazzo, Paul J. *Emily Dickinson*. Boston: Twayne, 1976.
    Print.

Griffith, Clark. *The Long Shadow: Emily Dickinson's
    Tragic Poetry*. Princeton: Princeton UP, 1964. Print.

Howard, William. "Emily Dickinson's Poetic Vocabulary."
    PMLA 72.2 (1957): 225-48. Print.

Johnson, Thomas H. *Emily Dickinson: An Interpretive
    Biography*. Cambridge: Harvard UP, 1955. Print.

Kher, Inder Nath. *The Landscape of Absence: Emily
    Dickinson's Poetry*. New Haven: Yale UP, 1974. Print.

Preparing the Manuscript

Sewall, Richard B. *The Life of Emily Dickinson.* 2 vols. New York: Farrar, 1974. Print.

Spiller, Robert E. *The Cycle of American Literature: An Essay in Historical Criticism.* 2nd ed. New York: Free, 1967. Print.

Thomas, Owen. "Father and Daughter: Edward and Emily Dickinson." *American Literature* 40.4 (1960): 510-23. Print.

Winters, Yvor. "Emily Dickinson and the Limits of Judgment." *Emily Dickinson: A Collection of Critical Essays.* Ed. Richard B. Sewall. Englewood Cliffs: Prentice, 1963. 38-56. Print.

Preparing the Manuscript

Solenopsis 1

Solenopsis invicta: Destroyer of Ecosystems

by

David Perez

Current Issues in Ecology

Section 1F

Professor Kim Harris

May 12, 2003

Preparing the Manuscript

Solenopsis 2

Abstract

Solenopsis invicta, a South American fire ant accidentally imported into the United States, is a notable example of the catastrophic destruction an aggressive alien species can cause when it invades an ecosystem. Since its appearance in Alabama in 1917, *S. invicta* has spread throughout the southern United States, outcompeting and outbreeding native ant species, as well as decimating other organisms. Ecologists are aware of *S. invicta*'s threat to biodiversity, and they fear the ant will eliminate some native species before science can fully study them for the potential benefits they may yield for humankind. As a result, scientists are studying possible methods for controlling *S. invicta*, including the importation of its natural enemies from South America. However, it is unlikely that an effective and safe program for controlling this fierce invader will be initiated very soon.

Solenopsis 3

***Solenopsis invicta*: Destroyer of Ecosystems**

History has shown us time and again the adverse
effects suffered by people whose world is invaded
by other people from an entirely different culture.
Europeans came to the New World bringing death and
destruction through their advanced technology and
through diseases such as smallpox for which the
native people had no defense. Later, industrial powers
invaded less technologically advanced societies
and turned them into colonies, debasing the lives
and cultures of the natives in the process. But human
beings are not alone in ravaging territories through
forceful aggression and occupation. Destruction of an
ecosystem by an invading species is fairly common
throughout nature.

Right now in the United States we are seeing a
dramatic example of an aggressive species causing
cataclysmic destruction as it becomes a major factor in
an ecosystem that it recently invaded. The culprit is a
red fire ant named *Solenopsis invicta*, which, since
moving to the United States from South America, has
wreaked havoc on the southern part of this country,
making life miserable or actually ending it for numerous
species that are native to the ecosystem (Mann, 1994).

In this paper, I will investigate how an aggressive
alien species that becomes transplanted to a new
ecosystem can do considerable damage to that system's
native inhabitants and, in some cases, pose a serious

Example of territorial aggression by human beings to provide general introduction to paper

Subject limited to single example of aggression

Date of Mann's work given according to APA style; complete information on this source appears on references page

Statement of purpose

Preparing the Manuscript

Solenopsis 4

threat to biodiversity. My subject for this study will be the red fire ant known as *Solenopsis invicta*.

Background information *S. invicta* came north accidentally just after World War I, entering the southeastern United States through the port of Mobile, Alabama. In the 1940s, according to B. Hölldobler, professor of zoology at the University of Würzburg, and E. O. Wilson, professor of science and curator of entomology at Harvard University (1990), the ant began a "rapid expansion that was to extend its **Page of book on which quotation appears** range over most of the United States by 1970" (p. 431). By the end of the century, "[i]solated colonies [had] been found as far west as California and as far north as Kansas City, Missouri" (California Department

Figure 1.   Current and possible future infestation areas of *S. invicta*.

Solenopsis 5

of Food and Agriculture [CDFA], 2000). Eventually, as shown in Figure 1, the ant may infest areas as far-flung as Puget Sound and Chesapeake Bay (CDFA, 2000).

If *S. invicta* had simply blended into its new surroundings and thrived as just another ant species in a biosystem that was home to numerous ant species, scientists would not regard it today as a significant ecological problem. But about twenty years after its arrival, *S. invicta* showed it had no intention of peacefully blending into its new ecosystem. And just as Europeans drastically reduced the native peoples after they invaded this land, so this foreign ant species has managed to devastate most of the native ants who had lived in harmony in the southern United States for millions of years.

A remarkable population density has been achieved by *S. invicta* in the last few decades. This change was brought about by a fairly recent development in the ant's reproductive practices. Mann (1994) explains that when it first entered the new ecosystem, *S. invicta* was a "monogyne" species, which means that each colony had a single egg-laying queen ant. In the 1980s, however, the species "increasingly appeared in a nonterritorial 'polygyne' form which creates interconnected 'super colonies' that may contain scores of egg-laying queens" (p. 1560). Obviously, when a colony includes multiple queens, each producing a

Solenopsis 6

colony of ants, it can rapidly outbreed, and thus conquer, the native single-queen species of ants.

S. Lutz, a wildlife ecologist at the University of Wisconsin-Madison, points out a further threat of the multi-queen system. "Ants are less territorial in the multi-queen mound system," allowing individual colonies to establish their mounds fairly close to one another, which leads to a large number of mounds in relatively small areas. Usually, Lutz explains, a single-queen system will produce anywhere from ten to twenty colonies, or mounds, per acre. But a multi-queen system can create from 600 to 700 mounds per acre (cited in Department of Agricultural Journalism, 1996, p. 2).

Further support for point made in preceding paragraph

It is not only its neighbor ants that are suffering from the aggressiveness of *S. invicta*. Recent findings show that creatures as large as fawns are being devastated as well, as the invaders spread ever more forcefully across the land (R. Jones, personal communication, December 22, 2003). Mann (1994) summarized an interview with S. D. Porter, an entomologist at the Insects Affecting Man and Animals Research Laboratory in Gainesville, Florida. Porter studied the effects of the polygyne *S. invicta*'s invasion of seventy acres in Texas. He found that after the invasion, the numbers of other ants had decreased by about 75 percent; other creatures, such as spiders and ticks, had decreased by about half. Porter painted a

***S. invicta*'s competitive dominance expanding threat to biodiversity**

Preparing the Manuscript

Solenopsis 7

rather grim picture of the destructive potential of
S. invicta: "The fire ants just seem to have outcompeted
everything else. The monogyne form is a nuisance
to people, but the polygyne form may pose a
significant threat to biodiversity" (as cited in Mann, **APA format**
1994, p. 1561). **for an author quoting another author**

We might wonder why scientists are deeply
concerned about, rather than merely interested in, the
destructive activities of this hostile immigrant. After all,
most of us are not overly fond of ants, spiders, ticks, or
other arthropods. E. Royte (1995), reporting on the
extinction and near extinction of flora and fauna
native to Hawaii as a result of invasions by alien **Reason for broad scientific interest in**
species, offers a practical reason for attempting to **S. invicta**
save species from extinction. "Conservationists . . .
stress that the loss of even one species may contribute to
the decline of entire ecosystems, and that native plants
and animals contain genetic information that could lead
to new food and medicines" (p. 14). Thus, *S. invicta*, by
wiping out native species, might well deprive us of
information that could enable us to lead healthier lives.

As the close scientific observation of *S. invicta*
continues, the fear that these fire ants may seriously
endanger biodiversity is becoming well justified. Lutz
discovered that large species such as birds are also
endangered. The northern bobwhite quail is one of **Support for**
the ant's latest victims. Lutz killed off large numbers **biodiversity threat introduced**
of fire ants in some areas inhabited by the quail while **earlier in paper**

Preparing the Manuscript

leaving other areas untouched. The quails quickly increased in the areas where the *S. invicta* population had been reduced, but no increase was seen in the areas where the ants were left in command. Lutz speculates that the fire ants either "sting chicks or adult birds to death" or "deprive the birds of a major food source when they eliminate the native insects upon which the quails feed" (as cited in Department of Agricultural Journalism, 1996, p. 1).

Oi and Koehler (1996) found that *S. invicta* can deliver a "burning sting" to human beings that leads to a "pustule and intense itching, which can persist for ten days." Some people with an allergy to the sting can suffer everything from rashes to infectious shock, and in rare cases an extreme allergic reaction can result in death. Despite these possibilities, *S. invicta* seems to pose no substantial threat to the quality of human life in the United States. However, news from South America is a little unsettling. Blount (1993) reported in the *Houston Chronicle* of a nightmarish possibility. An abstract of Blount's article states that nearly 7,000 people living in Elvira, Brazil, may be forced to leave town due to severe fire-ant infestation (p. A24). It would seem, then, that *S. invicta*'s territorial ambitions know no limits.

An obvious question at this point concerns efforts we should be making to control this destructive species. Actually, the federal government sponsored a serious

Real and possible threats to human beings

Solenopsis 9

attempt to control *S. invicta* during the 1960s. Mann (1994) tells us that the anti-fire-ant program included bombing large areas infested by *S. invicta*. The bombs, dropped by World War II bombers, consisted of a mixture of ant bait and ant poison. At first, *S. invicta* was stymied in its march across Dixie, but it soon recovered and came back stronger than ever. However, its victims, the native ant species, were permanently decimated. The result of this misguided strategy only made the world easier for *S. invicta* to conquer.

Attempts at control

Less dramatic plans for control are now being studied by scientists. Lutz tells of a fly species that preys on fire ants in their original South American habitat, thereby keeping the spread of *S. invicta* under control (cited in Department of Agricultural Journalism, 1996, p. 2). Lutz implies that these flies could be imported and turned loose in areas where *S. invicta* is spreading rapidly because it has no serious enemies. In the same vein, Mann (1994) discusses scientific interest in a parasite found in Argentina that has been known to reduce *S. invicta* populations drastically. However, it is unlikely that any such programs of fire-ant control will be implemented in the near future, because scientists must first make sure that by importing another alien species in an effort to control *S. invicta* they are not adding another, perhaps even greater, threat to the native ecosystems they hope to protect.

Preparing the Manuscript

Solenopsis 10

Conclusion

Taking a long-range view, we may find that nature will eventually resolve the problems caused by *S. invicta*, or any other aggressive invaders, through its own processes. "It is entirely possible that, given enough time, evolutionary and ecological changes will result in the 'taming' of such species and in their increasingly harmonious assimilation into the indigenous faunas" (Hölldobler & Wilson, 1990, p. 400). If all else fails, then we can hope that *Solenopsis invicta*, the accidental immigrant, will someday conclude that it has done quite well in the United States. At that time it may, much to everyone's relief, decide to settle down and join the system.

Preparing the Manuscript

References

Blount, J. (1993, September 19). Brazilian village trying to stamp out fire ants. *Houston Chronicle*, p. A24. Retrieved from DNEW database.

California Department of Food and Agriculture. (2000). *U.S. History*. Retrieved from http://www.cdfa.ca.gov/ pests/fire_ants/new/history.html

Department of Agricultural Journalism, University of Wisconsin-Madison. (1996). *Fire ants create problems for native wildlife* [Press release]. Madison, WI: Author.

Hölldobler, B., & Wilson, E. O. (1990). *The Ants*. Cambridge, MA: Belknap-Harvard University Press.

Mann, C. C. (1994, March 18). Fire ants parlay their queens into a threat to biodiversity. *Science, 263*(5153), 1560-1561. Retrieved from DPER database.

Oi, D. H., & Koehler, P. (1996). *Imported fire ants on lawns and turf*. Retrieved from University of Florida, Institute of Food and Agricultural Sciences website: http://edis.ifas.ufl.edu/LH059

Royte, E. (1995, September). On the brink: Hawaii's vanishing species. *National Geographic, 188*, 2-37.

Preparing the Manuscript

Cotton Mather's Necessary Witches

by

Fred Hutchins

History 57: Witchcraft in America

Professor Alfred Wintrol

November 13, 2003

Outline

Introduction

1. Historians have tried to learn about Mather's role in witchcraft hysteria and the Salem trials.

2. The old view of Mather as a cruel persecutor has given way to more favorable interpretations of his personality.

3. THESIS: Mather's belief in witchcraft was based on private religious beliefs.

I. Historians' opinions of Mather's role in the witch hunts and his motives for playing that role have changed in recent years.

   A. Mather's belief in witchcraft was normal for the time, and he was more humane than originally portrayed.

      1. The old harsh view of Mather was due to misinterpretation. (Murdock)

         a. He was actually more humane than most people think.

         b. Almost everyone in seventeenth-century America believed in witches.

      2. Modern historians may be biased against intellectuals of that era. (Hofstadter)

         a. They "encouraged greater tolerance."

         b. They opposed unenlightened trial judges.

      3. Mather tried to ensure fairness of trials. (Hansen)

Hutchins iii

      a. He warned against dangers of accepting "spectral evidence."

      b. He trusted judges to listen to him, but often they did not.

    4. Witchcraft really works in communities where everyone believes in it. (Hansen; long quotation)

    5. Mather also believed in witches because the Bible warns against them. (Levy)

  B. Whatever his motives, Mather played a critical role in the witch hunts.

    1. Mather's influence as preacher and writer may have encouraged the witch hunting. (Silverman)

    2. However, witch hunts began as local events, and probably would have occurred without Mather's pronouncements. (Silverman)

    3. Mather did not oppose the trials as such, and that implied approval. (Levin)

  C. Mather was deeply committed to maintaining the Puritan social order.

    1. Mather's book Wonders expressed concern for the Puritan church and the Devil's attempt to ruin it.

      a. He defended his friends, the judges. (Hansen)

      b. He later admitted some judges erred, but he never said the trials were wrong. (Levy)

Hutchins iv

2. Mather may have been an antifeminist. (Karlsen)

    a. History shows that accused witches were mainly women.

    b. He writes of "woman's complicity" in the Devil's plot against the Puritans.

3. Salem trials were symptomatic of women's problems in colonial America. (Karlsen)

    a. A "new woman" was called for; she should take care of the home so her husband could be free to succeed in business.

    b. Many women asserted their spiritual equality with men, based on Puritan creed.

    c. Men feared this equality might threaten their social dominance.

4. By defending the church against the Devil, Mather was defending male superiority. (Karlsen)

5. Puritans closely linked "church, state, and family," and saw the Devil attacking all three. (Pestana)

II. Mather's personal religious views necessitated his belief in witches.

    A. Mather believed he enjoyed a special relationship with God.

        1. Mather had to believe in witches to support belief in good supernatural beings.

            a. Witches were as real as angels. (Levin)

Hutchins v

    b. Witches, angels, spirit, God are all linked. (Silverman)

  2. Denying witches meant denying his whole faith.

    a. Mather believed he had been visited by an angel, who assured him he was righteous. (Levy)

    b. Witches proved atheism and doubt are evil. (Silverman)

B. Mather believed New England had a special part in God's plan.

  1. Mather saw the New England Puritan colony as the place where Christ would return to Earth. (Levy)

    a. The Bible said the Millennium would be preceded by evil days.

    b. So, the witchcraft outbreak seemed to signal Christ's immediate return.

  2. Mather focused on the American Puritan church's special role in God's plan for the world. (Middlekauff)

    a. It was purer than the English Puritan church.

    b. It deserved to be the site of Christ's return.

  3. The witchcraft epidemic brought good and bad news. (Miller)

    a. It pained individual sufferers.

    b. It foretold Christ's Second Coming.

Hutchins vi

Conclusion

1. All the social perspectives have some merit, but the role of Mather's personal beliefs seems to have been the basic source of his attitudes toward witches.

2. Afterthought: Mather may have found the conflict between the Devil's agents and God's followers a "thrilling" spectacle to participate in. (Starkey)

Hutchins 1

Cotton Mather's Necessary Witches

In 1692, a series of trials held in Salem,

Introduction of topic   Massachusetts, resulted in the execution of twenty

people for practicing witchcraft. Over the years, many

historians have tried to explain both the outbreak of

witchcraft hysteria at that time and the motives of

certain community leaders who played important roles

in hunting down and convicting people who were

Reference to source for background information   considered to be witches.[1] One such leader was Cotton

Mather, a prominent Puritan minister and theologian,

whose complex life and voluminous writings have

provided historians with ample material for attempting

to understand both the man and his times.

Early critics of Mather painted him as a cruel

witch hunter and tormentor of innocent people. And

while this negative image of Mather has not entirely

disappeared, modern historians have largely ruled out

the interpretation that Mather's involvement in witch

hunting stemmed from a deliberate desire to inflict

suffering upon innocent victims. Indeed, some historians

have all but absolved Mather of any unusual

responsibility for the trials. He was a person of the times,

these writers argue, and in late-seventeenth-century

America, it was a rare person who did not believe in and

fear the existence of witches. Other historians see

Mather's general support of the trials growing out of his

desire to defend the authority of the civil judges and

protect the Puritan social systems. Yet another

More background material

Nature of sources for this paper

Preparing the Manuscript

Hutchins 2

interpretation views Mather's role as that of a champion of the patriarchal social order. This idea may explain why Mather supported the trials of accused witches, the overwhelming majority of whom were women.

Cotton Mather was a complicated human being, and there may be some truth in all of these ideas. However, the ultimate explanation for his behavior during this fascinating if terrible moment in American history may well lie in his unique view of himself and the Puritan colony. His belief in witches, along with his need to identify and punish them, seems to have supported both his belief that he enjoyed a special, personal relationship with God, and his view that the New England Puritan colony was destined to play the central role in God's plan for the future of humanity.

The commonly accepted description of Cotton Mather shows a "bloodthirsty persecutor" who fanned the flames of the witchcraft hysteria that swept through New England during the last half of the seventeenth century. However, historians today claim that this inaccurate picture of Mather was based upon early misinterpretations of Mather's role in the proceedings. Kenneth Murdock, for example, says that Mather's writings and recent research "prove him to have been not less but more humane than his contemporaries."[2] Murdock accepts that Mather believed in witches, and he attributes that belief to the simple fact that most of Mather's contemporaries believed in them.[3]

Narrowing of chief argument

Statement of thesis

Subtopic: mistaken views of Mather

Mixture of paraphrase and quotation

Preparing the Manuscript

Hutchins 3

Further support for mistaken view of Mather

In the same vein, Richard Hofstadter sees an anti-intellectual bias in the way Mather and other educated leaders of that era have been treated by the "modern liberal mind." The charge that intellectual ministers were the "prime movers" of the Salem witch hunts does not take into account the social complexities of that period. According to Hofstadter, there is "ample evidence" that these ministers, including Cotton Mather, used their influence to "encourage greater tolerance" in the New England colony. In fact, in Hofstadter's view, these ministers wished to oppose the unenlightened actions of the civil judges who conducted the trials.[4]

Summary with partial quotations

The idea that Cotton Mather served as a moderating influence during the trials comes from a number of warnings he issued concerning the conduct of the trials. He said it was dangerous for a court to accept "spectral evidence" as decisive proof that a person was guilty of having made a contract with the Devil. Chadwick Hansen defines spectral evidence as "the appearance of the specter of a suspected person in the hallucinations of the afflicted."[5] People who claimed to be suffering from the torments of a witch would say in court that they could see the ghostly form of the person who was tormenting them. Although the form remained invisible to everyone else in the courtroom, at many trials this testimony was accepted as evidence against the accused. Mather reasoned that if spectral evidence

Quoted definition

Student's explanation of definition

Hutchins 4

were accepted as proof that someone was "trafficking with the Devil," then the way was clear for anyone to be accused by a personal enemy or a dreamer, with very little chance of refuting such evidence. Mather trusted in the wisdom of the civil judges to minimize the value of spectral evidence when evaluating the total evidence against an accused. However, the judges were far more willing to accept spectral evidence than Mather had expected, and, as a result, the number of imprisonments and executions increased.[6]

Summary of source material related to note 6

Hansen's discussion of witchcraft revolves around the idea that witchcraft <u>does</u> exist in societies that strongly believe in it. As Hansen explains it:

> We must bear in mind that in a society which believes in witchcraft, it works. If you believe in witchcraft and you discover that someone has been melting your wax image over a slow fire or muttering charms over your nail parings, the probability is that you will get extremely sick. To be sure, your symptoms will be psychosomatic rather than organic. But the fact that they are obviously not organic will make them only more terrible, since they will seem the result of malefic and demonic power. So it was in seventeenth-century Europe, and so it was in seventeenth-century Massachusetts.[7]

Long, direct quotation indented

From this point of view, Cotton Mather was a product of his society; for Mather and the Salem

Preparing the Manuscript

community, the strange behavior of the people who claimed they were being attacked by witches could only be due to the influence of the Devil. And, as Babette Levy says, Mather would have taken seriously the warnings in the Bible against witches and recognized the need to put such sinners to death.[8]

It appears, then, that Cotton Mather's belief in witches reflected the commonly accepted beliefs of seventeenth-century New England. And, to the extent that he tried to influence people's attitudes toward the judgment of accused witches, he was more enlightened and humane than most Puritans of that time.

However, the evidence also indicates that Mather was not simply a person of his times who got caught up in a sudden awareness of the Devil's activity in New England. Kenneth Silverman, one of Mather's biographers, says that Mather may have contributed to the outbreak of witch hunting. For many months before the witchcraft trials, Mather "kept calling public attention to the existence of devils and witches." As the leader of a large congregation, Mather preached frequently, and he was a prolific writer. The wide circulation of his ideas could have led to the general fear of an evil "invisible world" that threatened the very existence of the Puritan colony.[9]

Silverman suggests, however, that the persecution of witches stemmed from a number of factors. Such outbreaks were "distinctly community events," in that

Student summarizes paper to this point

Subtopic: Mather heavily involved in witchcraft events

Preparing the Manuscript

Hutchins 6

members of the community had to start accusing each
other of being witches. And taking these accused
witches to trial and punishing them could only occur
with the consent of the community as a whole. Thus, the
witchcraft mania might have broken out in New England
at that time whether or not Cotton Mather had spoken
out against the danger.[10]

David Levin, in another biography, offers a
stronger criticism of Mather. Levin asserts that a
study of Mather's role "will not allow even the most
sympathetic biographer the pleasure of casting Mather
as a defeated hero in this affair." Levin points out that
even though Mather criticized the courts for relying on
spectral evidence as grounds for convictions, he did not
strongly oppose the witch hunts, thereby allowing the
hunts to continue with his apparent approval. Levin warns
against viewing Mather as a noble hero challenging the
established order over the issue of spectral evidence.
Instead, we should realize that Mather's doubts about the
conduct of the trials were clearly secondary to deeper
religious beliefs that touched his personal sense of God
and of the way God's will works in the world.[11]

In 1692 Cotton Mather wrote Wonders of the
Invisible World, an account of five witchcraft trials. In
this book, he expressed great concern for New England
and its Puritan church, saying that his goal was "to
countermine the whole Plot of the Devil against New
England, in every Branch of it, as far as one of my

Mather's involvement tended toward approval of the trials

Hutchins 7

darkness can comprehend such a work of darkness."[12] Without doubt, Mather showed concern for the colony and the Puritan church, but Chadwick Hansen senses another purpose behind this book. He regards Wonders as a defense of the court, in which Mather went out of his way "to defend his friends," the judges of the court, from the increasing criticism of their methods. In this view, Mather becomes the "chief apologist" for a group of men whose methods he had earlier criticized.[13] Later in life, Mather acknowledged that the judges had made some mistakes that resulted in innocent people being hanged; however, as Levy explains, Mather attributed those errors to human weakness, not to "intentional evil." Yet, despite questioning the judges' methods and admitting their mistakes, Mather never repudiated his belief that the witchcraft peril had been substantial and that therefore the trials were fully justified.[14]

Carol Karlsen also sees Wonders as Mather's defense of the social order, but from a slightly different point of view. Calling Wonders Mather's "chief" justification for the witchcraft trials and executions,[15] Karlsen goes on to connect the events at Salem to the history of witchcraft, which she sees as "primarily the story of women." She places considerable emphasis on the fact that throughout history a great many more women than men were executed as witches (ibid., xii). Further, Karlsen traces a long tradition of female suppression in Christianity, starting with the concept of Eve as the "main

---

Preparing the Manuscript

Subtopic: Mather as defender of Puritan social order

Another aspect of Mather's defense of social order

Parenthetical citation referring to previously cited source to avoid succession of *ibid.* endnotes

Hutchins 8

symbol of woman-as-evil . . . in many ways, the
archetypal witch (ibid., 177). Applying this view of history
to her evaluation of Cotton Mather, Karlsen claims that
he focused in Wonders on "women's complicity" in the
Devil's plot to destroy the Puritan church (ibid., 179).

Karlsen regards the Salem trials as a symptom of
problems growing out of the role of women in the New
World. The growth of capitalism in the New England
colony had led its leaders to call for a "new woman," one
who would relieve her husband of most domestic
responsibilities so he could direct his energies toward
success in business. It was woman's duty to bolster her
husband's sense of self-importance (ibid., 180). Back in
England, and during the earliest days of the colony,
women had come to assert that they were the spiritual
equals of men, basing their argument on parts of the
Puritan creed. However, once the Puritan church became
established in New England, church leaders questioned
this idea of spiritual equality because they feared it
would spill over into the social order as well and call
into question the tradition of male superiority, a tradition
which, according to the male leaders, was divinely
ordained (ibid., 172).

Mather, in his defense of the "true Church"
against the Devil's assaults, was, according to Karlsen's
interpretation, equally ready to defend the Puritan social
structure against the Devil's wily attempts to use women
as tools for subversion of that social order. The divine

Summary of source material

Church and social order linked

Hutchins 9

order that began with God, the all-knowing, all-powerful
father, established the model for men as fathers on earth,
both within the family and within the church. This order
had to be preserved at all costs, in Mather's view, and
witchcraft, which was primarily a woman's crime,
threatened that order (ibid., 181).

Surely the question of what role the fear of
women's influence upon the social order played in the
Salem witch trials will continue to be investigated,
but Karlsen's study calls our attention to the close
connection between the religious and the civil power
structures in the Puritan colony. Along these lines, Carla
Pestana shows how the Puritan leaders had "shaped all
their social institutions--the church, the state, the
family--into weapons to be used in the cause of good."
The Puritans, says Pestana, "expected Satan to attempt
to undermine their holy commonwealth in countless
ways," and, as a result, they were constantly on the alert
for his disciples and agents, who could appear in their
midst at any time.[16] According to religious teachings of
the period, Satan undermined the good in three ways--
temptation, obsession, and possession--and possession
was almost always associated with witchcraft.[17]

These various interpretations of Cotton Mather's
role in the tragic occurrence at Salem leave us with the
fundamental question "How did Mather come to believe
so strongly in the Devil and witchcraft?" Levin tells us
that Mather's belief in the Devil was derived, through a

Preparing the Manuscript (side margin)

Depths of Puritan regard for social order supported (margin note)

Student's interpretation (margin note)

Hutchins 10

kind of religious logic, from his belief in good
supernatural entities. For Mather, "denial of the Devil's
power in this world implied the denial of other spirits,
including angels. . . ."[18] Such denials would, of course,
strike at the heart of Mather's religious beliefs and
destroy the faith upon which his whole life was based.
Kenneth Silverman expresses much the same idea in
saying that Mather thought that a disbelief in witches
"threatened to deny the reality of Spirit itself." As
Silverman states: "No witches, no Spirit, no God."[19]

In fact, as Babette Levy points out, for Mather to
deny the existence of witches, he would have to deny his
"totality of faith." And that would mean denying that he
had been visited by his "guardian angel" on a number of
occasions following extended periods of fasting and
prayer.[20] Mather needed to believe the angel's
appearances were real because those visits assured him
that he was predestined for salvation and that he was
performing his clerical duties in a manner that was
pleasing to God. Belief in angels compelled him to
believe in witches, for both are part of the supernatural
world in which good and evil spirits operate in
inexplicable ways. Silverman notes that Cotton Mather
looked upon instances of witchcraft as "Letters of Thanks
from Hell"--signs of a supernatural order that disproved
atheism and theories of religious doubt.[21]

To a large extent, then, Cotton Mather wanted
to believe in witches. Their existence justified both

Ellipsis points in quotation indicate omitted text

Support for thesis

Support for thesis

Subtopic: Mather's special relationship to God

Restatement of thesis

Preparing the Manuscript

Hutchins 11

his view of himself as a God-chosen person and the traditions of his Puritan faith. In addition, as part of this system of belief, Mather had formed a concept of the Puritan colony's special role in God's eternal plan.

Further support for thesis

According to Levy, Mather believed that New England was a "likely site for the New Jerusalem," the place where "Christ would rule the Earth in a kingdom with his saints for a thousand years before the final Day of Judgment," as foretold in Revelation. This last book of the New Testament spoke of signs that would appear when the Millennium (Christ's thousand-year reign) was close at hand. The major sign would be a "period of deepening corruption . . . when the Devil would make

Mixture of paraphrase and quotation

more violent assaults than usual" on humankind. In the 1690s, Mather and other Puritan leaders thought the Millennium was about to begin, probably in the early 1700s. The outbreak of witchcraft fit neatly into this view.[22]

New England's special place in God's plan dominated Cotton Mather's thinking throughout most of his life, according to Robert Middlekauff. The Puritan church in New England was the "true church," having escaped from the corruption of the original Puritan church in England, as well as from the corruption that plagued all other religions. Mather believed it was his duty to "preserve the Church," and thus the "true faith," until Christ returned to make all things right and just.[23]

Hutchins 12

But if the Devil's assault on New England through witchcraft was painful to witness and called for a courageous counterattack, the situation also offered opportunity for optimism, since it meant Christ would be returning soon. In analyzing Wonders, Perry Miller notes that "the discourse plunges into chiliastic ecstasy. The witches are signs of the times, of the death pangs of the Devil; mischievous powers prevail for the moment, but only because his rule is nearing extinction."[24] Thus, for Cotton Mather, the outbreak of witchcraft was bad news and good news at the same time.

Further support for thesis

It seems, then, that Mather was a complicated person, and that, in all likelihood, the beliefs of his time, his concept of social and religious order, and his view of women's place within that order all played parts in shaping his attitude toward witchcraft and the Salem trials. However, these factors seem to provide only secondary motives for his belief in witches and for his general support of the witchcraft trials. Looked at one way, the witches represented Satan's insidious plot to throw the Puritan church and its community into disorder. On the other hand, the witches' presence confirmed Mather's concept of a supernatural world populated with good and bad spirits, a concept that supported Mather's understanding of his personal relationship with God. From yet another viewpoint, the Devil's use of witches marked the final days before

Conclusion

Restatement of major points of paper

Student's summary of his research

Preparing the Manuscript

Hutchins 13

Christ's glorious return to Earth to reign in New England, the New Jerusalem.

In addition, recognizing that the Salem witchcraft crisis provided a time of high excitement for the New England colony, and that Cotton Mather was profoundly involved in the event, intellectually, emotionally, and spiritually, one might wonder, along with Marion Starkey, about the poetically dramatic "thrill" that may have been "unconsciously submerged" in this great religious figure as he witnessed "a collision between heaven and hell."[25]

Interesting afterthought speculating on Mather's "dramatic" view of the witchcraft events

Preparing the Manuscript

Hutchins 14

Notes

1. This paper draws mainly on sources that focus in depth on Cotton Mather's role in the witch hunts. Although most of these sources were published decades ago, they are still the most authoritative, comprehensive studies on Mather. For an overview of more general, current interpretations of causes leading to the New England witchcraft outbreak, see Mary Beth Norton, In the Devil's Snare: The Salem Witchcraft Crisis of 1692 (New York: Knopf, 2002).

2. Kenneth B. Murdock, ed., introduction to Cotton Mather: Selections, by Cotton Mather (1926; repr. New York: Hafner, 1965), xv.

3. Ibid., xvi.

4. Richard Hofstadter, Anti-intellectualism in American Life (New York: Knopf, 1963), 62-63.

5. Chadwick Hansen, Witchcraft at Salem (New York: Braziller, 1969), 101.

6. Ibid., 101-04.

7. Ibid., 10.

8. Babette M. Levy, Cotton Mather (Boston: Twayne, 1979), 59-60.

9. Kenneth Silverman, The Life and Times of Cotton Mather (New York: Harper, 1984), 87-88.

10. Ibid., 89-90.

11. David Levin, Cotton Mather: The Young Life of the Lord's Remembrancer (Cambridge: Harvard University Press, 1978), 200.

Hutchins 15

12. Cotton Mather, Wonders of the Invisible World, in Narratives of the Witchcraft Cases 1648-1706, ed. George Lincoln Burr (1914; repr. New York: Barnes, 1975), 211.

13. Hansen, Witchcraft, 171.

14. Levy, Cotton Mather, 64.

15. Carol F. Karlsen, The Devil in the Shape of a Woman: Witchcraft in Colonial New England (New York: Norton, 1987), 180.

16. Carla G. Pestana, "The City upon a Hill under Siege: The Puritan Perception of the Quaker Threat to Massachusetts Bay, 1656-1661," New England Quarterly 56 (September 1983): 353.

17. David Harley, "Explaining Salem: Calvinist Psychology and the Diagnosis of Possession," The American Historical Review 101, no. 2 (1996), http://www.ebscohost.com.

18. Levin, Young Life, 200.

19. Silverman, Life and Times, 92.

20. Levy, Cotton Mather, 59.

21. Silverman, Life and Times, 92-93.

22. Levy, Cotton Mather, 33-34.

23. Robert Middlekauff, The Mathers: Three Generations of Puritan Intellectuals, 1596-1728 (New York: Oxford University Press, 1971), 200.

24. Perry Miller, The New England Mind from Colony to Provinces (Cambridge: Harvard University Press, 1962), 203.

Hutchins 16

25. Marion L. Starkey, The Devil in Massachusetts:
A Modern Inquiry into the Salem Witch Trials (1949; repr.
New York: Anchor, 1969), 239.

Preparing the Manuscript

Hutchins 17

Bibliography

Hansen, Chadwick. Witchcraft at Salem. New York:
Braziller, 1969.

Harley, David. "Explaining Salem: Calvinist Psychology
and the Diagnosis of Possession." The American
Historical Review 101, no. 2 (1996). http://www.
ebscohost.com.

Hofstadter, Richard. Anti-intellectualism in American
Life. New York: Knopf, 1963.

Karlsen, Carol F. The Devil in the Shape of a Woman:
Witchcraft in Colonial New England. New York:
Norton, 1987.

Levin, David. Cotton Mather: The Young Life of the Lord's
Remembrancer. Cambridge: Harvard University
Press, 1978.

Levy, Babette M. Cotton Mather. Boston: Twayne, 1979.

Mather, Cotton. Wonders of the Invisible World. In
Narratives of the Witchcraft Cases 1648-1706, edited
by George Lincoln Burr. 1914. Reprint, New York:
Barnes, 1975.

Middlekauff, Robert. The Mathers: Three Generations of
Puritan Intellectuals, 1596-1728. New York: Oxford
University Press, 1971.

Miller, Perry. The New England Mind from Colony to
Provinces. Cambridge: Harvard University Press,
1962.

Murdock, Kenneth B., ed. Introduction to Cotton Mather:
Selections. 1926. Reprint, New York: Hafner, 1965.

Hutchins 18

Norton, Mary Beth. In the Devil's Snare: The Salem
    Witchcraft Crisis of 1692. New York: Knopf, 2002.

Pestana, Carla G. "The City upon a Hill under Siege:
    The Puritan Perception of the Quaker Threat to
    Massachusetts Bay, 1656-1661." New England
    Quarterly 56 (September 1983): 323-53.

Silverman, Kenneth. The Life and Times of Cotton
    Mather. New York: Harper, 1984.

Starkey, Marion L. The Devil in Massachusetts: A Modern
    Inquiry into the Salem Witch Trials. 1949. Reprint,
    New York: Anchor, 1969.

Preparing the Manuscript

Appendix

Reference Sources

The first section of this appendix, lists general reference sources — encyclopedias, periodical indexes and databases, and biographical sources. The second section, lists the most important sources within a wide range of disciplines. Because these reference works are more often known by their titles than by their authors or editors, we have listed them all by title. Within each discipline, we list first the major reference books, then the main indexes and databases, and finally some useful Web sites that you might explore. Note that many titles are available in more than one format (for example, print, microfilm, CD-ROM, or online). Conversion from one format to another is occurring continually, and accessibility will vary considerably among libraries.

General Sources

Encyclopedias and General Reference Sources

Academic American Encyclopedia. 21 vols. Revised annually.
Dictionary of the History of Ideas. Ed. Phillip P. Wiener. 4 vols., plus index. New York: Scribner's, 1973.
Encyclopedia of Associations. Separate editions for regional, national, and international data. Revised frequently. Also available online.
Encyclopaedia Britannica. 32 vols. Updated annually.
Facts on File: News Digest. 1941–; weekly.
McGraw-Hill Encyclopedia of Science and Technology. 9th ed. New York: McGraw-Hill, 2002.

Social Science Encyclopedia. Ed. Paul Kegan. 2nd ed. London: Routledge, 1996.
Statistical Abstracts of the United States. 1878–; annual.

General Periodical Indexes and Databases

Academic Index
Alternative Press Index
American Statistics Index (ASI)
Arts and Humanities Citation Index
Bibliographic Index
Book Review Digest
Dissertation Abstracts
EBSCOhost
Essay and General Literature Index
Ethnic Newswatch

Expanded Academic ASAP
General Science Index
Humanities Index. Online version is
    Humanities Abstracts.
LexisNexis Academic Universe
National Newspaper Index
Newspaper Abstracts
New York Times Index. 1913–.
Periodical Abstracts
ProQuest Direct
Readers' Guide to Periodical Literature
Science Citation Index
Social Sciences Citation Index
Social Sciences Index

General Research Web Sites

Academic Info at <http://academic
    info.net>
The Columbia Encyclopedia. 6th ed.
    2001–04. *Bartleby.com: Great Books
    Online* at <.www.bartleby.com/65>
*Infomine: Scholarly Internet Resource
    Collections* at <http://infomine.
    ucr.edu>
The Internet Public Library at
    <www.ipl.org>
Social Science Internet Gateway at
    <http://sosig.ac.uk>
*Voice of the Shuttle: Web Site for
    Humanities Research* at
    <http://vos.ucsb.edu>
The World Wide Web Virtual Library at
    <http://vlib.org>

Biographical Sources

Chambers Biographical Dictionary. Edited
    by J. O. Thorne. Rev. ed. Melanie
    Parry. 6th ed. New York: Larousse,
    1997.
Contemporary Authors. Various editions.
    Detroit: Gale, 1967–. Also available
    on CD-ROM.
Contemporary Black Biography. Detroit:
    Gale, 1992–.
Current Biography. New York: Wilson,
    1940–. Monthly, with annual
    accumulations.

Dictionary of American Biography.
    17 vols., plus supplements. New
    York: Scribner's, 1927–. Also avail-
    able on CD-ROM. Includes only
    deceased Americans.
Dictionary of Literary Biography. Various
    editions, with frequent supple-
    ments. Detroit: Gale, 1978–.
Dictionary of National Biography. Ed.
    Leslie Stephen and Sidney Lee.
    22 vols., plus supplements. New
    York: Oxford University Press,
    1882–. Also available on CD-ROM.
Dictionary of Scientific Biography. 8 vols.,
    plus supplements. New York:
    Macmillan, 1981–.
Who's Who. 1849–. Many editions (*Who's
    Who of Black Americans, Who's Who
    of American Women*, and so on).

Indexes and Databases
Biography and Genealogy Master Index
Biography Index
Biography Resource Center

Web Sites
Biography.com at <www.biography.com>
Chambers Reference Online at
    <www.chambersharrap.co.uk/
    chambers/chref/chref.py/main>
Lives: The Biography Resource at
    <http://amillionlives.com>
The Time 100 at <www.time.com/
    time/time100/leaders/index.html>

Sources in the Disciplines
Art and Architecture

*Art Through the Ages: The Western
    Perspective.* Fred S. Kleiner, Christ-
    ian J. Mamiya, and Richard G.
    Tansey. 11th ed. Belmont, CA:
    Thomson/Wadsworth, 2003.
*The Concise Oxford Dictionary of Art and
    Artists.* Ed. Ian Chilvers. 2nd ed.
    Oxford: Oxford University Press,
    1996.

Contemporary Artists. Ed. Sara Pendergast and Tom Pendergast. 5th ed. 2 vols. Detroit, MI: St. James, 2002. A biographical dictionary revised every five years.

Dictionary of Art. Ed. Jane Turner. 34 vols. New York: Grove, 1996.

Encyclopedia of American Art before 1914. Ed. Jane Turner. New York: Grove's Dictionaries, 2000.

Encyclopedia of Architecture. Ed. Joseph A. Wilkes and Robert T. Packard. 5 vols. New York: Wiley, 1988–90.

Encyclopedia of World Art. 17 vols. New York: McGraw, 1959–87.

Macmillan Encyclopedia of Architects. Ed. Adolf K. Placzek. 4 vols. New York: Free, 1982.

Indexes and Databases

Art Index. Online version is *Art Abstracts.*
ARTBibliographies Modern
Bibliography of the History of Art (BHA)
Grove Art Online

Web Sites

Architecture.com at <www.architecture.com>
A Digital Archive of Architecture at <www.bc.edu/bc_org/av/cas/fnart/arch>
Art History Resources on the Web at <http://witcombe.bcpw.sbc.edu/ARTHLinks.html>
The Mother of All Art and Art History Links Pages at <www.art-design.umich.edu/mother>

Astronomy

Astronomical Almanac. Nautical Almanac Office. Washington, DC: GPO. Annually.

Astronomy and Astrophysics Encyclopedia. Ed. Stephen Maran. New York: Van Nostrand, 1992.

Encyclopedia of Astronomy and Astrophysics. Ed. Paul Murdin. 4 vols. London, New York: Nature Publishing Group, 2001.

Facts on File Dictionary of Astronomy. Ed. Valerie Illingworth and John O. E. Clark. 4th ed. New York: Facts on File, 2000.

Indexes and Databases

Astronomy and Astrophysics Abstracts

Web Sites

The Astronomy Net at <www.astronomy.net>
AstroWeb at <www.stsci.edu/astroweb/astronomy.html>
NASA Web at <www.nasa.gov>
Open Directory's Astronomy Directory at <http://dmoz.org/Science/Astronomy>

Biological Sciences

Atlas of Human Anatomy. Frank H. Netter. Consulting Ed. John T. Hansen. 3rd ed. Teterboro, NJ: Icon Learning Systems, 2003.

Facts on File Dictionary of Biology. Ed. Robert Hine. 3rd ed. New York: Facts on File, 1999.

Grzimek's Animal Life Encyclopedia. Gale Research Staff. 2nd ed. 13 vols. Detroit: Gale, 2002.

Oxford Dictionary of Biology. 4th ed. Oxford: Oxford University Press, 2000.

Indexes and Databases

Biological Abstracts. Online version is *BIOSIS.*
Biological & Agricultural Index
Zoological Record

Web Sites

BioNetbook at <www.pasteur.fr/recherche/BNB/bnb-en.html>
Centers for Disease Control and Prevention at <www.cdc.gov>

*National Center for Biotechnology
Information* at <www.ncbi.nlm.
nih.gov>
National Institutes of Health at
<www.nih.gov>
*The WWW Virtual Library—
Biosciences* at <http://vlib.org/
Biosciences.html>

Business and Economics

Business Information Sources. Lorna M.
Daniells. 3rd ed. Berkeley: Univer-
sity of California Press, 1993.
Companion Encyclopedia of Marketing.
Ed. Michael J. Baker. New York:
Routledge, 1995.
Dictionary of Business and Economics.
Christine Ammer and Dean S.
Ammer. Rev. and enl. ed. New
York: Free, 1986.
Encyclopedia of Economics. Ed. Douglas
Greenwald. 2nd ed. New York:
McGraw, 1994.
*International Encyclopedia of Business
and Management.* Ed. Malcolm
Warner. 2nd ed. 8 vols. London:
Thomson Learning, 2002.
*The New Palgrave: A Dictionary of Eco-
nomics.* Ed. John Eatwell, Murray
Milgate, and Peter Newman.
4 vols. New York: Stockton, 1987.

Indexes and Databases*

ABI/Inform
Banking Information Source
Business Abstracts
Business Periodicals Index
EconLit
Gale Business Resources
Wilson Business Abstracts

Web Sites

Business Week Online at
<www.businessweek.com>
Hoover's Online at <www.hoovers.com>

*Internet Public Library—Business and
Economics* at <www.ipl.org/div/
subject/browse/bus00.00.00>
*Securities and Exchange Commission:
EDGAR Database of Corporate
Information* at <www.sec.gov/
edgarhp.htm>
WebEc at <www.helsinki.fi/WebEc/
WebEc.html>
*WWW Virtual Library: Resources for
Economists on the Internet* at
<http://rfe.wustl.edu>

Chemistry

Facts on File Dictionary of Chemistry. Ed.
John Daintith. 3rd ed. New York:
Facts on File, 1999.
Hawley's Condensed Chemical Dictionary.
Ed. Richard J. Lewis. 14th ed. New
York: Wiley, 2002.
*How to Find Chemical Information: A
Guide for Practicing Chemists, Teach-
ers, and Students.* Robert E. Maizell.
3rd ed. New York: Wiley, 1998.
Macmillan Encyclopedia of Chemistry. Ed.
Joseph J. Lagowski. 4 vols. New
York: Macmillan Reference, 1997.

Indexes and Databases

Analytical Abstracts
Chemical Abstracts

Web Sites

Academic Info—Chemistry Gateway at
<http://academicinfo.net/chem.
html>
*Chemistry.org: The Web Site of the
American Chemical Society* at
<www.chemistry.org>
ChemWeb—Beilstein Abstracts at
<www.chemweb.com/databases/
belabs>
*WWW Virtual Library—Links for
Chemists* at <www.liv.ac.uk/
chemistry/links/links.html>

* Standard business sources such as Dun's, Thomas, and Moody's offer many of their directories and publicaitons as databases.

Computer Sciences

Encyclopedia of Computer Science. Ed.
Anthony Ralston, Edwin D. Reilly,
and David Hemmendinger. 4th
ed. New York: Wiley, 2003
*Encyclopedia of Computer Science and
Technology.* Harry Henderson.
New York: Facts on File, 2003.
*Webster's New World Computer Dictio-
nary.* Bryan Pfaffenberger. 10th ed.
Indianapolis, IN: Wiley, 2003.

Indexes and Databases

ACM Guide to Computing Literature
Applied Science & Technology Index.
Online version is *Applied Science
and Technology Abstracts.*
Computer Abstracts

Web Sites

*The Collection of Computer Science Bibli-
ographies* at <http://liinwww.ira.
uka.de/bibliography/index.html>
ElsevierComputerScience at <www.
elseviercomputerscience.com/
compsciweb/show/Index.htt>
*FOLDOC: Free Online Dictionary of
Computing* at <http://foldoc.doc.
ic.ac.uk/foldoc/index.html>
*LSU Libraries—Computer Science Subject
Guide* at <www.lib.lsu.edu/sci/
compsci.html>

Drama

*The Concise Oxford Companion to the
Theater.* Ed. Phyllis Hartnoll and
Peter Found. 2nd ed. New York:
Oxford University Press, 1992.
A Guide to Critical Reviews. James M.
Salem. 3rd ed. Metuchen, NJ:
Scarecrow, 1984–91.
*McGraw-Hill Encyclopedia of World
Drama.* Ed. Stanley Hochman.
5 vols. 2nd ed. New York:
McGraw, 1984.
*Modern Dramatists: A Casebook of the
Major British, Irish, and American*

Playwrights. Ed. Kimball King.
New York, Routledge, 2001.
*The Oxford Companion to the American
Theater.* Ed. Gerald Martin Bord-
man. 2nd ed. New York: Oxford
University Press, 1992.
*World Encyclopedia of Contemporary
Theater.* Ed. Don Rubin. 6 vols.
London: Routledge, 2000.

Indexes and Databases

*Dramatic Criticism Index: A Bibliography
of Commentaries on Playwrights from
Ibsen to the Avant Garde*
International Index to the Performing Arts

Web Sites

*Brief Guide to Internet Resources in
Theatre and Performance* at <www.
stetson.edu/csata/thr_guid.html>
Theatre History Sites on the WWW at
<www.win.net/~kudzu/history.
html>
*WWW Virtual Library—Theatre and
Drama* at <www.vl-theatre.com>

Earth Sciences

Encyclopedia of Earth System Science. Ed.
William A. Nierenberg. 4 vols. San
Diego: Adacemic Press, 1992.
McGraw-Hill Dictionary of Earth Science.
2nd ed. New York: McGraw-Hill,
2003.
*McGraw-Hill Dictionary of Geology and
Mineralogy.* 2nd ed. New York:
McGraw-Hill, 2003.

Indexes and Databases

Bibliography and Index of Geology.
Online version is *GeoRef.*

Web Sites

American Geological Institute at
<www.agiweb.org>
Geology.com at <www.geology.com>
U.S. Geological Survey at
<www.usgs.gov>

The WWW Virtual Library—Earth Science at <www.vlib.org/Earth Science.html>

Education

Education: A Guide to Reference and Information Sources. Nancy P. O'Brien. 2nd ed. Englewood, CO: Libraries Unlimited, 2000.

Encyclopedia of American Education. Ed. Harlow G. Unger. 2nd ed. New York: Facts on File, 2001.

Encyclopedia of Education. Ed. James W. Guthrie. 2nd ed. 8 vols. New York: Macmillan, 2003.

Encyclopedia of Educational Research. American Educational Research Association. Ed. Marvin C. Alkin. 6th ed. New York: Macmillan, 1992.

The Facts on File Dictionary of Education. Jay M. Shafritz et al. New York: Facts on File, 1989.

Indexes and Databases

Education Abstracts
Education Index
ERIC: Educational Resources Information Center

Web Sites

Education Index at <www.educationindex.com>
Education Week on the Web at <www.edweek.org/ew>
The Educator's Reference Desk at <www.eduref.org>
National Center for Education Statistics at <http://nces.ed.gov>
U.S. Department of Education at <www.ed.gov>

Environmental Science

Encyclopedia of Environmental Issues. Ed. Craig W. Allin. 3 vols. Pasadena, CA: Salem, 2000.

Encyclopedia of Environmental Science. Ed. David E. Alexander and Rhodes W. Fairbridge. Boston: Kluwer, 1999.

Indexes and Databases

Ecology Abstracts
Envirofacts (U.S. Environmental Protection Agency)
Environment Abstracts. Online version is called *Enviroline.*
Environmental Periodicals Bibliography
Pollution Abstracts

Web Sites

The Ecology WWW Page at <http://pbil.univ-lyon1.fr/Ecology/Ecology-WWW.html>
EnviroLink at <www.envirolink.org/>
Environmental Protection Agency at <www.epa.gov>
The Nature Conservancy at <http://nature.org>
World Resources Institute at <www.wri.org>

Ethnic Studies

African American Encyclopedia. Ed. R. Kent Rasmussen. 2nd ed. 10 vols. New York: Marshall Cavendish, 2001.

American Immigrant Cultures: Builders of a Nation. Ed. David Levinson and Melvin Ember. 2 vols. New York: Macmillan, 1997.

Asian American Encyclopedia. Ed. Franklin Ng. 6 vols. New York: Marshall Cavendish, 1995.

Encyclopedia of Multicultural America. Ed. Julie Galens et al. 2 vols. Detroit: Gale Group, 1999.

Gale Encyclopedia of Native American Tribes. 4 vols. Detroit: Gale Group, 1998.

Guide to Multicultural Resources. Madison, WI: Praxis, 1985–1998.

Handbook of Hispanic Culture in the United States. 4 vols. Houston: Arte Publico, 1993.

Reference Encyclopedia of the American Indian. Ed. Barry T. Klein.10th ed. West Nyack, NY: Todd, 2003.

Indexes and Databases

Ethnic NewsWatch
Hispanic American Periodicals Index (HAPI)
Index to Black Periodicals
Index to Literature on the American Indian
Sociological Abstracts. Online version is called *SocioFile.*

Web Sites

The African American Mosaic: A Library of Congress Resource Guide for the Study of Black History and Culture at <http://lcweb.loc.gov/exhibits/african/intro.html>

American Indian History and Related Issues at <www.csulb.edu/projects/ais/>

Asian American Studies Resources at <http://sun3.lib.uci.edu/~dtsang/aas2.htm>

Diversity and Ethnic Studies: Recommended Web Sites and Research Guides at <www.public.iastate.edu/~savega/divweb2.htm>

Library of Congress HLAS Online: Handbook of Latin American Studies at <http://lcweb2.loc.gov/hlas>

The WWW Virtual Library—Migration and Ethnic Relations at <www.ercomer.org/wwwvl>

Film

The Complete Film Dictionary. Ira Konigsberg. 2nd ed. New York: Penguin, 1997.

The Film Encyclopedia. Ephraim Katz. 4th ed. New York: HarperCollins, 2001.

Halliwell's Who's Who in the Movies. Leslie Halliwell. 13th ed. New York: HarperPerennial, 1999.

International Dictionary of Film and Film-makers. Ed. Tom Pendergast and Sara Pendergast. 4th ed. Detroit: St. James, 2000.

Indexes and Databases

Film Literature Index
International Index to Film Periodicals

Web Sites

The Internet Movie Database at <www.imdb.com>

ScreenSite at <www.tcf.ua.edu/ss>

Voice of the Shuttle—Film/Video at <http://vos.ucsb.edu/browse.asp?id=2720#id917>

Yale University Library's Research Guide in Film Studies at <www.library.yale.edu/humanities/film/>

Health and Medicine

Companion Encyclopedia of the History of Medicine. Ed. W. F. Bynum and Roy Porter. 2 vols. New York: Routledge, 1993.

Gale Encyclopedia of Medicine. Ed. Jacqueline L. Longe. 2nd ed. 5 vols. Detroit, MI: Gale Group, 2002.

Introduction to Reference Sources in the Health Sciences. Ed. F. Roper and J. Boorkman. 3rd ed. Chicago: MLA, 1994.

Stedman's Medical Dictionary. Ed. Thomas Stedman. 27th ed. Philadelphia: Lippincott Williams and Wilkins, 2000.

Indexes and Databases

Cumulative Index to Nursing and Allied Health Literature (CINAHL)

Index Medicus. Online version is *MEDLINE* (U.S. National Library of Medicine).

Web Sites

Centers for Disease Control and
Prevention at <www.cdc.gov>
HealthWeb at <www.healthweb.org>
National Library of Medicine: PubMed at
<www.ncbi.nlm.nih.gov/entrez/
query.fcgi>
WWW Virtual Library—Medicine
and Health at <www.vlib.org/
Medicine.html>

History

The Cambridge Ancient History. Ed.
Averil Cameron and Peter Garnsey.
14 vols. Cambridge: Cambridge
University Press, 1970–2000.
Cambridge Medieval History. Eds. H. M.
Gwathin et al. 2nd ed. 9 vols. New
York: Cambridge UP, 1966–.
Dictionary of American History. Ed.
Stanley I. Kutler. 3rd ed. 10 vols.
New York: Scribner's, 2003.
An Encyclopedia of World History:
Ancient, Medieval, and Modern,
Chronologically Arranged. Ed.
Peter N. Stearns. 6th ed. Boston:
Houghton, 2001.
Guide to Historical Literature. Ed.
George F. Howe et al. 3rd ed. New
York: American Historical Associa-
tion, 1995.
New Cambridge Modern History. 14 vols.
Cambridge: Cambridge University
Press, 1957–79.

Indexes and Databases

America: History & Life
Historical Abstracts

Web Sites

American Memory: Historical Collections
for the National Digital Library at
<http://memory.loc.gov/ammem/
amhome.html>
Bedford/St. Martin's History Links Library
at <www.bedfordstmartins.com/
historylinks>

Historical Text Archive at
<http://historicaltextarchive.com>
TheHistoryNet at
Internet Modern History Sourcebook at
<www.fordham.edu/halsall/mod/
modsbook.html>
World History Archives at <www.
hartford-hwp.com/archives>
World Wide Web Virtual Library: History
at <www.ukans.edu/history/VL/>

Language and Linguistics

Dictionary of Linguistics and Phonetics.
5th ed. Cambridge, MA: Blackwell, 2003.
International Encyclopedia of Linguistics.
Ed. William J. Frawley. 2nd ed.
4 vols. New York: Oxford University Press, 2003.
The Major Languages of South Asia, the
Middle East, and Africa. Ed. Bernard
Comrie. London: Routledge, 1990.
The Origins and Development of the English Language. Thomas Pyles. 4th
ed. New York: Harcourt, 1993.

Indexes and Databases

Linguistics Abstracts
Linguistics and Language Behavior
Abstracts (LLBA)
MLA International Bibliography

Web Sites

EServer.org—Language and Linguistics at
<http://eserver.org/langs>
In Other Words: A Lexicon of the
Humanities at <www.sil.org/
~radneyr/humanities>
Linguistics Resources on the Internet at
<www.sil.org/linguistics/topical.
html>

Literature

Annual Bibliography of English Language
and Literature. Modern Humanities

Research Association. New York: Cambridge University Press, 1921–.

Black Authors: A Selected Annotated Bibliography. James Edward Newby. New York: Garland, 1991.

The Bloomsbury Guide to Women's Literature. Ed. Claire Buck. New York: Prentice Hall, 1992.

The Cambridge History of American Literature. Ed. Sacvan Bercovitch. New York: Cambridge University Press, 1994–2003.

The Concise Oxford Companion to African American Literature. Ed. William L. Andrews, Frances Smith Foster, Trudier Harris. New York: Oxford University Press, 2001.

The Concise Oxford Companion to Classical Literature. Ed. M. C. Howatson and Ian Chilvers. New York: Oxford University Press, 1993.

Contemporary Literary Criticism. Series. Detroit: Gale, 1973–.

Dictionary of Literary Biography. Series. Detroit: Gale, 1978–.

Encyclopedia of Folklore and Literature. Ed. Mary Ellen Brown and Bruce A. Rosenberg. Santa Barbara, CA: ABC-CLIO, 1998.

Encyclopedia of World Literature in the 20th Century. Ed. Steven R. Serafin. 3rd ed. 4 vols. Detroit, MI: St. James, 1999.

Literary Research Guide: An Annotated Listing of Reference Sources in English Literary Studies. James L. Harner. 4th ed. New York: MLA, 2002.

New Cambridge Bibliography of English Literature. Ed. Joanne Shattock. 3rd ed. New York: Cambridge University Press, 1999–

Nineteenth-Century Literary Criticism. Detroit: Gale, 1981–.

The Oxford Companion to American Literature. Ed. James David Hart. 6th ed. New York: Oxford University Press, 1995.

The Oxford Companion to English Literature. Ed. Margaret Drabble.

6th ed. New York: Oxford University Press, 2000.

The Oxford History of English Literature. 15 vols. New York: Oxford University Press, 1947–90.

A Research Guide for Undergraduate Students: English and American Literature. Nancy L. Baker and Nancy Huling. 5th ed. New York: MLA, 2000.

Indexes and Databases

Contemporary Authors
Essay and General Literature Index
MLA International Bibliography
World Authors

Web Sites

Bartleby.com: Great Books Online at <www.bartleby.com>
EServer.org at <http://eserver.org>
Internet Public Library—Literary Criticism at <www.ipl.org/div/litcrit>
Voice of the Shuttle—Literature at <http://vos.ucsb.edu/browse.asp?id=3>

Mathematics

CRC Concise Encyclopedia of Mathematics. Eric W. Weisstein. 2nd ed. Boca Raton, FL: Chapman & Hall/CRC, 2003.

Elsevier's Dictionary of Mathematics. Ed. K. Peeva. New York: Elsevier, 2000.

Encyclopedic Dictionary of Mathematics. Ed. K. Ito. 2nd ed. 4 vols. Cambridge: MIT Press, 1987.

Indexes and Databases

MathSciNet

Web Sites

American Mathematical Society: Mathematics on the Web at <www.ams.org/mathweb>

MathWorld at <http://mathworld. wolfram.com>

The WWW Virtual Library—Mathematics at <www.math.fsu.edu/Virtual>

Media

Biographical Dictionary of American Journalism. Ed. Joseph P. McKerns. New York: Greenwood, 1989.

Communication Yearbook. New Brunswick, NJ: National Communication Association. 1977–.

History of the Mass Media in the United States. Ed. Margaret A. Blanchard. Chicago: Fitzroy Dearborn, 1998.

Webster's New World Dictionary of Media and Communications. Richard Weiner. Rev. and updated ed. New York: Macmillan, 1996.

Indexes and Databases

Communications Abstracts

Gale Database of Publications and Broadcast Media

Index to Journals in Communication Studies

Web Sites

The American Communication Association at <www.americancomm.org>

Columbia Journalism Review at <www.cjr.org>

The Media and Communications Studies Site at <www.aber.ac.uk/media/medmenu.html>

Media Research Center at <www.mediaresearch.org>

Newswatch.org: Views on the News at <www.newswatch.org>

Poynter Online at <www.poynter.org>

Music

Baker's Biographical Dictionary of Musicians. Nicolas Slonimsky. Centennial ed. New York: Schirmer, 2001.

Garland Encyclopedia of World Music. Ed. Bruno Nettl, Ruth M. Stone, James Porter, and Timothy Rice. New York: Garland, 1998–2002.

Music Reference and Research Materials: An Annotated Bibliography. Vincent Duckles and Michael A. Keller. 5th ed. New York: Schirmer, 1997.

New Grove Dictionary of American Music. Ed. H. Wiley Hitchcock and Stanley Sadie. 4 vols. New York: Grove's, 1986.

New Grove Dictionary of Music and Musicians. Ed. Stanley Sadie. 2nd ed. 29 vols. New York: Grove, 2001. (Also available online by subscription.)

New Oxford Companion to Music. Ed. Denis Arnold. New York: Oxford University Press, 1983.

New Oxford History of Music. 2nd ed. New York: Oxford University Press, 1990–2001.

Indexes and Databases

The Music Index

RLM Abstracts of Musical Literature

Web Sites

The Classical Music Pages at <http://w3.rz-berlin.mpg.de/cmp>

Web Resources for Research in Music at <www.music.ucc.ie/wrrm>

Worldwide Internet Music Resources at <www.music.indiana.edu/music_resources>

The WWW Virtual Library—Classical Music at <www.gprep.org/classical>

Philosophy

Dictionary of Philosophy. Ed. Anthony Flew. Rev. 2nd ed. New York: Gramercy, 1999.

A History of Philosophy. Frederick Copleston. New York: Image, 1993.

History of Western Philosophy. Bertrand Russell. 2nd ed. New York: Routledge, 1991.

Oxford Dictionary of Philosophy. Simon Blackburn. New York: Oxford University Press, 1996.

Routledge Encyclopedia of Philosophy. Ed. Edward Craig. 10 vols. New York: Routledge, 1998. (Also available online by subscription.)

Women Philosophers: A Bio-Critical Source Book. Ethel M. Dersey. Westport, CT: Greenwood, 1989.

Indexes and Databases

The Philosopher's Index

Web Sites

The Internet Encyclopedia of Philosophy at <www.utm.edu/research/iep>

Philosophy in Cyberspace at <www-personal.monash.edu.au/~dey/phil>

Stanford Encyclopedia of Philosophy at <http://plato.stanford.edu>

The WWW Virtual Library—Philosophy at <www.bris.ac.uk/Depts/Philosophy/VL>

Physics

Encyclopedia of Modern Physics. Ed. Robert A. Meyers. San Diego: Academic, 1990.

Encyclopedia of Physics. Ed. Robert M. Besancon. 3rd ed. New York: Chapman, 1990.

The Facts on File Dictionary of Physics. Ed. John Daintith and John Clark. 3rd ed. New York: Facts on File, 1999.

Macmillan Encyclopedia of Physics. Ed. John S. Rigden. 4 vols. New York: Simon & Schuster Macmillan, 1996.

Indexes and Databases

Physics Abstracts. Online version is INSPEC.

SPIN (Searchable Physics Information Notices)

Web Sites

American Institute of Physics—Center for History of Physics at <www.aip.org/history/index.html>

Physics News at <www.het.brown.edu/news/index.html>

PhysLink.com at <www.physlink.com>

The WWW Virtual Library of Physics at <www.vlib.org/Physics.html>

Political Science

American Political Dictionary. Jack C. Plano and Milton Greenberg. 11th ed. Fort Worth, TX: Harcourt College, 2001.

Congressional Quarterly Almanac. Washington, DC: Congressional Quarterly News Features, 1948–2001.

Encyclopedia of Crime and Justice. Ed. Joshua Dressler. 2nd ed. 4 vols. New York: Macmillan, 2002.

Oxford Companion to Politics of the World. Ed. Joel Krieger. 2nd ed. New York: Oxford University Press, 2001.

The Statesman's Yearbook. New York: St. Martin's, 1964–.

Worldmark Encyclopedia of the Nations. 10th ed. 6 vols. Detroit: Gale, 2001.

Yearbook of World Affairs. London Institute of World Affairs. Boulder, CO: Praeger, 1978—.

Indexes and Databases

ABC Pol Sci

International Political Science Abstracts

U.S. Political Science Documents

Web Sites

CNN.com—Inside Politics at <www.cnn.com/ALLPOLITICS>

Political Information: A Search Engine for Politics, Policy, and Political News at <www.politicalinformation.com>

Political Science Resources on the Web at
<www.lib.umich.edu/govdocs/
polisci.html>
United Nations at <www.un.org>

Psychology

Baker Encyclopedia of Psychology. Ed.
David G. Benner and Peter C. Hill.
2nd ed. Grand Rapids, MI: Baker,
1999.
*The Corsini Encyclopedia of Psychology
and Behavioral Science*. Ed. W.
Edward Craighead and Charles B.
Nemeroff. 3rd ed. 4 vols. New
York: Wiley, 2001.
A Dictionary of Psychology. Ed. Andrew
M. Colman. New York: Oxford
University Press, 2001.
Encyclopedia of Psychology. Ed. Ray-
mond J. Corsini. 2nd ed. 4 vols.
New York: Wiley, 1994.

Indexes and Databases

PsycARTICLES
Psychological Abstracts
PsycINFO

Web Sites

American Psychological Association at
<www.politicalinformation.com>
Encyclopedia of Psychology at
<www.psychology.org>
Psych Web at <www.psywww.com>
*Social Science Information Gateway—
Psychology Gateway* at
<http://sosig.ac.uk/Psychology>

Religion

The Anchor Bible Dictionary. Ed. David
Noel Freedman. 6 vols. New York:
Doubleday, 1992.
Contemporary American Religion. Ed.
Wade Clark Roof. 2 vols. New
York: Macmillan, 2000.
*Dictionary of Philosophy and Religion:
Eastern and Western Thought*.

William L. Reese. Exp. ed.
Amherst, NY: Humanity, 1999.
Encyclopaedia Judaica. 16 vols.
Jerusalem: Encyclopaedia Judaica;
New York: Macmillan, 1971–72.
Encyclopedia of Religion. Ed. Mircea
Eliade. Comp. and unabridged ed.
16 vols. New York: Macmillan,
1993.
*The Oxford Encyclopedia of the Modern
Islamic World*. Ed. John L. Esposito.
4 vols. New York: Oxford Univer-
sity Press, 1995
The Penguin Dictionary of Religions. Ed.
John R. Hinnells. Exp. new ed.
New York: Penguin, 1997.
World Religions. New York: Macmillan,
1998.

Indexes and Databases

Religion Index
Religious and Theological Abstracts

Web Sites

Internet History Sourcebooks Project at
<www.fordham.edu/halsall/
index.html>
Religion, Religions, Religious Studies at
<www.clas.ufl.edu/users/
gthursby/rel>
Sacred and Religious Texts at <http://
davidwiley.com/religion.html>
Virtual Religion Index at
<http://religion.rutgers.edu/vri/
index.html>

Sociology and Social Work

*The Blackwell Encyclopaedia of Social
Work*. Ed. Martin Davies. Malden,
MA: Blackwell, 2000.
Encyclopedia of Social Work. Ed. Richard
L. Edwards. 19th ed. New York:
National Association of Social
Workers, 1995.
Encyclopedia of Sociology. Ed. Edgar F.
Borgatta. 2nd ed. 5 vols. New
York: Macmillan, 2000.

Encyclopedic Dictionary of Sociology. Ed. adviser Richard Lachmann. 4th ed. Guilford, CT: Dushkin, 1991.
International Encyclopedia of Sociology. Ed. Frank N. Magill. 2 vols. Chicago: Fitzroy Dearborn, 1995.
The Social Work Dictionary. Ed. Robert L. Barker. Washington, DC: NASW Press, 2003.

Indexes and Databases

Criminal Justice Abstracts
Social Sciences Index
Sociological Abstracts. Online version is *SocioFile.*

Web Sites

American Sociological Society at <www.asanet.org>
Electronic Journal of Sociology at <www.sociology.org>
Social Science Information Gateway—Sociology at <http://sosig.ac.uk/sociology>
Social Work and Social Services Web Sites at <www.gwbweb.wustl.edu/websites.html>
The SocioWeb at <www.socioweb.com/~markbl/socioweb>

Women's Studies

Black Women in White America: A Documentary History. Gerda Lerner. New York: Vintage, 1992.

A Concise Glossary of Feminist Theory. Sonya Andermahr, Terry Lovell, and Carol Wolkowitz. New York: St. Martin's, 1997.
From Suffrage to the Senate: An Encyclopedia of American Women in Politics. Suzanne O'Dea Schenken. 2 vols. Santa Barbara, CA: ABC-CLIO, 1999.
A Reader's Guide to Women's Studies. Ed. Eleanor B. Amico. Chicago: Fitzroy Dearborn, 1998.
Women in World History: A Biographical Encyclopedia. Ed. Anne Commire and Deborah Klezmer. 17 vols. Waterford, CT: Yorkin, 1999–2002.
Women's Studies Encyclopedia. Ed. Helen Tierney. Rev. and exp. ed. 3 vols. Westport, CT: Greenwood, 1999.

Indexes and Databases

Contemporary Women's Issues
Women's Studies Abstracts
Women's Studies Index

Web Sites

Documents from the Women's Liberation Movement: An Online Archival Collection at <http://scriptorium.lib.duke.edu/wlm>
Feminist Majority Foundation at <www.feminist.org>
Institute for Women's Policy Research at <www.iwpr.org>
Women's Studies Database at <www.mith2.umd.edu/WomensStudies>

Natalie Angier. "Gene Hunters Pursue Elusive and Complex Traits of Mind." From *The New York Times,* October 31, 1995. Copyright © The New York Times. Reprinted by permission.

Malcolm W. Browne. "Russian Spy Plane Is Turning Its Sights from U.S. to Ozone." From *The New York Times,* October 17, 1995. Copyright © 1995 The New York Times. Reprinted by permission.

"Mary Cassatt." From *The New Columbia Encyclopedia.* Copyright © 1975 by Columbia University Press. Reprinted by permission.

Emily Dickinson. "Fame is the one that does not stay" (1475) & "Some — work for immortality" (#406). From *The Poems of Emily Dickinson,* Thomas H. Johnson, ed., Cambridge, Mass.: The Belknap Press of Harvard University Press. Copyright © 1951, 1955, 1979, 1983 by the President and Fellows of Harvard College. Reprinted by permission of the publishers and the Trustees of Amherst College.

Dynix. A telnet library catalog on the Seattle Public Library website (Figure 5.4). Software created by Dynix. © 1997 Dynix Corporation. All rights reserved. Reprinted by permission.

EBSCO Publishing Information Services screen shots (Figures 6.1 and 6.2). List of databases and a basic keyword search on a periodical database. Courtesy of EBSCO Information Services. www.ebsco.com

Excerpt from *The New York Times Index,* June 1, 2003, p. 61. © The New York Times. Reprinted by permission.

"Emma Goldman, Biographical Essay." From *Feminist Writers* (Gale Group, Biography Resource Center), by St. James Press. © 1996, St. James Press. Reprinted by permission of the Gale Group.

Google's basic and advanced search templates (Figures 7.1 and 7.2). © 2004 Google. Reprinted by permission. www.google.com.

"Cotton Mather." Excerpt by Kenneth Murdock. From *Encyclopedia Americana,* 1992 edition. © Grolier. Reprinted by permission of Scholastic Library Publishing Company, Inc.

Roger D. McGrath. "The Myth of Frontier Violence." Excerpt from a lecture delivered at California State University, Long Beach, on November 1984. Reprinted by permission of the author.

New York University Libraries screen grabs. (Figures 4.1, 4.2, and 5.1.) © Copyright 2004 New York University. Reprinted by permission.

ProQuest screen shots (Figures 6.3 and 6.4). An advanced search on a periodical database and evaluating the results of a database search. © ProQuest Information and Learning Company, a division of ProQuest Company. All rights reserved. Inquiries may be made to: ProQuest Information and Learning Company, 300 North Zeeb Road, Ann Arbor, MI 48106-1346 USA. Telephone 733-761-7400. Email: Infor@il.proquest.com Web page: www.il.proquest.com. Reprinted by permission.

Readers' Guide to Periodical Literature. Figure 6-5, Vol. 103, #6 (August 2003), p. 481. Reprinted with permission from The H.W. Wilson Company.

William K. Stevens. "Study of Cloud Patterns Points to Many Areas Exposed to Big Rises in Ultraviolet Radiation." From *The New York Times,* November 21, 1995. Copyright © 1995 The New York Times. Reprinted by permission.

University of Michigan School of Information. Internet Public Library screen shot (Figure 7.3). Result of a subject directory search. © 1995–2004 The Regents of the University of Michigan. All rights reserved. Reprinted by permission.

Index

Points to Consider as You Plan and Write Your Research Paper

- Do you understand the difference between a subject and a topic?

- What methods can you use to develop possible topics and to select one for your paper?

- Is your topic neither too limited nor too broad to satisfy the requirements of your research project?

- Have you thought of a preliminary hypothesis to guide your early research and to focus your thoughts?

- Have you learned how to take advantage of the various research opportunities in your library, including computerized facilities?

- Have you investigated the Internet as a possible source of material for your paper?

- Have you acquired an adequate number and variety of sources for your paper?

- Have you evaluated your sources?

- Have you developed an efficient method for taking notes from your sources? Are you able to record direct quotations correctly? Can you paraphrase and summarize adequately?

- Do you understand what constitutes plagiarism? Can you distinguish between general knowledge and material that must be documented?

- Has your hypothesis evolved into a thesis statement? Is the thesis clearly stated in your paper? Does it appear early in the manuscript?

- Have you provided yourself with an outline or a statement of purpose to guide the organization of your paper?

- In your preliminary drafts, have you worked at integrating your sources into a smooth and coherent presentation? Have you revised for organization, support, language, and documentation?

- Have you carefully applied the documentation style appropriate for your paper?

- Have you proofread your final manuscript to catch and correct any remaining writing or documentation errors?

- Have you followed your instructor's specifications for preparing your final manuscript?

CONTENTS